EASTERN SHORE ROAD TRIPS #2

26 More One-Day Adventures on Delmarva

EASTERN SHORE ROAD TRIPS #2

26 More One-Day Adventures on Delmarva

A Secrets of the Eastern Shore Guide

BY JIM DUFFY

Published by Secrets of the Eastern Shore
Cambridge, Maryland

Publishing Services by Happy Self Publishing
www.happyselfpublishing.com

Cover Photo: Jill Jasuta Photography
Cover Design: Jill Jasuta
Interior Design: Happy Self Publishing

ISBN: 978-0-9978005-4-8

Also by Jim Duffy:
Eastern Shore Road Trips: 27 One-Day Adventures on Delmarva
Tubman Travels: 32 Underground Railroad Journeys on Delmarva

More Eastern Shore Stories & Travels:
secretsoftheeasternshore.com
facebook.com/secretsoftheeasternshore

Feedback:
secretsoftheeasternshore@gmail.com
443.477.4490

CONTENTS

CLASSICS

BEACHES

BACKROADS

CONTENTS BY REGION

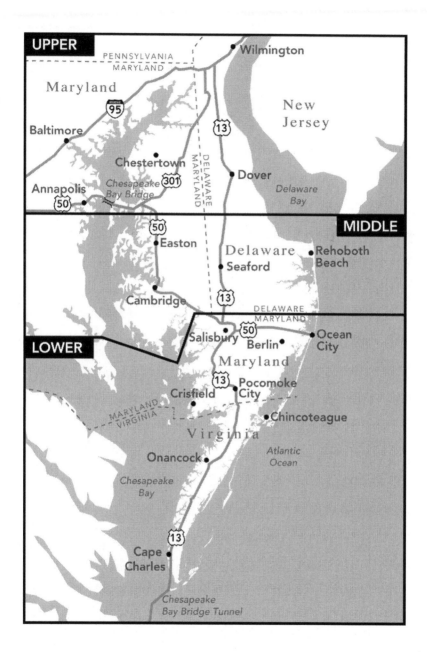

INTRODUCTION

People ask sometimes if I'm ever going to *finish* the work at hand. Will I get to a point where I've been to all the great places and told all the great stories the Delmarva Peninsula has to tell? The question makes me laugh. Thinking it over in this particular moment, I find my mind wandering to the midsummer morning when I rolled into Laurel, Del.

Life had been complicated that week, so I hadn't done much in the way of preliminary research before showing up to meet local history buffs Ed and Norma Jean Fowler. Laurel doesn't rank among the peninsula's most famous or storied destinations. Tourists don't flock there the way they do to St. Michaels, with its patriots, or Chincoteague, with its ponies, or Rehoboth Beach, with its culinary charms.

But the Fowlers started telling stories that day, tying each new tale in with one tidbit or another in the collection at the local historical society. They insisted I climb in their car so we could go see some sights in and around town. The hours flew by. The stories kept coming—and oh, they were *good ones*.

I had similar experiences in quite a few of other places that most folks fly by in their travels—Eastville and Pungoteague and Preston and Snow Hill and Port Penn and beyond. So no, the business at hand will never be *done*. I'd need another lifetime to cross that finish line.

The only thing to do about this predicament is to get out and go: Keep exploring, keep learning, and keep marveling over what an American treasure we have here in the Delmarva Peninsula. I hope the itineraries and stories in this book help to inspire you to get out and make some new discoveries.

Happy wandering!

Jim Duffy, Secrets of the Eastern Shore

ROAD TRIP #1

ST. MICHAELS, MD.

As a history nerd, I pay pretty close attention to the line between fact and folklore. But facts can be fuzzy affairs, especially after a century or two goes by. So it goes with the sign along Route 33 that will welcome you on your way into St. Michaels by proclaiming this as the "Town That Fooled the British."

As we'll see, that story might well be true, but then again it might be false. Or it could be a little of both, a spoonful of truth stirred into a bowl full of exaggeration. Either way, however, the story is fun and interesting. One thing I've learned while wandering the Delmarva Peninsula is that legends sometimes deserve a place in the history books, too.

When fuzzy stories from days gone by find their way into the hearts and minds of local people, they take on a significance independent of the veracity of this or that particular fact. Stories that manage this trick often say something in the end about what a place is all about and what sort of character its people possess. A folklorist named Dick Peskin put it this way when talking a while back about this "Town That Fooled the British" business:

When you study folklore, the truth of such stories doesn't really matter. You are trying to understand how people see the world.

The Lay of the Land

St. Michaels is thick with history. Eighteen buildings here today were standing when the British troops attacked in 1813. You will see quickly while making your way into the downtown why the place ranks as one of the Eastern Shore's most popular tourist destinations. Talbot Street is chock full of picturesque old storefronts. The sidewalks are usually bustling with happy travelers.

The town's centerpiece attraction is a waterfront maritime museum that ranks among the best such facilities in the country. Its luxury resort, the Inn at Perry Cabin, is steeped in local lore. The Miles River is gorgeous. Shopping is first-rate, a mix of upscale clothing boutiques, idiosyncratic gift shops, and artist-run galleries. St. Michaels is a great dining town, too, with eateries that cater to most every taste, from elegant French bistros to down-home barbecue. There is a winery, a brewery, and a distillery, all of which offer tours and tastings. You could easily pass a whole long day here just browsing and grazing.

To some, the scene is almost too idyllic. Mention St. Michaels in certain circles, and you might hear a snide comment about how the place is touristy and fake. But the roots of this town are as hardscrabble and authentic as any other on Delmarva. The stories you can explore here unfold in shipyards, seafood-packing houses, and rough-and-tumble taverns.

Those shipyards dominated this scene in the years leading up to the War of 1812. Those were tense times for American vessels on the Atlantic Ocean, where the British Navy harassed American ships relentlessly, even going so far as "impressing" American sailors—basically, seizing them in the name of the Crown and forcing them into service as grunts.

Demand was high back then for "Baltimore Clippers," sleek and speedy schooners known for their ability to outrun British ships. They were a specialty of the shipyards in St. Michaels.

The story behind the town's slogan dates to Aug. 10, 1813. Enemy Brits had sailed up the Miles River, sparking panic. Most women, children, and livestock were moved outside of town. When the attack came, the Brits made a couple of overland advances, only to be turned back to their boats. Eventually, they moved into position to bombard the town. That's when the clever defenders of St. Michaels supposedly gathered up a bunch of lanterns and hung them high up in trees and atop ship masts while simultaneously extinguishing all ground-level lights.

It was, as the saying goes, a dark and stormy night. When the bad guys took aim at those lanterns, their cannonballs overshot their mark, flying over the town.

This much is true: The British attacked, and that attack failed. The good guys reported a grand total of one casualty—a rooster that got thwacked by a cannonball after climbing atop a stump to crow at dawn. This alone ranks as heroic stuff. Things turned out much worse in other Eastern Shore locales around this time. Several were burned to the ground; others were occupied by the Brits.

But the record on that lantern business is dicey. Historians have been unable to locate any mention of this stroke of strategic genius until many decades after the battle. Why wasn't anyone bragging about it in letters and diaries written in the weeks after the Brits sailed away in disgrace?

A similar fuzziness surrounds a related legend from the Battle of St. Michaels. This tale involved one of the few cannonballs that actually landed in town that night. Supposedly, it crashed through a wall or a chimney in a building at 200 Mulberry St. that's now known as "The Cannonball House." That cannonball then rolled right into the house and down a flight of interior steps in full view of a couple of wide-eyed older ladies, or a mother carrying an infant daughter, or … someone.

The Facts of the Matter

Are these stories exaggerated? Possibly. Are they out-and-out falsehoods? Maybe. Battlefields are always confusing places, and the Battle of St. Michaels was no exception. There was a ton of confusion afterward about what, exactly, happened. Which units ran away from the fight? Which ones stood tall and fought? Who were the heroes? Who were the cowards?

One clever historian has dubbed all this post-battle fog of war "The Second Battle of St. Michaels." The battlefield this time was in taverns and restaurants all over town, where arguments broke out over who, exactly, did what on that dark and stormy night.

Many were the black eyes and bloody noses of the warriors of St. Michaels [in this second battle].

The first mention of that fuzzy business with the lanterns comes many years later, in the late 1800s. That's when a couple of locals were quoted remembering the tale as something their now-deceased parents told them. These stories bubbled along into the early 1900s, when it came time for St. Michaels to mark the centennial of the big battle.

That's when the town went all in on the lantern story. The timing is interesting. St. Michaels spent most of the 1800s mired in a long economic tailspin. Boom times didn't really return in earnest until the market for Chesapeake Bay oysters exploded in the last years of that century. This, then, is when those colorful stories about the heroes of the War of 1812 moved front and center.

It's probably no coincidence that the townspeople would embrace those fuzzy lantern tales just as their town was regaining its mojo. Towns on the revitalization trail today often engage in a similar sort of "rebranding," adopting new slogans and logos and printing up new brochures that reframe the history of the place and reflect a mood of resurgence.

What better way to rebrand than as a town chock full of patriotic bravery and civic ingenuity? So, as the sign says, "Welcome to St. Michaels: The Town that Fooled the British."

You should explore the hardscrabble roots of St. Michaels at two museums while in town. The Chesapeake Bay Maritime Museum sprawls across 18 acres and 10 exhibit buildings. The collection includes 85 historic boats as well, so this is the place to learn about all of those colorfully named vessel types in the annals of the Chesapeake Bay—shallops, sloops, bateaus, schooners, log canoes, bugeyes, skipjacks, deadrises, and more.

The museum also has a working boatyard where you can watch artisans at work restoring one or another of these old vessels. You could even look into opportunities that come along now and again to sign up and do a little woodworking yourself under their tutelage. The fact that admission tickets are good for two consecutive days should give you an idea of just how much there is to see here.

Where the maritime museum has a region-wide Chesapeake focus, the smaller St. Michaels Museum at St. Mary's Square stays closer to home. Set on the original 1771 town center, it encompasses three buildings from the 1800s that are full of old-time gadgets, historical artifacts, and exhibit panels. In the warmer months, the museum offers a slate of walking tours, with different themes set for different weekends of the month.

If you prefer self-guided wandering, no worries. Stroll down the various side streets that run to the riverfront. Houses here show their age in ways that will be a joy for both architecture buffs fluent in fancy terminology and regular folks who simply enjoy ogling pretty houses with sweet flowerbeds. Here and there, you will find reminders of the rough-and-tumble days of yore.

In the late 1700s, a stretch of Cherry Street was known as "Hell's Crossing" because of all the brawls that broke out among hard-drinking sailors and factory workers as they made their way between waterfront shipyards and downtown taverns. Pedestrians have been crossing a stretch of water at the end of Cherry Street along the pretty "Honeymoon Bridge" since the late 1800s. A poetically named "Small Frame House" stands near the intersection of Carpenter and Locust streets— homes like this were selling for $200 when Thomas Jefferson was president.

Cute little Muskrat Park, 100 Green St., has a lovely gazebo, sweet views of the Miles River, and a couple of replica cannons that evoke the Battle of St. Michaels. Farther south, on the water between Mulberry and Chestnut streets, is Church Cove Park. Shipyards were operating here clear back in the 1600s; the park stands on ground that used to be underwater, part of a big harbor that got filled in with dredge materials during the 1800s.

Back up on Talbot Street, an interpretive marker pays tribute to the town's most famous resident. No one living here in the 1830s would have predicted that history would award that honor to a then-enslaved young man named Fred Bailey. He had a reputation around town as a teenage troublemaker, but he would grow up to become the famed abolitionist writer and orator Frederick Douglass.

Several keystone experiences in Douglass's early life unfolded in and around St. Michaels, including his first escape attempt, a dismal failure that ended with him and several co-conspirators getting arrested and being led through St. Michaels on foot, their hands bound, en route to a stint in jail in nearby Easton. It was here, too, that an aging Douglass returned after the Civil War for a fascinating visit with his former owner, Thomas Auld, as Auld lay on his deathbed in a home now occupied by the Dr. Dodson House Bed & Breakfast, 200 Cherry St. (These stories and more are told in detail in my book, *Tubman Travels: 32 Underground Railroad Journeys on Delmarva*.)

Getting out on the water will be easy as can be during the warmer months. As of this writing, the 150-passenger *Patriot*, a replica of a 1930s ferryboat, offers daily narrated tours, as well as themed "cocktail cruises" and the like. Other public-sail options include the skipjack *H.M. Krentz* and the luxury yacht *Selina II*. The maritime museum offers small boat rentals. Kayaks should be readily available from a local outfitter, too.

One last suggestion: The backroads outside St. Michaels are fabulous for aimless cruising. North of town, try taking Claiborne Road out to the pretty little burg of that name and find your way to the boat launch that has an itty bitty little park and a view of the old steamboat wharf on Eastern Bay. Bozman-Neavitt Road is another gem, winding past some glorious waterfront estates on its way to a dead end into a boat launch at the tip of the peninsula where Broad Creek and Harris Creek run into the wide Choptank River. South of town, the street to find is Royal Oak Road, from which you'll turn onto Bellevue Road to reach the Oxford-Bellevue Ferry, an operation that dates to 1683. You can still ride it today across the Tred Avon River and into Oxford (see Chapter 16).

CONNECTIONS
• St. Michaels Business Association
stmichaelsmd.org; 800.808.7622
• Talbot County Tourism
tourtalbot.org; 410.770.8000
• Chesapeake Bay Maritime Museum
cbmm.org; 410.745.2916
213 N. Talbot St., St. Michaels, Md.
• St. Michaels Museum at St. Mary's Square
stmichaelsmuseum.org; 410.745.9561
201 East Chestnut St., St. Michaels, Md.

NEARBY TRIPS: A list of other trips on the middle Delmarva Peninsula is on page 7.

Way Back Machine
Michener in St. Michaels
By the time *Chesapeake* was published in June of 1978, James Michener was richer than God. This is a guy who sold 75 million books during his lifetime. He confessed to a journalist once that he could have retired on the earnings of his first book, *Tales of the South Pacific* (1947), which was the source material for a certain Broadway hit.

Michener and his wife, Mari, moved to St. Michaels for a couple of years during the mid-1970s, living first right in town on Railroad Avenue and later on a waterfront spread outside of town. Here's the odd thing: Visitors to the Michener abode were surprised by the ragtag character of the place. A swivel armchair in the study was "in shreds." The desk was a makeshift contraption, "two borrowed tables pushed together." Michener's typewriter was "a sorry contraption with the front cover gone." He kept a cache of safety pins on his desk to help unstick stubborn keys.

And here's the odder thing: In the kitchen, the freezer was stacked floor to ceiling with boxes of Mrs. Paul's Fish Sticks. Another friend from those days recalls seeing "cases—literally, *cases*—of canned fruit, everywhere." When Mari and James served up fish sticks, they did so on a table stocked with packets of ketchup and other condiments that had been liberated from area restaurants. In an interview later in life, Michener confessed:

> I still worry about having enough money. I live every day as if the [Depression-era Works Progress Administration] were coming back again.

As famous as Michener was for the exhaustive research that went into his novels, he never got to the bottom of his own story. Abandoned as an infant by a mother he would never meet, he landed in the care of one Mabel Michener in Doylestown, Pa. For a long time he thought Mabel was his mother. She ran a makeshift orphanage out of her house. Mabel took in laundry and did some sewing to help make ends meet. On three occasions that Michener could remember, she (and he) landed in the poorhouse, unable to keep up with the bills. "It's a real American experience," Michener recalled. "If you come through it, it's not a bad experience."

What could be good about it? Well, there were evenings when Mabel would read to her young charges from books by the greatest of storytellers—Homer, Dickens, and others. There was the local library—by age 10, Michener had read every book in the children's section. Then there was the old Victrola:

> I am one of the few people around who grew up in abject poverty, listening to [opera singer Enrico] Caruso.

The valedictorian of his high school class, Michener earned a scholarship to Swarthmore College. While there, he received a string of mean-spirited, anonymous letters from someone in Mabel's family, informing him that Mabel was not his biological mother and telling him he was not a "real" Michener.

> It was a bad bit for a week. I suffered. But then I just said, "Screw it."

Tossing that heartbreak aside, Michener got about living a life that turned into quite an adventure. After graduating from Swarthmore College in 1929, he studied for a bit in Scotland, then burned through jobs as a teacher, a Chautauqua actor, and a coal-ship laborer. When World War II came along, Michener served with the Navy. He received a plum assignment by accident—his superiors mistook him for a VIP, the son of an admiral with the sound-alike name of Marc Mitscher. That job had him writing human interest stories for military publications about the lives of various groups of sailors he followed around in the Pacific theater. Back home and living in New York City, he transformed that material into his first novel. *Tales of the South Pacific* won the Pulitzer Prize in 1947.

What drew Michener to the Eastern Shore in the 1970s were memories of sailing the upper bay in his college days. He conducted countless interviews for *Chesapeake* and spent more than his share of time hunched over manuscripts in the Maryland Room of the Talbot County Free Library in Easton. His research went on for one year, then two, and into a third.

Finally, he planted himself in that shabby chair in front of that raggedy typewriter and started knocking out the book. By this time in life, his childhood love for Caruso had given way to a different sort of musical passion. The song that Michener listened to over and over again while writing *Chesapeake* was "Yakety Yak," by the Coasters.

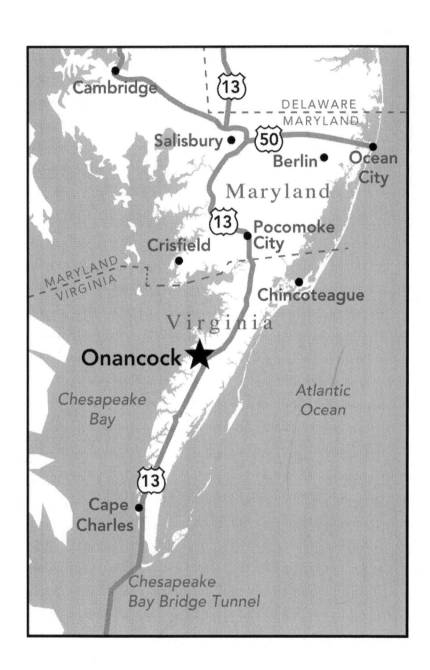

ROAD TRIP #2

ONANCOCK, VA.

I hope you have better luck when visiting Onancock, Va. than Captain John Smith did. If all goes well for you, the town will live up to its name and show itself on the morning of your visit through a gloriously photogenic mist. Like so many places on Virginia's Eastern Shore, Onancock traces its name to Indian times—the word means "foggy place."

Smith and his crew missed out on the sweet scenery because of Mother Nature. They were headed somewhere else altogether during their 1608 voyage of discovery, out toward a couple of islands in the Chesapeake Bay, when …

> … ere we could obtain them, such an extreame gust of wind, rayne, thunder, and lightening happened, that with great danger we escaped the vnmercifull raging of that Ocean-like water. The highest land on the mayne, yet it was but low, we called Keales hill.

Most of the experts who've studied Smith's voyages think he found his way into Onancock Creek in search of shelter from that storm. The English name he gave the place honored a crew member, Richard Keale, who served as his "fishmonger." That job title says something about just how new the New World was during that historic voyage, as Keale was in charge of figuring out which of the strange creatures in these uncharted waters might be edible. The 15-member crew on Smith's cramped shallop disembarked at Keales hill and went looking for much-needed fresh drinking water, but they came up empty.

Inspiration on the Creek
It shouldn't be nearly as hard to find what you're looking for in Onancock today, especially if your tastes run to art and history. Located at the midpoint of Virginia's Eastern Shore, the town of 1,500 has ranked for quite some time now among Delmarva's top little artist enclaves.

As of this writing, there are key galleries downtown showcasing the wildlife art of Tangier Islander Willie Crockett, the vibrant folk-art paintings of native Virginia shoreman Danny Doughty, and the rich landscape paintings of big-city transplant Jack Richardson. Then there is the Eastern Shore Art League, which has a co-op space at 59 Market St. The Historic Onancock School building at 6 College Ave. has a good number of artist studios as well.

The arts beat goes on: One of the better local theater companies around makes its home in the North Street Playhouse at 34 Market St. The 1854 Cokesbury Church at 75 Market St. does double duty nowadays as a community center and performance hall.

Last but not least: A few miles south of town, you will find Turner Sculpture at 27316 Lankford Hwy. This 4,000-square-foot facility showcases the bronze wildlife sculptures of brothers Bill and David Turner, the latter a five-time winner of the Ward World Championship of Wildfowl Carving. The Turners have quite the big-time operation going, with 20-plus artisans working in eight buildings as they employ the traditional method known as "lost wax" in creating casting molds and then transforming them into finished bronze birds posed in spectacular detail.

A word of caution to you art lovers: Don't get so caught up in admiring the way these Onancock artists view their natural surroundings that you run out of time to go see those surroundings for yourself.

A picture-perfect starting point is Onancock Wharf at the end of Market Street. If you put your imagination to work here, the centuries will unfold in your mind's eye while you look out on Onancock Creek. Most of us modern visitors arrive in town via overland roads, of course, but this waterfront served as the town's front door in times when goods and people were much more likely to move by water than land.

Native Americans used paddle-powered canoes to navigate these waters, but those canoes were nothing like the banana-shaped little things that bear the name today. Some tribes in the lower Chesapeake had "canoes" that ran to 50 feet long and carried 30 people. John Smith's shallop, which launched the age of sail in these waters, could fit only half that number.

Once the Indians here actually got to know some of the European newcomers that followed in Smith's wake, they developed an interesting way of describing them, according to the journalist Charles Wheat:

The bones of our area's Indian dwellers show the effects of few if any bouts of disease, and one good cause might be the fact that the ... Indians in general believed in a daily bath. That was foreign to Europeans, leading to several recorded examples of Indians complaining that the Englishmen *stanck*.

Seven decades passed between John Smith's arrival at Keales hill and the establishment of a significant trading port on Onancock Creek in the 1680s. From that point through colonial times and beyond, schooners chock full of cargo sailed in and out of these waters. Sadly, a handful of slave ships delivered "cargo" through the port here as well.

John Sergeant Wise lived on the other side of the creek as a young boy in the years before the Civil War. In a memoir written later in life, he recalls the scene he witnessed almost every day in the 1850s while looking out toward the distant town.

> [T]he whole shore was at that time strewn with grain houses ... and there was a wharf at each grain house. From the creek, could be seen the village of Onancock, with its steeples, and sandy streets, and red-topped houses, and wharves swarming with boats of all sizes, from the schooner to the skiff.

Wise also recalls heading into town one day to meet his father "at old Captain Hopkins's store at the wharf." The mailboat his father arrived on also brought news of the results of the 1852 presidential election. A "throng" of local people had gathered at the store in anticipation of those results, and they "cheered vociferously" when told that pro-slavery Democrat Franklin Pierce would be the next president.

It's been moved a couple of times since then, but the same store building now stands on the wharf at 2 Market St. Incredibly, this sweet sentinel from the past stayed in the hands of the Hopkins family from opening day in 1842 all the way into the 1960s. A restaurant is located inside nowadays. You'll also find some exhibit materials and old photos put up by the Historical Society of the Eastern Shore of Virginia.

There is lots more fuel for the imagination as you look out over the creek. Can you see all the different styles of workboats through the years, from log canoes to bugeyes to skipjacks and right on up to modern-day deadrises? Can you picture an old Eastern Shore Steamboat Company vessel from the late 19th or early 20th century? Those boats weren't just chock full of passengers — they carried local potatoes, tomatoes, strawberries, oysters, and more to big-city markets. Those steamboat days were boom times here in Onancock.

An old steamboat ticket office stands next to former Hopkins Store — the last time I visited, it housed a kayak-rental operation that also offers guided paddling tours. The wharf retains one other touch of those busy times — this is the departure point for ferryboats that shuttle tourists and residents out to remote Tangier Island, Va. in the middle of the Chesapeake Bay (see Chapter 10).

Of Cowardice and Bravery
The walk along Market Street from the wharf back to downtown will take you past a bevy of sweet old homes and end in an old-school commercial district. The pretty swath of green space between East and West streets served as the original town square when Onancock was first laid out in the late 1600s. Nearby, at 14 Market St., is a now-private home that was originally built in 1878 to serve as the town hall.

The oldest house in town is next door, at 12 Market St. Scott Hall dates to around 1770. Out back is a quaint little graveyard that's the final resting place of Zedekiah Whaley, whose name occasionally pops up in history books through an interesting footnote to the Revolutionary War.

We all learned back in grade school about how that war ended with the surrender of Cornwallis at Yorktown, Va. in 1781, but things were actually more complicated. Another year would pass before a formal peace deal got written up covering all the proper bureaucratic terms and arrangements. It wasn't until 1784 that the Treaty of Paris was finally ratified by the new Continental Congress.

In the meantime, hostilities still flared up now and again. On Delmarva, the troubles centered on a flotilla of small, flat-bottomed ships under the command of British loyalists clinging to their all-but-lost cause. Commodore Whaley was trying to put a stop to those raids when he sailed up Onancock Creek in late 1782 and asked local militia members to join him in going after the marauders.

The so-called "Battle of the Barges" that followed out in the waters of Pocomoke Sound was a disaster for the good guys. Several American vessels ran away from the fight while under fire, leaving Whaley and his crew aboard the *Protector* alone and exposed. The commodore was among 24 killed on the patriot side of the ledger.

One Virginian who stood his ground on the *Protector* and ended up getting knocked unconscious during the affair summed up the dismal turn of events this way:

There was never before upon a like occasion so much cowardice exhibited.

Local history takes a braver turn not far from Whaley's final resting place. The house at 9 Market St. is known as Holden nowadays, but an earlier building near this site was home in the late 1600s to a local girl named Naomi Anderson. One night she heard a young Irish immigrant named Francis Makemie talk about his faith and found herself wondering:

> Was not that a noble young man? ... I wonder what is the young minister's name?

Known now as "Father of American Presbyterianism," Francis Makemie soon married Naomi, and the two lived in Onancock in their early years together. Makemie made his living as an itinerant merchant, but his true passion was spreading a new kind of religion. His courage surfaced not in physical battles, but in the fight for religious freedom. Virginia was basically a one-faith-allowed place at the time, with little or no toleration for any beliefs not sanctioned by the Anglican Church of England.

Makemie helped to establish two of the earliest Presbyterian congregations in America on the Maryland side of the Eastern Shore, in Westover and Snow Hill. The most famous incident in his life happened in 1707 while traveling through territory in New York that was under the control of a sheriff named Cornbury, who had been making a name for himself by jailing any and all preachers whose words strayed from the Anglican straight and narrow.

In a provocative move, Makemie went out of his way to do some public preaching, seemingly hoping to get arrested. Then, serving as his own lawyer, Makemie bested the sheriff in the courtroom confrontation that ensued—that case is regarded even today as a landmark in the development of religious liberty. Makemie died in 1708. He is buried on the upper part of the Virginia shore, in a park on the site of the home where he and Naomi spent their later years.

Rich Man, Working Man, Watermen

Downtown Onancock covers about four blocks in all, with stretches of Market, North, and King streets serving up a modest mix of shops, services and eateries amid those art galleries I mentioned earlier. The signature historical attraction downtown is Ker Place, a Federal-style home that dates to about 1800 and has been dubbed "one of the Shore's major architectural landmarks."

It now serves as home base for the Historical Society of the Eastern Shore of Virginia, so you will find exhibits and gallery space in addition to rooms adorned with fine woodwork and period furnishings. The society's collection includes a 1904 oystering log canoe, the *Annie C.*; an extensive collection of silver pieces; and military memorabilia from two leading citizens back in the day, Gen. John Cropper and Henry Wise, who served a term as governor just before the Civil War.

Farther out toward the highway is a more modest structure that honors the working-class heritage of Onancock. As of this writing, the transformation of the Samuel D. Outlaw Blacksmith Shop into a little museum is still a work in progress, so be sure to check in advance about getting access. A native of North Carolina, Outlaw moved to Onancock in 1926, fresh out of college. He toiled here for many decades as a metalworker, fixing everything from the horse-drawn wagons used by farmers to the rudders and crab scrapes needed by local watermen.

Those watermen are the focus of the small but interesting Eastern Shore Watermen's Museum and Research Center, located in the Historic Onancock School. Open on Saturdays as of this writing, the museum features an idiosyncratic array of artifacts and memorabilia from days gone by and is often staffed by folks with long firsthand experience in the fishing, oystering, and crabbing trades that were so important in the development of this town.

CONNECTIONS
• Eastern Shore of Virginia Tourism
visitesva.com; 757.331.1660
• Accomack County Tourism
co.accomack.va.us/visitors; 757.787.5700
• Town of Onancock
onancock.com/community/page/visit-onancock; 757.787.3363
• Ker Place/Historical Society of the Eastern Shore of Virginia
shorehistory.org/ker-place; 757.787.8012
69 Market St., Onancock, Va.
• Eastern Shore Watermen's Museum and Research Center
esvawatermen.org; 757-665-5771
6 College Ave., Onancock, Va.

NEARBY TRIPS: A list of other trips on the lower Delmarva Peninsula is on page 7.

Way Back Machine
The 'Horse-Frightening Machine'

In her 1988 book, *The Eastern Shore of Virginia: 1603-1964*, Nora Miller Turman recounts the tumultuous days when automobiles first arrived on Virginia's Eastern Shore:

> The first [car] was owned by Claude Nottingham of Onancock about 1906. It has been said that ladies would not go out in their carriages until the said Nottingham was consulted to see if he expected to use that horse frightening machine that day. ...
>
> ... On March 17, 1906, the General Assembly approved an Act for operating automobiles. ... The rate of speed was fixed at fifteen miles per hour in the open country and eight miles per hour for going around curves, up and down hills, and in villages, towns, or cities.
>
> The driver was to watch for the approach of horseback riders and vehicles drawn by animals. If the driver or rider found his animal frightened, he was to signal the driver of the horseless carriage to stop until the frightened animal passed. If such driver were a man, he could be asked to lead the frightened animal past his horseless carriage.

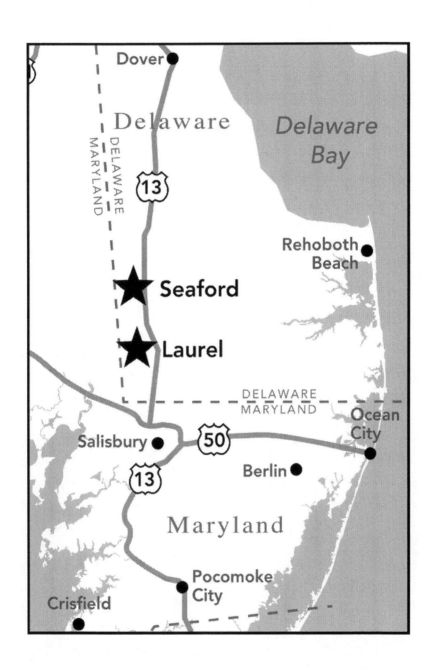

Dover

Delaware

Delaware
Bay

DELAWARE
MARYLAND

(13)

Rehoboth
Beach

★ Seaford

★ Laurel

DELAWARE
MARYLAND

Salisbury (50) Ocean
City

(13) Berlin

Maryland

Pocomoke
City

Crisfield

ROAD TRIP #3

LAUREL & SEAFORD, DEL.

I was in the back seat that July morning. Up front were Ed and Norma Jean Fowler, who wanted me to see an interesting old church in the countryside outside of Laurel, Del. The scenery along the way was lush Sussex County farmland, bright green and shimmering after a recent run of rains. Norma Jean gasped: "Ooooh!"

She pointed toward a dozen or so men working a patch of produce, their broad-brimmed hats bobbing this way and that through the field of green. The men were scooping watermelons up and loading them onto a school bus parked in the midst of that field. The bus was a tattered affair, its roof gone except for some strips of metal stretched atop it like scaffolding. Its body had been painted graffiti style, in bold colors that dropped a splash of Mexican street art into this Delaware field.

One thing I've learned to appreciate in my travels around Delmarva is how different places have different iconic scenes. Over in St. Michaels, Md. the sort of gasp that came from Norma Jean that morning might have signaled a skipjack sighting. Down at Assateague, it might have been a pony. Up on the Delaware Bay, it might have been a horseshoe crab.

Here in western Sussex County, the midsummer watermelon harvest is what makes folks go weak at the knees. Agriculture is still the king here, as we will discover while wandering the streets, parks, and little museums in and around Laurel and nearby Seaford.

19th-Century Marvil

Fair warning: Neither town in this road trip has managed at this point to get all gussied up for the 21st-century tourist trade. Both boast some interesting shops and restaurants, but have vacant storefronts, too. Neither is awash in the sort of high-end eateries and boutiques that adorn some more famous destinations.

But both of these works in progress have plenty of interesting stories to tell and sites to see. Laurel got off to a late start by Delmarva standards, incorporating in 1883. One reason for that tardy arrival is that this landscape was a Nanticoke Indian reservation for much of the 1700s—something that impacted the town's early development in a fascinating way.

Those Indians didn't chase the tobacco boom of colonial times, which turned out to be a good thing for Laurel. Tobacco is a beast when it comes to wearing out farmland. Planted over a course of years, it turns healthy fields into tired, lifeless affairs. When Laurel finally took shape, it had soils much richer and more productive than its tobacco-addled neighbors.

Reservation life didn't work out for the Nanticokes. The beginning of the end came in a shadowy incident during the 1740s, when rumors surfaced that local tribes were planning an armed rebellion. Colonial leaders clamped down on Indian freedoms, limiting their travel rights and banning the ownership of the guns that the Indians had come to rely on for hunting.

In the years that followed, most Nanticokes gave up on their homeland and began moving north to live among the Iroquois in Pennsylvania. Here is a sad scene to put in mind as you admire the way pretty Broad Creek winds through downtown Laurel. After that Indian exodus, small groups of Nanticokes would return now and again in dugout canoes to tackle the grisly work of digging up the bones of their ancestors for transport up to their new home.

That creek is the focus of modern-day redevelopment efforts in Laurel. Several little parks now lie along its banks, offering boat ramps, kayak launches, playgrounds, and picnic benches. A number of old warehouses stand there as well — and they tell the story of how Laurel became a basket case.

On that July morning, I met the Fowlers at the Cook House, one of two little museums run by the Laurel Historical Society (with a third and more ambitious project in the works as of this writing). The Cook House is not an especially noteworthy specimen of architecture, but it's chock full of artifacts and memorabilia.

Keep your eye out for one item in particular there, though it might look to untrained eyes like just another humble bushel basket. The story behind that basket begins in 1825, when Joshua Hopkins Marvil was born. His father died when Joshua was nine or 10, leaving a widow and six children. Marvil worked aboard cargo ships for a bit, traveling to distant ports. Back home, he got a job with a shipbuilder and dabbled in carpentry and cabinetmaking.

He was in his late 20s when he turned his attention to the local farm economy and set his sights on becoming an inventor. The first railroad line through southern Delaware was under construction at that point—in fact, it's the same line that you'll see crossing Broad Creek today.

Before that railroad arrived, the farm economy of lower Sussex County was built on grains. Perishable fruits and vegetables couldn't survive the long, bumpy ride to market on overland roads. Sail transport took too long as well—the journey involved going out Broad Creek, then down the long Nanticoke River, and back up the Chesapeake Bay to Annapolis and Baltimore.

Once rail transport changed that, the fields outside Laurel filled with strawberry plants and peach trees. This is the market Joshua Marvil conquered. His Marvil Package Company made wooden baskets for peaches and smaller trays for strawberries. His products were sturdy enough to withstand the rigors of loading and unloading, but they were also dirt cheap. Marvil baskets were so cheap, in fact, that business historians today regard the company's products as a groundbreaking early example of disposable packaging.

The company made 600,000 baskets in its first year. By the 1880s, it was making 2 million baskets a year. By the early 1900s, it was churning out 35,000 baskets *every day*. Some old Marvil warehouses still stand along Broad Creek. So, too, does Marvil's magnificent old house, at 606 West St. If you find your way to pretty Fisher Park, keep an eye out while standing alongside the creek for some old pilings under the surface—those, too, are remnants of the Marvil empire.

Other companies flourished in Laurel as well—there were canneries, fertilizer plants, fruit evaporators, and more. But Marvil was the big dog for a long stretch. His company was the main reason why Laurel ranked during the 1880s as the richest town in Delaware. His executives were the folks who built many of the Queen Anne Revival, Victorian Gothic, and

Colonial Revival houses that dot the town's sprawling historic district.

Marvil himself became quite a celebrity. He turned down several pleas to run for governor before finally running, and winning, in 1894. Alas, he died a few months into that term. His son, Joshua Dallas Marvil, carried on, expanding company operations into baskets for tomatoes, apples, potatoes, beans, and onions. The company closed in 1959, after a century in business.

Natural Diversions

That, then, is the story behind just one of the hundreds of artifacts on display at the Cook House. Keep an eye out there for the superb corner cupboards, done up in a style unique to the area. I also enjoyed the room filled with mid-20th-century memories of Laurel's thriving, Norman Rockwellish downtown, with its full array of restaurants, movie theaters, dance halls, clothing stores, hardware stores, drugstores, butcher shops, and soda fountains.

Downtown Laurel has a more modest mix of businesses today. The work-in-progress revitalization effort is looking to reorient the town visually around Broad Creek and position Laurel in the tourism market as a base camp for outdoorsy types interested in exploring Trap Pond State Park and the Nanticoke Wildlife Area nearby, or going fishing at popular Phillips Landing.

Those parks offer a window into the area's fascinating natural history. Much of inland Sussex County used to be part of a vast, spooky Great Cypress Swamp, which covered 50,000 acres. You can explore remnants of that swamp at Trap Pond, which has 12 miles of water trails in addition to hiking paths and a nature center. Adventurous paddlers might want to look into exploring nearby James Creek—the Fowlers told me that a challenging route there leads to a cypress tree estimated at more than 500 years old.

Before leaving downtown, be sure to stop by the second museum operated by the Laurel Historical Society. Housed in an old train station, it's a showcase for the society's impressive collection of photos by the local Waller Studios, founded in the early 1900s by Albert H. Waller and run later by his son, Norman. The museum doubles as a visitors center, so you'll also be able to pick up a brochure to guide you along a stroll of the historic district.

Before heading off toward Seaford here, I should get back to where I started. On that ride into the countryside, the Fowlers drove east of town on Laurel Road, then turned up Christ Church Road, which dead ends at a remarkable remnant of colonial times, a 40-foot-by-60-foot frame church that dates to 1772.

A good number of brick churches from that era are still standing, but just a handful of frame churches have managed to avoid the ravages of fire, wind, dampness, and insects. The color of the aging heart-of-pine wood here explains the building's nickname, "Old Lightwood." The place has never been plumbed or electrified. Only a few window sashes have ever been painted. The interior manages to be both nothing fancy and thoroughly gorgeous, with its boxed pews, a double pulpit, and an upstairs "slave gallery."

The local Episcopal church still holds services here on the first Sunday of warmer months, as well as on special holidays. They often use a prayer book from the 1790s during those occasions.

On the way back into town, the Fowlers drove me past a centerpiece of today's agricultural economy, the Laurel Auction

Market. Known as "The Block," it's where buyers come to load up on local watermelons. If you visit during the midsummer harvest, you'll want to pull over here and watch while workers roll conveyor belts onto those tattered old school buses to get the melons started on their journey to shops and restaurants in big cities.

Sea Captains and Sailing Rams

Take the roundabout way to Seaford, leaving Laurel along Bethel Road, whose name soon changes to Woodland Ferry Road as it tracks the course of Broad Creek on its way to the Nanticoke River. Turn south onto Route 493, which then becomes Main Street in Bethel, a town of 200 souls.

Winding your way along the narrow streets here, you will pass a bunch of homes that were built by sea captains and shipbuilders in the late 1800s and early 1900s. You can grab a sandwich or snack at the throwback Bethel Store. You might also want to take a stroll through one or both of Bethel's historic graveyards.

The volunteer-run Bethel Heritage Museum has limited public hours, so you will want to check on those or make a special appointment. The most fascinating of the stories told inside this former public school concerns the Broad Creek shipyard that specialized in building "Bethel rams," workhorses that rank among the biggest sailing schooners ever built on the Delmarva Peninsula.

More than 30 rams were built here between 1871 and 1918. These flat-bottomed, three-masted vessels were designed to store more cargo than other ships while requiring smaller crews. Another key thing: They were built to just barely squeeze through the Chesapeake & Delaware Canal. According to one legend, the name Ram comes from the day an observer watched one of these behemoths entering a canal lock and cried out, "That ship is pushing through just like a ram!"

Only two ships built at this Bethel yard still survive. You can see the tugboat *Delaware* at the Chesapeake Bay Maritime Museum in St. Michaels, Md. You can sail aboard the other, *Victory Chimes*, but that will involve a long trip — it's serving as a tourist boat up in Rockland, Me. In fact, that old ram is such a big deal in Maine that the state put its likeness on the back of its official quarter.

If you're in the mood for another natural detour, find your way across Broad Creek to Shell Bridge Road and then turn right onto Phillips Landing Road, which runs through the Nanticoke Wildlife Area and ends in the Phillips Landing Recreation Area — both are popular spots with paddlers, anglers, and birders. The park straddles the shores of both Broad Creek and the Nanticoke River. A historic marker here commemorates Captain John Smith's journey up the Nanticoke during his famous "voyage of discovery" in 1608.

The Nylon Capital of the World

When you're ready to head to Seaford, you'll have two choices. If you turn from Bethel onto westbound Woodland Ferry Road, you'll cross the Nanticoke River atop the little ferry of that name (see Chapter 16) and make your way into town from the west. For a quicker, ferry-less trip, find your way to Seaford Road or Sussex Highway and come into town from the south.

Either way, Seaford isn't going to appear as the kind of place that puts its best face forward. Instead, you'll arrive through a mishmash of gas stations, fast-food outlets, and strip shopping centers. Things get more interesting off of those main drags.

A good starting point is the Gov. Ross Plantation, which occupies 20 of the 1,400 acres that belonged to William Henry

Harrison Ross in the years around the Civil War. Ross was born in nearby Laurel. It was there, as a young man, that he first played around with growing peach trees, an experiment that did not bear full fruit until he moved to Seaford. At one point, peach trees would cover more than 800 acres on this plantation.

Ross was elected governor of Delaware in 1851 at the tender age of 36. He still ranks as the youngest man ever elected to that post. It's no coincidence that the construction of the first railroad line through Sussex County began during his time in office, or that those tracks ran straight through this plantation. There was even a trackside station house on the property—a replica of that building was recently constructed on the plantation.

A slave owner, Ross became one of Delaware's most ardent supporters of the South and its "peculiar institution." One of his sons signed up to fight for the Confederacy. Ross himself has been linked in history books to some rather unsavory activities, including running guns to Virginia and intimidating members of a local black church. Fearing arrest by Union troops at one point, Ross fled to England, where he sat out the war years lamenting what he regarded as the "madness and fanaticism" of those who wanted to bring slavery to an end.

Today, the Gov. Ross Plantation ranks as the best place in Delaware to get a full sense for plantation life in those Civil War times. The centerpiece of the property is an elaborate, three-story Italianate mansion that dates to the 1850s. You can sign on for guided tours of the interior, which is full of period furnishings and art. The grounds boast a number of interesting outbuildings, including a rare surviving slave quarter.

The peach boom that helped make Ross a rich man came to a slow, painful end in the early decades of the 1900s, as a deadly disease called "the yellows" moved slowly but surely through

Delmarva's orchards. The Depression fell soon thereafter, leaving towns like Seaford trapped in a downward spiral.

Then came Oct. 19, 1938, the day the humongous DuPont Corporation announced that it had selected a site west of town on the Nanticoke River for a factory dedicated to producing a newfangled synthetic material, nylon. Local newspaper accounts describe the town as "almost hysterical with joy" over the news. An impromptu parade broke out that night, with fire trucks from Seaford and nearby towns rolling through the downtown, sirens blaring. High school marching bands scrambled together and joined in the parade as well.

The whole town was a riot of color, noise, laughter, and happy smiling faces.

The joy was well founded. The Seaford plant produced 4 million pounds of nylon in its first year of operation. That number soon grew to an astounding 270 million pounds annually as demand skyrocketed for stockings and other nylon products. At its peak in the 1970s, the nylon plant employed more than 4,500 people, a number nearly equal to the town's population at that time. Seaford adopted a new slogan: "The Nylon Capital of the World."

Those glory days are distant memories now, as you'll see when you find your way down Nylon Boulevard to check out the old plant. You'll pass a lush golf course that dates to the nylon boom times, but the boulevard ends in a different sort of scene, with overgrown shrubs obscuring your view of the decaying hulk of a factory as it rises up behind a fence topped with rusting barbed wire.

Operating as Invista, the plant was still open and producing nylon as of this writing—but barely, with a workforce of less than 100. That loss of more than 4,000 jobs in a town with a current population of 7,000 helps put those vacant storefronts around town into proper perspective.

You are unlikely nowadays to encounter traffic troubles as you make your way along Pennsylvania Avenue, which becomes High Street as it approaches old downtown Seaford. But this wasn't always the case—horrendous rush-hour backups occurred nearly every time a shift let out back in the heyday of the nylon factory.

Cars would crawl down eastbound High Street, stopping en masse at each stoplight along the way. At some point in the 1970s, journalist William Wright Robinson got a bright idea— his *Seaford News* floated a suggestion: Why not let cars turn right at red lights when the coast was clear? The concept that Seaford helped launch slowly spread to other towns and states before becoming legal most everywhere in the country by the 1990s.

That is one of the stories you will get in touch with at the sizable Seaford Museum, housed in an old downtown post office. Other displays here touch on slavery times, seafaring days, and many other topics. Take some time afterward to stroll through the streets of Seaford's pleasant old downtown. As of this writing, those streets offered a few shops of interest, some Latin-flavored eateries, and a fancy French bistro.

Be sure to walk down the hill along Market Street, which will lead to a short "Riverwalk" along the Nanticoke River at a spot where steamboats used to land. This brings us back to our Seaford starting point, slavery times. One October day in 1856, Harriet Tubman and an enslaved woman named Tilly disembarked from the steamboat *Kent* here after a journey from Baltimore. They had a couple of close calls on that journey, but in the end, Tilly joined the ranks of the estimated 70 slaves that

Tubman led to freedom during the years she spent working along the Underground Railroad.

CONNECTIONS
• Sussex County Tourism
visitsoutherndelaware.com; 800.357.1818
• Town of Laurel
townoflaurel.net; 302.875.2277
• Laurel Historical Society
laureldehistoricalsociety.org; 302.875.1344
Cook House Museum: 502 E. 4th St., Laurel, Del.
Laurel Heritage Museum (in the old train station): 215 Mechanic St., Laurel, Del.
• Trap Pond State Park
destateparks.com/pondsrivers/trappond; 302.875.5153
33587 Baldcypress Ln., Laurel, Del.
• Phillips Landing/Nanticoke Wildlife Area
visitdelaware.com/listings/phillips-landing-nanticoke-wildlife-area/2414; 302.539.3160
End of Phillips Landing Road, Laurel, Del.
• Town of Bethel
bethel.delaware.gov; 302.877.8139
• Bethel Museum
bethel-historical-society.weebly.com
312 First St., Bethel, Del.
• Town of Seaford
seafordde.com; 302.629.9173
• Seaford Historical Society
seafordhistoricalsociety.com; 302.628.9828
Ross Mansion: 23669 Ross Station Rd., Seaford, Del.
Seaford Museum: 203 High St., Seaford, Del.

NEARBY TRIPS: A list of other trips on the middle Delmarva Peninsula is on page 7.

Way Back Machine
Launch Days in Bethel

Whenever a newly built Bethel Ram was ready for launching in Broad Creek, the occasion was a public holiday. The whole town would turn out and line the shores of the creek. Some of the people would climb aboard and crowd onto the deck of the new ram.

That boat would be sitting up on greased skids, perched so as to slide right into the creek when set free from the various lines and blocks holding it in place. Every once in a while, however, a freed boat stayed stuck up on the skids, refusing to budge. In those cases, the hundred-plus passengers would be herded back to the bow and ordered to sprint up to the stern in unison and stop dead in their tracks. Invariably, the boat would then rock forward and flop into the creek.

At one launching in 1896, a woman named Amelia Gordy fell overboard. No worries: She happened to be wearing several layers of then-fashionable petticoats under her dress, and when she landed feet first, those petticoats gave her enough buoyancy to stay afloat. She landed like a duck, her torso never dipping below the waterline.

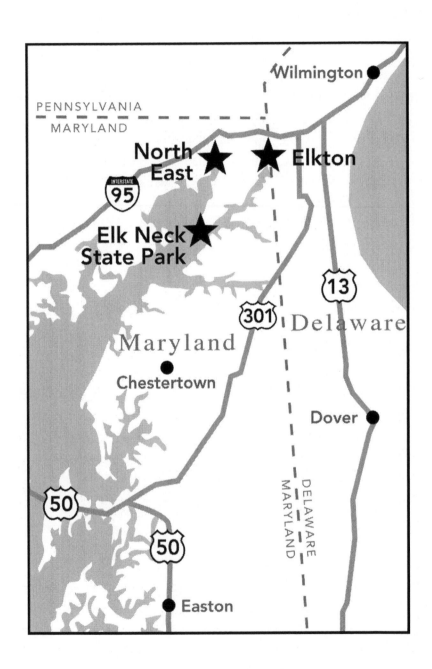

ROAD TRIP #4

ELKTON & NORTH EAST, MD.

Personally, I never grow tired of wandering the flatlands that cover nearly all of the Delmarva Peninsula, but I can understand how some folks might yearn for a touch of vertical relief now and again. Good news: You don't have to venture up into the hills of Pennsylvania or Western Maryland to find what you're looking for.

The Elk Neck peninsula, which drops down into the top of the Chesapeake Bay between the North East and Elk rivers, is a generously hilly affair where you can find heart-pumping hikes and bluff-top vistas, then visit a trio of interesting and historic towns in Cecil County, Md.

Standin' at the Top of the Bay
The most beautiful of those overlooks lies at the end of a 12-or-so-mile drive down Turkey Point Road (Route 272). This winding, hilly affair runs through the 2,500-acre Elk Neck State Park, which offers 12 miles of hiking trails and an array of park

facilities, some of which date from the Great Depression days of the Civilian Conservation Corps.

The park's most famous attraction dates back even further, by a full century. Turkey Point Light was built in 1833 to alert mariners of the turn into the Elk River that would lead them into the Chesapeake & Delaware Canal, a then-brand-new shortcut to the Delaware River and its prosperous urban markets of Wilmington and Philadelphia.

That beacon still stands here, wrapped in white stucco and topped by a black roof and a glass light chamber. Getting to the lighthouse involves following Turkey Point Road clear down to its dead end and then embarking on a reasonably easy stroll of three-quarters of a mile. As of this writing, the interior of the lighthouse is open for a few hours on Saturdays and Sundays in the warmer months, which is when you will have the opportunity to climb the 31 steps inside and visit a little gift shack outside.

But the trail is open every day, and the scenery out here will be worth the walk whether the beacon's interior is open or not. Turkey Point is just 35 feet tall, but it's perched atop a 100-foot-high bluff. Measuring from the water, it ranks as the third tallest of the 82 beacons that have done duty on the Chesapeake Bay over the centuries. The views are out of this world.

Turkey Point Light has a second claim to fame as well. During the 19th- and 20th-century periods when men dominated the lighthouse-keeper game, this light had four different female keepers. Women were in charge here for 89 of the 115 years that the facility was, um, manned on a 24/7 basis.

All four women snuck into the post by way of family connections. Elizabeth Lusby took over after her husband died in 1844. Rebecca Crouch got the job the same way in 1873 and was succeeded by her daughter, Georgiana Brumfield. The fourth distaff keeper, Fanny May Salter, took over for her late husband in 1925 and served for 22 years, at which point the light became an automated affair, with no need for a keeper to live on the grounds. At her retirement, Salter offered this nonchalant summary of her service:

Oh, it was an easy-like chore, but my feet got tired, and climbing the tower has given me fallen arches.

It's one thing to note that these women were gender pioneers in a male-dominated field, but think, too, while wandering that bluff, about the sort of work they took on. Turkey Point was isolated as can be through the 1800s and into the 1900s. The roads from the closest towns, North East and Elkton, were bumpy, muddy messes. Most supplies arrived by boat, from Havre de Grace.

Those vessels would come ashore at the bottom of the bluff. A rickety stairway rose from there, 137 steps in all. For some of this period, keepers and their deliverymen hauled supplies up the hill along a chute by way of a windlass contraption powered by a hand-spun wheel. Farming, hunting, and fishing were part of day-to-day life. Keepers raised their own chickens, sheep, and turkeys.

A fog bell mechanism needed to be wound up every three hours, day and night. During one stupendous stretch of haze, that mechanism failed, leaving Salter to pull a rope that sounded the bell at precise 15-second intervals for nearly a full hour, until she was certain that a steamship down below had made it safely into the C&D Canal.

Even life's routine affairs were challenges for those keepers. Take sleeping, for example. Salter lived in a house that once stood on this bluff. She set up her bedroom in a way that allowed the light to blink directly into her face as she lay in bed—she trained herself to wake up in an instant if the blinking ever stopped.

The social isolation out here on Turkey Point could be quite intense. Salter found solace in word games:

I never seem to get enough of crossword puzzles. My friends send me hundreds, but I'm always fresh out.

The last time I made the walk out to the lighthouse at Turkey Point, the wide trail up and back was awash in birds and deer. Heading back up Turkey Point Road, you'll pass the Elk Neck State Park office, which is where you can get more information about other parts of the park you might want to explore. If you're looking to get the heart pumping on the most ambitious of the uphills, take the White Banks Trail, a three-mile round trip that offers more spectacular overviews of the bay.

Go with the Flow in North East

The first Europeans to settle on the banks of the North East River did so because the inland streams flow a little faster through this hilly terrain. The town that bears the river's name sprung up around early gristmills and ironworks powered by the force of that moving water.

Water remains the main attraction here today, of course, but the business at hand in the 21st century is recreation. Boaters, anglers, and hunters visit North East in big numbers, as you'll see if you take a perch on a bench or picnic table at North East Community Park and watch the boats come and go on the pretty riverfront. The park is located at the end of Walnut Street.

The Upper Bay Museum, which is right in the park, sets another nice stage, with displays that trace the history of and show off artifacts from the area's hunting and fishing heritage. The museum boasts an exceptional array of old decoys, as well as a top-notch collection of vintage marine engines. They are working to keep those traditions alive, too, by offering classes in which local teens and interested adults learn to build wooden boats in old-school fashion.

Main Street in North East is a one-way affair, so you will need to cross over it on the way out of the park and then head north on Mauldin Road before circling around by way of Philadelphia Road to come back southbound into the town's main array of shops and restaurants. The dining scene along these few blocks is dominated by comfort foods — steaks, seafood, and ice cream abound. Antiques lovers will find plenty of browsing interest in the shops.

If you need to walk off that comfort food, stroll south past the shopping district to St. Mary Anne's Episcopal Church. The building here dates to 1743, and the expansive graveyard is well worth wandering. Legend has it that some of the small stones behind the old vestry house mark the graves of Susquehannock Indians who converted to Christianity.

This scene here wasn't always so serene, however. Stores and saloons once stood on the edges of this churchyard. Early on, the job description for pastors at St. Mary Anne's included venturing out at 10pm on Saturday nights to clear out all of the townsfolk who partook of "too much of the evil beverages."

The little town of Charlestown is worth the short detour to the west of North East along Old Philadelphia Road. Another sweet piece of waterfront history, the place was born of big dreams that never panned out. The men who founded the place in 1742 were supremely confident that Charlestown would soon outpace then-13-year-old Baltimore and become *the* metropolis of the upper bay.

Nothing remotely metropolitan ever developed here, however, unless you count the fact that this town of 1,500 people boasts four different marinas as of this writing. Here, you'll get to enjoy more sweet views of the North East River, especially out by a replica of the old wharf at Water and Conestoga streets. The original wharf was built in 1744 and served as a supply depot for the Continental Army during the Revolutionary War. Historic markers nearby tell the stories of Nathanial Ramsay and Michael Rudolph, a couple of local heroes who served in that war. Stroll up the street and through town if you're in the mood, so as to admire more than two dozen old homes, taverns, inns, and other buildings that date to the 1700s and 1800s.

Down the Falls and Over to Elkton
Before heading to Elkton, take a little detour to see the longest of the surviving covered bridges in Maryland. Gilpin's Falls Bridge stands a few miles north of downtown North East along Route 272 (called North East Road up here) in a rather odd and unattractive spot, hard up against the shoulder of a noisy four-lane highway. But step under that roof and start admiring the rafters above, and you will find instant refuge from that traffic.

In days gone by, more than 100 of these covered bridges dotted the landscape statewide. It's easy for us to lament the disappearance of these beauties, but the truth is, the good old days weren't all that good for the roadway engineers who built and maintained structures like this. Wooden bridges were highly susceptible to fire, rot, and insects, which is why they went out of style so quickly once metal and concrete alternatives came along.

The story of Gilpin's Falls Bridge dates to the Civil War. Completed in 1860, the 119-foot-long span carried the nearby (and now non-existent) Nottingham Road over North East Creek. The bridge takes its name from a stretch of the creek that doesn't qualify as a full-fledged waterfall, but drops in a more gradual, sloping fashion for a run of 106 feet just below where the covered bridge stands today.

Samuel Gilpin bought this land in the early 1730s and tapped into the power of that falling current to operate a gristmill and a sawmill. A dam breast, a sluice, and some foundation walls from those operations remain visible today, ruins lying deep in the woods that line the streambed.

Finding those ruins is a bit of a challenge, but it's worth the effort. A public trail leading to the old mill site runs down through those woods from the edge of the Cecil Community College campus, which is located back to the south on Route 272. No signs that I am aware of point the way to this trail, so what you need to do is follow the signs to the campus athletic fields, then park nearby. From there, make your way toward the most distant of the baseball diamonds, the one that backs up to the woods. You'll find the trail I took to those ruins in back of the right-field foul pole.

On the way to Elkton, you will probably get a congested sense for the fact that the towns here at the top of the bay qualify nowadays as distant suburbs of Baltimore and Wilmington. A gazillion commuters make their way to and from work along two major thoroughfares, Route 40 and Interstate 95. Fast food outlets and chain stores abound.

Such a crossroads role isn't new for Elkton. Back in colonial times when the area was known as "Head of Elk," the land that would become Elkton served as a way station on a different kind of highway. Revolutionary-War-era VIPs traveling from Norfolk, Annapolis, and other western shore locales would make their way to Philadelphia by sailing across the bay and up the Elk River, then traveling overland from here to the Delaware River.

In point of fact, the seat of modern-day Cecil County was born through an act of treason. In the summer of 1777, George Washington got word that British troops were about to roll through Head of Elk. When he came from Pennsylvania to scout the scene, he visited with a landowner named Robert Alexander, who must have seemed a trustworthy sort, having served in the patriot-dominated Continental Congress.

When the Brits arrived three days later, Alexander also offered his hospitality to their general, William Howe. Legend has it that some Continental troops didn't like that gesture and busted into Alexander's house while the owner was out greeting Howe's ship. They even stole the meal Alexander's servants had prepared for his second visiting general.

Alexander packed up and left Head of Elk immediately after that, skedaddling so fast that he left his wife behind. He found his way aboard a ship bound for England and never returned to these shores. In 1780, the Maryland legislature convicted Alexander in absentia of treason and seized most of his land, though they were thoughtful enough to leave a little slice of it in the hands of Alexander's abandoned spouse.

Elkton stands today on Alexander's old property. The historic downtown here has a touch of Western Maryland about it, with a winding, slightly hilly Main Street serving up views of distant church steeples. A decent number of shops, restaurants, and galleries lie along a three-block stretch here. The Cecil County Historical Society always seems to have something interesting on display.

Ironically, given its treasonous roots, Elkton has a wealth of patriotic stories to tell. The Mitchell House (1769) at 131 E. Main St. served as a makeshift hospital for wounded soldiers during the Revolutionary War. George Washington passed along Main Street here on a second occasion, this time en route to a triumphant encounter at Yorktown.

War came calling again a few decades after that, but the people of Elkton proved themselves up to the challenge. During the War of 1812, British ships wandered here, there, and everywhere on the upper Chesapeake Bay, burning the nearby towns of Georgetown, Fredericktown, and Havre de Grace.

But they failed on two tries to turn the same trick in Elkton. On one occasion, locals erected a makeshift barrier across the Elk River to stop a British ship in its tracks. The enemy then tried to attack by land, but that was repelled as well. Legend has it that an enslaved woman named Hettie Boulden cleverly led those British troops right into a fortified line of defense.

The key to Elkton's success in those dangerous days was the diligence and generosity of its own citizens. In the spring of 1813, some 200 locals gathered at the courthouse here to discuss the risks of a British attack. Those folks then put their money where their mouths were, donating $1,000 toward the construction of a "fort," by which they really meant a fortified breastwork to provide cover for a small battery of guns.

Three such "forts" went up hereabouts—Fort Hollingsworth, Fort Defiance, and Fort Frederick. You can visit the site of long-gone Fort Hollingsworth on select summer weekend days when the fledgling tourist attraction of Elk Landing is open for tours. The 15-acre site, which has a couple of significant old homes that are being restored, is a work in progress run by a local nonprofit that has visions of developing a significant living-history destination.

Throughout much of the 1800s, Elkton continued to play its role as an important crossroads town. One of the first steamboats to serve on the Chesapeake Bay, *The Eagle*, ran between Baltimore and Elkton on Tuesdays, Thursdays, and Sundays starting in 1815. Passengers from the big city would then take a stagecoach to Wilmington, where they boarded another ship that carried them on to Philadelphia.

The railroad arrived in 1831. Early on, trains were pulled by horses, but steam-powered engines started rolling into town soon enough. Nearly a century later, those same trains would help give Elkton another claim to fame, as the quickie wedding capital of the East Coast. There is more about that in the Way Back Machine section at the end of this chapter.

CONNECTIONS
• Cecil County Tourism
seececil.org; 800.232.4595
• Elk Neck State Park
dnr.maryland.gov/publiclands/pages/central/elkneck.aspx;
410.287.5333
• Turkey Point Light Station
tpls.org
• Town of North East
northeastmd.org/north-east-maryland-tourism; 410.287.5801
• Upper Bay Museum
upperbaymuseum.org; 410.287.2675
219 W. Walnut St., North East, Md.
• Town of Charlestown
charlestownmd.org; 410.287.6173
• Gilpin's Falls Bridge
mdcoveredbridges.com/gilpinsfalls.html
• Elkton Chamber of Commerce
elktonalliance.org; 410.398.5076
• Cecil County Historical Society
cecilhistory.org; 410.398.1790

135 E. Main St., Elkton, Md.

NEARBY TRIPS: A list of other trips on the upper Delmarva Peninsula is on page 7.

Way Back Machine
The Quickie-Wedding Capital

In 1913, the state of Delaware adopted a new law requiring that couples planning to get hitched endure a four-day waiting period between getting a license and having a ceremony. By that point, New York and Pennsylvania required waiting periods, too.

What's a couple in a rush to do when faced with such obstacles? Back then, they found an answer in Elkton, the closest county seat in Maryland to the Delaware border, as well as a super convenient destination by car and train.

In June of 1913, Elkton issued 60 wedding licenses. The whole year before, it had issued 18. There was a lot more of that yet to come — in 1936 Elkton issued 11,791 marriage licenses, an average of 32 nuptials every day.

There were a couple of colorful idiosyncrasies about this elopement trade. Maryland back then required that weddings involve an official religious ceremony, so couples couldn't get hitched at the courthouse, which is why more than 20 wedding chapels lined Elkton's Main Street at the height of the quickie wedding boom.

The state also had a law that prohibited the active "solicitation" of wedding business, so these chapels were not allowed to advertise or otherwise reach out to prospective newlyweds. Elkton's taxi drivers stepped into that void, many of them cutting under-the-table deals with this or that chapel and then prowling the train station in search of freshly arrived lovebirds. Oral history has it that fistfights broke out with regularity among cabbies arguing over who spotted which pair of lovebirds first.

On the Secrets of the Eastern Shore website, reader Andrea Boulden-Gagliano shared some family memories about this period. Describing her native Elkton as a "sweet Mayberry kind of town," she went on to describe shenanigans that seem a little un-Mayberryish:

> My aunt Pauline Boulden, was married to Harry "Hedgey" Woolman, who would later become a fairly well-known stunt man in Hollywood. During the Elkton chapel heyday, they would ride [on motorcycles in front of] the potential and just-married couples, with my aunt riding on Hedgey's shoulders and doing all kinds of tricks. She said times were tough and that was a quick way to make a buck.

Hedgey Woolman had a bunch of fun tricks up his sleeve. He was also known to lead couples through the downtown while seated backward on his motorcycle, or while doing a handstand. Lots of famous people got married in Elkton — actors Cornel Wilde, Joan Fontaine, Martha Raye, and Debbie Reynolds among them. One of them turned out to be a big-time promoter who lured Woolman to Hollywood, where he became a well-known stuntman in numerous movies and television shows. If you ever watch the classic "Hunchback of Notre Dame" starring Charles Laughton, that's not Laughton swinging down on a rope from a bell tower and swooping up a condemned girl from the gallows — that's Hedgey from Elkton.

Back in Hedgey's hometown, Elkton's 25-year-long reign as the quickie-wedding capital of the region started to come to an end in 1938, when a statewide referendum mandating a 48-hour waiting period passed by a wide margin. (In Cecil County, the vote was overwhelmingly against that measure.)

Many of the chapels on Main Street managed to live off of the town's wedding-bells reputation for quite some time to come, however. As late as the 1970s Elkton was still marrying 6,000 couples a year. More recently, celebrities who have tied the knot there include Watergate-era Attorney General John Mitchell, basketball star Charles Barkley, and evangelical minister Pat Robertson. Alas, the last wedding chapel in downtown Elkton closed in 2017.

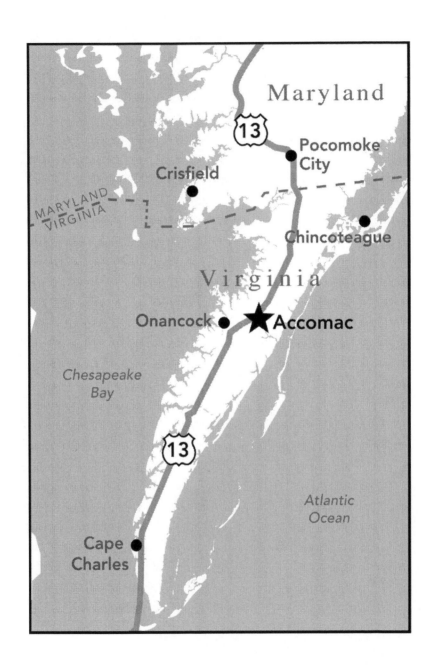

ROAD TRIP #5

ACCOMAC, VA.

Does the Eastern Shore of Virginia have more churches per capita than any other place in the country? I haven't seen statistics on this, but the question definitely has popped into my head while making journeys like the one here, in which we'll stroll through the historic burg of Accomac. Places of worship come in all shapes and sizes here, from stately old structures with spots of honor on the National Register of Historic Places to ramshackle storefronts retrofitted to serve fledgling congregations.

This religious abundance has a heartwarming aspect, giving the landscape a sense that old-fashioned notions of faith and community still run as deep as ever in this neck of the woods. But here's the thing: The backstories on many of these churches are filled with conflict and contention. We're not talking about genteel theological debates, either: We're talking fisticuffs, kidnapping, and jail time.

The Baptist on Trial

The Anglican Church of England ruled the religious roost on Virginia's Eastern Shore in colonial times. People had to pay taxes to support their Anglican preacher. They could get in trouble if they declined to take an oath of religious loyalty. Eventually, Virginia would come around and sign on to the key American notion of religious freedom, but it was a bumpy ride for a while.

Accomac is a great place to discover how interesting that journey was — and to meet the various brave characters who helped make it happen. Home to just 500 people, the town is the seat of Accomack County. (Believe it or not, that extra "k" is not a typo; the two jurisdictions have different spellings.)

A beautiful old town square is Accomac's most famous attraction. The residential back streets are nearly as sweet, awash in pretty old houses with gorgeous gardens. On my last visit, a single restaurant was open — and only at lunchtime, so you might want to do a little advance meal planning.

Early on, Accomac was known as Metompkin, after an Indian tribe. The first white settler, John Dye, arrived in the 1660s. Circuit-riding judges were stopping in town to hear cases by the 1690s, at which point the place had taken the name of Drummondtown, after a prominent landowner.

A courthouse went up in 1756. The red-brick successor that frames the town square today dates to 1899. The county clerk's office just west of that holds court records running back to 1663, the second oldest continuous collection of such documents in the country, behind nearby Eastville.

The most famous structure on the square is the Debtor's Prison, a small and rather nondescript brick affair built in 1783 to stand inside of a walled prison yard. It served as a home for jailers until the early 1800s, when it morphed into the place where people landed if they fell behind on their finances and couldn't pay a court fee or a tax bill.

A man named Elijah Baker spent some quality time in the Drummondtown jail before that old building even went up. Born in 1742 on the western shore of Virginia, Baker took a wayward, sinful path through his younger years, until, as a biographer put it:

> [God] who is rich in mercy, checked him in his course of sensuality, and gave a new direction to his desires.

Baker was 27 years old when he took the plunge in the sort of full-immersion ceremony that gave the then-fledgling Baptist faith its name. After that,

> Churches sprang up wherever he went.

A friend from the Eastern Shore invited Baker to sail over and spread some Good News on this side of the Chesapeake Bay. He arrived on Easter Sunday in the momentous year of 1776. By that point, the religious revolution known as the First Great Awakening had already rolled through other colonies. Here in Virginia, however, the Methodist, Presbyterian, and Baptist faiths were still mostly unknown—and decidedly unwelcome.

Baker intended to keep things low key that day by quietly attending an Easter service at a church on Old Plantation Creek, near Cape Charles. But when that church's traveling rector failed to show, Baker told the disappointed faithful that he would preach if anyone wanted to listen.

He headed into some nearby woods, where, depending on which account you read, he either stepped atop a big old tree stump or used a sawhorse as a makeshift pulpit. The locals who ventured into those woods were accustomed to preaching by ministers who came from the upper crust of society. Baker didn't offer much in the way of sophistication and education.

[He was] a man of low parentage, small learning, and confined abilities. But with one talent he did more than many did with five.

Most of those locals were appalled by what they heard, but a handful seemed intrigued. Baker promised to come back and celebrate Pentecost with them. After that second crossing of the Chesapeake Bay, he never again went back to his home turf on the western shore, devoting the rest of his days to "planting" an astounding 15 churches on Delmarva—six in Virginia, five in Maryland, and four in Delaware.

First on that list was Lower Northampton Baptist Church in that Cape Charles area, where he baptized five believers in 1778. He came to Drummondtown next, but the Anglican powers that be sprang into action here. Arrested on trumped-up charges of vagrancy and unable to pay bail, he spent 56 days locked up here that summer, awaiting trial.

Baker didn't let that predicament keep him from pursuing his calling. He preached through windows with metal bars, hoping someone might be within earshot. By some accounts, he was pelted with rocks or fruit while engaged in this work.

When his trial date finally arrived in August, those Anglican powers that be didn't bother to show up and press their iffy case. But Baker's Accomac ordeal wasn't quite over. None too pleased about the release of this heretic, local men kidnapped the Baptist and dumped him aboard a ship bound for Europe, telling the captain to take this troublemaker across the ocean.

Several legends have grown up around Baker's escape from this predicament—the simplest of the stories is that when the ship's captain heard Baker preaching to crew members, he decided not to play a part in kidnapping a decent, faithful man.

For the rest of his days, Baker wandered the Delmarva Peninsula, planting those churches. He was about that work in Salisbury, Md. when he died at 56 years of age in 1798. No one knows today where the faithful Baptists of Salisbury buried their leader, but it's still possible to pay respects by finding your way to a marker here in Accomac that honors his legacy. We'll get there after strolling past a couple of other spots in this pretty and historic burg.

Methodist Muscle

Across the way, as you walk west from the town square along Front Street, there is a marker outside a private home located on the former site of a tavern where Henry A. Wise was born in 1806. Until recently, Wise ranked as the only governor in Virginia's history to hail from the Eastern Shore, serving in that post during the tense pre-Civil-War years of 1856 to 1860.

Turn south at Drummondtown Road and you'll come back to the main Accomac storyline of religious freedom. Built in 1838, St. James Episcopal Church, 23319 Back St., is probably the finest example of Greek Revival architecture on the Virginia shore. The congregation here is much older than the building, going back to those colonial days when Anglicans ruled the roost.

Those days came to an end after the Revolutionary War, when pretty much all things British fell into disrepute. Eventually, the Anglicans would reinvent themselves as all-American Episcopalians.

Up ahead, past an intersection with Back Street, is Drummondtown United Methodist Church, 23457 Drummondtown Rd., which represents the most lasting and important chapter in the story of the area's religious transformation. Methodism started out as a reform movement housed inside that Anglican church. When the Revolutionary War broke out, most Methodist ministers fled back to England, fearing for their safety.

Francis Asbury was not the fleeing type. He holed up at Barratt's Chapel just north of Frederica, Del., and set about reinventing Methodism as an all-American movement completely separate from those British Anglicans.

This new faith didn't go after rich and educated converts. Asbury recruited homegrown missionaries who spoke the language of common people and knew their culture and traditions. The first of those missionaries sent to visit this part of Virginia gave up after getting lost in the vast, spooky cypress swamp that then covered much of Maryland's lower Eastern Shore. A second preacher, Freeborn Garrettson, got lost there as well, but he didn't give up. Legend has it that he came across a local man in that swamp and asked him if he knew Jesus Christ.

Sir, I don't know that man, and can't tell you where he lives.

Garrettson preached here in Accomac while the Revolutionary War was still going strong, in 1778. Asbury visited in 1783 and 1784. During this period, he was often accompanied on his travels by Black Harry Hosier. Born into slavery, Hosier was given his freedom by his owner, a Methodist convert. He landed at Asbury's side after that, at first taking on the duties of a paid servant. He was illiterate, but he had a wondrous gift. During long travels together, Asbury would read scripture aloud, and his every word was instantly imprinted on Hosier's photographic memory — or audiographic, to be more precise.

In time, Asbury started letting Hosier preach to black audiences. Then he had Hosier address white audiences, too, as a kind of warm-up act. On more than a few occasions, Hosier proved the more popular of the two. He was probably the first black man to ever preach in white churches in this country.

[Black Harry] possessed a most musical voice, which he could modulate with the skill of a master, and use with the most complete success in the pathetic, terrible, or persuasive parts of a discourse. ... He was never at a loss in preaching, ... and few of the white preachers could equal him.

The Methodism preached by Asbury, Garrettson, and Hosier was really the heart and soul of that Second Great Awakening, a nationwide revival that grew so intense that many people were certain the Second Coming was nigh. But early on here in Virginia, such Methodist ministers endured a less than welcoming atmosphere. In the town of Belle Haven, Rev. Joseph Everett found himself face to face one day with a crowd that had a surly, inhospitable look. He took off his coat, rolled up his sleeves, and flexed a bare bicep.

Men of Virginia, this is old Everett. Look at him. He has large arms and willing muscles, and always feels ready to stand up for the cause in which, by the grace of God, he is now enlisted.

Everett went on to preach without interruption. In the end, the message he and his Methodist colleagues delivered won the day on the Eastern Shore of Virginia, where Methodism would soon become the most popular faith by far—a status it retains today.

If you backtrack a bit from Drummondtown United Methodist, you will return to that intersection with Back Street. To the east, beyond a run of gorgeous old houses, is the 1838 Makemie Presbyterian Church, 23355 Back St. The place was trashed by Union soldiers in the 1860s, but has since been restored to its pre-Civil War glory. In the yard out back stands a statue of another interesting religious pioneer, Francis Makemie. There is more about "The Father of American Presbyterianism" in Chapter 2, set in Onancock, Va.

Eventually, Back Street will meet up with Front Street. That's where you'll find that marker honoring Rev. Elijah Baker, in the graveyard outside of Drummondtown Baptist Church.

CONNECTIONS
• Eastern Shore of Virginia Tourism
visitesva.com; 757.331.1660
• Accomack County Tourism
co.accomack.va.us/visitors; 757.787.5700
• Town of Accomac
accomac.org; 757.789.5171

NEARBY TRIPS: A list of other trips on the lower Delmarva Peninsula is on page 7.

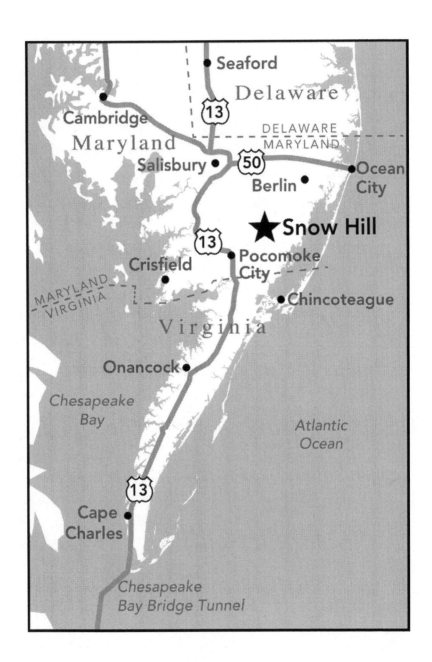

Seaford

Delaware

Cambridge

Maryland

Salisbury

DELAWARE
MARYLAND

Berlin

Ocean City

★ Snow Hill

Crisfield

Pocomoke City

MARYLAND
VIRGINIA

Chincoteague

Virginia

Onancock

Chesapeake Bay

Atlantic Ocean

Cape Charles

Chesapeake Bay Bridge Tunnel

ROAD TRIP #6

SNOW HILL, MD.

I no longer remember the name of the woman who came up with my favorite description of life in Snow Hill. More than a dozen years have passed since I first visited this town on Maryland's lower Eastern Shore while writing an article about "The Best Small Towns in Maryland" for a magazine in Baltimore.

At one point during that project I landed in the office of a local businesswoman. What I needed from her was a fun quote about the joys of living in a place that would seem so remote and exotic to my big-city readers. I tried the question one way, but the woman's answer was boring. I tried it another way, but her next reply was even more pedestrian. When I rephrased the question a third way, the voice of a stranger jumped in. The receptionist seated in a waiting area outside the office had been eavesdropping.

"Tell him it's more like living in a big family than a small town!" she shouted. Welcome to Snow Hill, population 2,100.

Remnants on the Outskirts

Founded in 1684, the seat of Worcester County ranks among the oldest towns on the Delmarva Peninsula. Situated along the base of a geographic triangle formed by Salisbury, Berlin, and Pocomoke City, it's right next door to the abundant natural wonders of Pocomoke River State Park and Forest. The slogan they've adopted here in recent years is, "Small Town, Big Adventure."

Before heading into town, I recommend pausing over a couple of remnants from the days when Snow Hill was just taking shape. Indians still roamed here in the late 1600s, clinging to old, semi-nomadic ways that had them moving with hunting, fishing, and gathering seasons among various settlements between ocean and bay. Just north of town, where Route 12 meets Whiton/Nassawango Road (Route 354), a marker stands at the site of Askiminokonson, or Indian Town.

In the 1670s this was one of those settlements, the now-and-again home of a mix of Pocomokes, Annamessexes, Manokins, Nassawattexes, and Acquinticas. Nothing remains of Indian Town except the marker, but there is a lot to think about while surveying the farm landscape where its campfires once burned.

Seventy short years after Captain John Smith's arrival in the Chesapeake Bay in 1607, times were already getting tough for Native Americans. European diseases were tearing through tribal populations. Hunting grounds had begun shrinking as more and more white people settled in for the long haul. Colonial authorities tried now and again to set aside swaths of land so the Indians could continue living in traditional ways, but one by one those territories dwindled and eventually disappeared in the face of ever-growing settlement pressure from new white arrivals.

There would be no reversing the trends under way for people in places like Askiminokonson. In the end, the ones who survived the long run of death and disappointment would fade into the general population and try as best they could to make their way in the strange New World that overtook their native lands.

Another remnant of past centuries lies a little farther north. Unlike Askiminokonson, there is plenty to see and explore at the Furnace Town Living Heritage Village. The story here is an entrepreneurial affair, rooted in the natural resources of the vast cypress swamp that dominated this landscape for centuries.

Such swamps are beehives of biochemical activity, and one byproduct of that activity is "bog iron." This goop is too full of impurities to be usable in its natural state, but humans have been figuring out various ways to extract the good stuff from that muck since before the days of the Roman Empire.

Local farm families were the first to turn that trick here near Snow Hill, transforming bog iron into nails and other little household items. In time, bigger operations started snooping around the swamp. One of those, the Maryland Iron Company, set up shop in the 1830s along Nassawango Creek, the longest tributary of the Pocomoke River.

The furnace they built went through several technological iterations, but is most famous for the period when it employed a then newly invented technique, the "hot blast." A mix of bog ore, oyster shells, clam shells, and charcoal was loaded into a humongous furnace equipped with a gargantuan bellows. When the blaze in that furnace hit 3,000 degrees, two different liquids would begin oozing out from the bottom. One was slag, which was left to cool and then thrown away. The other was the real iron deal, which was poured into molds and shipped to cities as far away as Philadelphia and New York.

The operation was successful for a stretch—at one point, 300 people lived in the company town that surrounded the furnace. But bog iron deposits are notoriously unpredictable, delivering scads of product for one stretch of time and then all of a sudden not so much. The Maryland Iron Company sold the operation, which eventually landed under the control of a local lawyer, Thomas Spence, but he couldn't make it work either.

After the company went bankrupt around 1850, the town went to ruin. Legend has it that a free black man, Sampson Harmon, stayed on, living at the furnace with his family long after everyone else had left. Lots of spooky stories have sprung up around Harmon, whose ghost supposedly always wears a hat, never wears shoes, and takes care of a collection of stray cats.

During the last half of the 20th century, various civic groups set out to rescue the site from oblivion, a process that in the end gave birth to the modern-day incarnation of Furnace Town. In addition to the furnace ruins, this "historical village" boasts a restored blacksmith shop, a one-room schoolhouse, a woodworking shop, a church, and other buildings from various historical periods. The first time I visited that schoolhouse, the volunteer on duty was quite insistent for some mysterious reason that I don a humongous, cone-shaped dunce cap.

The best part of visiting Furnace Town is the title attraction. When you walk up to the top of the old iron furnace, think about the combination of ingenuity and backbreaking labor that went into turning the raw materials of the swamp into 700 tons of iron a year.

Keep your eyes peeled inside the village for the entrance to the Paul Liefer Trail, which leads through the Nature Conservancy's Nassawango Creek Preserve. At 9,000 acres, the preserve is nearly as big as nearby Pocomoke State Park. But it draws fewer visitors and thus gives a better flavor for just how isolated and forbidding a wilderness this swampland used to be—and why the tales of Sampson Harmon and quite a few other ghost stories might spring up around it. Another plus: The preserve boasts 14 species of orchids.

A Town on the Rebound

Entering downtown Snow Hill from the north along Route 12, the first thing you'll see is a sprawling old warehouse on the left—as of this writing, it houses the Pocomoke River Canoe Company. It was originally built by the Corddry Company, a forestry operation. This pairing of past and present seems quite fitting: A building where men once worked in an industry that cleared forestland now serves as a base station for men and women eager to get out on the Pocomoke River and paddle their way through remnants of those woods.

Like many other towns on the Eastern Shore, Snow Hill has endured its share of lean times in recent decades. But a turnaround seems well under way now, thanks to pioneering entrepreneurs like Ann Coates, whose Bishop's Stock gallery sparked the development of an interesting little arts scene that the town celebrates monthly during "Arts on the River" weekends. New shops and eateries have been popping up as well. On my most recent stroll through town, the new arrivals included a coffee shop here, a specialty candy shop there, and a sprawling toy store around the corner.

Snow Hill is blessed with some remarkable old architecture. Fire roared through the downtown area on two different occasions in the late 1800s, so the most interesting commercial buildings date to the early 1900s. A walking-tour brochure should be readily available around town. Be sure to find your way to the one-time home of John Walter Smith, who served as governor of Maryland from 1900 to 1904 and built a Queen Anne-style gem for his family at 104 S. Church St.

Just around the corner at 109 W. Market St. is All Hallows Episcopal Church, which went up in the 1750s. Some graves in the cemetery there date back to that early period, but the one that made me stop and think on a recent visit dates to a century after that. The Hudson stone has four names listed prominently—up top are parents Moses and Mary Hudson, followed by son Aaron and daughter-in-law Anne Allen. Then, all the way at the bottom, is this bit of small print:

Handy Hudson Their Faithful Slave 1805-1856.

This was quite unusual—as far as anyone knows, Handy is the only black person from slave times buried here in a "white" cemetery. It's funny, how an affectionate small-print memorial like that can leave you pondering the fates of so many men and women in his generation, who almost—but not quite—made it long enough in life to see slavery come to an end.

A little way up at 208 W. Market St. is the interesting Julia Purnell Museum, which has a wonderfully idiosyncratic collection of local artifacts and ephemera. There is more on that in the Way Back Machine section at the end of this chapter.

Snow Hill boasts a pair of sweet parks along the Pocomoke River. The one closest to downtown is Sturgis Park, built on the former site of an old fertilizer plant. Today, the Pocomoke is a thin stretch of water here in town. That wasn't always the case—shipbuilding operations thrived in Snow Hill during the days when that river ran much deeper and wider than it does today. The town's library is nearby, at 307 N. Washington St. A marker went up there recently honoring native son Judy

Johnson, whose phenomenal athletic accomplishments landed him in baseball's Hall of Fame (see Chapter 15).

Be sure to check the civic calendar before you visit, as Snow Hill serves up a generous parade of annual events. The one at the top of my recommended list is the "Blessing of the Combines," which has the downtown streets thronged with flag-waving locals as area farmers roll in on a Saturday morning in August atop their biggest vehicles, so as to receive a pre-harvest-season blessing. Many of those combines stay parked square in the middle of downtown all day, serving as the climbing-friendly centerpiece for a family-oriented street festival.

A Visit to the Swamp

Much of the land near Snow Hill was once part of a 50,000-plus swath of swampland that stretched from here up into southern Delaware. You can explore remnants of that old natural wonder at Pocomoke River State Park, which awaits three or so miles outside of town. The park's Shad Landing and Milburn areas are full of the expected amenities—hiking trails, boat rentals, campsites, playgrounds, and more.

The star attraction here is the bald cypress tree, a strange creature that looks like a pine tree but drops all of its needle-like leaves every fall as surely as a maple or an oak. It thrives in flood-prone places where most other trees would drown.

And what is up with all those knobby little "knees" rising up around the trunk? They look like a gaggle of little kids gathered around an old storyteller. Experts used to theorize that these knees were all about facilitating the tree's oxygen supply, but now they seem to prefer the idea that they are about structural stability, protecting the bald cypress against high winds during hurricanes and tropical storms.

A couple of historians have speculated over the years that the surviving remnants of the old cypress swamp—there is another one up in Trap Pond State Park near Laurel, Del.—might be about as close as you can get on the modern-day Delmarva Peninsula to seeing something that still looks pretty similar to the way it did when Captain John Smith and his crew were wandering around in the early 1600s.

These places can be quite spooky. They have a Deep South look, with sphagnum moss hanging here, there, and everywhere. Cypress swamps never really see the full light of day—it's always somewhere between dark and semi-dark—"one of the most frightful labyrinths you can imagine," in the words of a traveler in 1809. It should come as no surprise, then, that the swamp has served as a popular hiding place over the centuries for everyone from British loyalists and runaway slaves to moonshiners and criminals on the run.

What happened to the old swamp is a familiar chapter in the story of European development over the centuries. The bald cypress is a valuable source of hardwood, so lots of trees came down, their wood bound for use in shipbuilding, as roof shingles, and even in coffins. As the trees disappeared, farmers moved in, clearing out what was left of the old forest.

The oldest trees here today are perhaps 100 years old, a far cry from the days when visitors talked about much older and bigger trees, with wider trunks and knees reaching heights of 10 feet. Those trees, by the way, are where the Pocomoke River gets its name. Pocomoke is an old Indian word meaning "dark water"—and a key source of that coloring is the tannic acid found in cypress needles.

CONNECTIONS

• Worcester County Tourism
visitworcester.org; 800.852.0335
• Furnace Town Living Heritage Village
furnacetown.org; 410.632.2032
3816 Old Furnace Rd., Snow Hill, Md.
• Town of Snow Hill
snowhillmd.gov/visitors; 410.632.2080
• Julia Purnell Museum
purnellmuseum.org; 410.632.0515
208 W. Market St., Snow Hill, Md.
• Pocomoke River State Park
dnr.maryland.gov/publiclands/pages/eastern/pocomokeriver.
aspx; 410.632.2566
Milburn Landing Area: 3036 Nassawango Rd., Pocomoke City,
Md.
Shad Landing Area: 3461 Worcester Hwy., Snow Hill, Md.

NEARBY TRIPS: A list of other trips on the lower Delmarva Peninsula is on page 7.

Way Back Machine
Julia Purnell: It's Never Too Late

When Julia Purnell landed in a wheelchair after a bad fall, she could have given up on an active life. She was 85 years old, after all. We've all heard stories about older people who let despair get the best of them in the face of such setbacks. Not Purnell: She decided to start making art, and the work she turned out over the 15 years that followed is the reason her name adorns a museum in her hometown of Snow Hill.

Purnell was born in 1843 as Julia Anne LeCompte. Her parents, James and Henrietta, ran a general store in Snow Hill.

Julia learned to sew early in life, as most young women did back then. The last time I stopped by the Julia Purnell Museum, historian Linda Duyer told me about oral-history speculation that had Purnell developing her skills at an early age by sewing satin sheets destined to go inside the coffins sold at the general store.

She probably did lots of needlework through her later married years, but it would have been functional stuff — mending clothes, making quilts, and the like. Only after that fall at age 85 did she start approaching embroidery with the mindset of a painter, creating detailed depictions of the homes, churches, and gardens of Snow Hill. She had no formal training, so her work falls into the category of folk art that is often dubbed "outsider" or "visionary" in museum circles. There is an aspect of historical preservation to her output as well — the scenes she embroidered document buildings that no longer stand.

Purnell was incredibly prolific, making more than 1,000 works over a 15-year period. She gave away most of those pieces to friends and neighbors. Today, the museum has about 100 of her artworks — not just street scenes but quilts, dolls, and appliqué compositions as well.

Many "outsider" artists toil in anonymity during their lifetimes, but Purnell managed to enjoy a measure of acclaim. When she was 97, her son William sent a batch of her artworks to the prestigious Philadelphia Hobby Show. She was awarded a grand prize. She was inducted into the Hobby Hall of Fame in the early 1940s.

Purnell died just after her 100th birthday, in 1943. The year before, William had opened the Julia Purnell Museum in an outbuilding at his Snow Hill home. Eventually, the museum was moved into a former Catholic Church at 208 W. Market St.

The needleworks on display there have Victorian-style walnut frames built by William himself, who made his living as a commercial flower grower.

William's real passion, however, was a hobby that lay somewhere on the border between "collector" and "hoarder." His stuff, too, is on display in the museum. A bizarre model of an easy chair assembled from itty-bitty spruce twigs is attributed to an unnamed inmate in a New Jersey prison. The three "dressed fleas" on display are exactly that—tiny flea carcasses decked out in elaborate costumes, as per the practice of a bizarre folk-art phenomenon native to Mexico. There is a magnifying glass to help visitors inspect the piece, which consists of three flea dioramas, each about the size of a penny.

Other items have found their way to the museum over the years as well. The old steamship whistle from the *Morro Castle* is here—the vessel wrecked off the coast of New Jersey in 1934, killing 137 in an infamous disaster. The old projector from Snow Hill's long-gone Outten Theater is here, too—an interpretive note nearby says that Westerns played at the theater on Fridays and Saturdays, while Mondays and Tuesdays were reserved for "better movies." Personal aside: I actually didn't know until reading this that there were "better movies" than old Westerns.

THE WILMINGTON, DEL. RIVERFRONT

Jamestown, Plymouth Rock, St. Mary's City, ... Wilmington? Bear with me: The notion isn't as farfetched as you might think. At first glance, the journey at hand here appears a thoroughly 21st-century affair, seeing as it involves a leisurely stroll along the gleaming Riverwalk development that has taken shape in recent decades along the Christina River in Delaware's biggest city. There will be modern diversions aplenty along the way—big museums, fancy eateries, green spaces, even miniature golf.

But echoes of the past abound as well. Riverwalk meanders in the footsteps of shipbuilders, railroad titans, and immigrant laborers from centuries gone by. The river it follows once presented a key, nerve-racking obstacle for slaves on the run toward freedom along the Underground Railroad. And then there is the most distant echo, from the very first wave of

European adventurers who sailed far from home hoping to settle a wild New World.

How Swede It Is

First, an introductory detour: A few blocks east of the Riverwalk, along residential Church Street, stands an old stone church of "rugged strength," surrounded on four sides by a sprawling graveyard full of shade trees. Known as "Old Swedes," it ranks as the oldest church in the country that's still standing as originally built and still being used as a house of worship. The walnut pulpit inside is the nation's oldest without any qualification.

Those landmark rankings get at an underappreciated truth: Wilmington is one of our country's oldest cities, neck and neck with Boston and a length ahead of Philadelphia. The back story on Old Swedes leads right back to the Christina River, which takes its name from Queen Christina of Sweden.

One of the best-educated women of the 17th century, she danced to her own tune in life. Women back then were expected to marry, especially women in royal families. Christina refused to tie the knot. Women back then were expected to dress like, well, women. Christina preferred men's clothing. Her most dramatic detour came late in life, when she walked away from her throne voluntarily, converting to Catholicism and moving to Rome.

Sweden ranked as a fairly big global power in Christina's day. At first, the young queen and her court watched from a distance as England, Holland, and France started sending ships and colonists across the ocean. But eventually, they decided that Sweden, too, deserved a piece of the New World pie.

In the fall of 1637, the Swedish South Company launched two ships, *Fogel Grip* and *Kalmar Nyckel*, that landed on our shores 18 short years after the *Mayflower's* famous arrival in Massachusetts. I tell the story of that momentous voyage in Chapter 17, which is focused on old-school tall ships, including a replica of that *Kalmar Nyckel*.

For now, suffice it to say that the colony didn't stick. The Dutch took control of New Sweden in 1654. A decade after that, the British moved in. These big-picture regime changes are what history texts tend to focus on, but sometimes all that hullabaloo among the higher-ups doesn't have that much of an impact on the "little" people.

The Dutch did give the boot to the governor of the Swedish colony, but "otherwise life was little changed." Things actually got better when the English arrived, as they lightened the regulatory and tax loads around the shipping trade. Those original Swedish settlers just kept on keeping on, making their way by farming, fur trading, and whatever else needed doing.

Eventually, folks back in the mother country took notice of their resilience. In 1698, Sweden sent missionaries to help out their American brethren, and that's when everyone got about the business of building a proper Swedish church. Today, visitors enter the Old Swedes property through a small museum and gift shop located in Hendrickson House, a typical Swedish homestead from the early 1700s. A tour guide leads the way through the graveyard and into the church, pointing out lots of interesting details along the way. A smidgeon of colonial-era graffiti is kinda sorta still visible on one wall. So, too, are the names of donors carved into that ancient walnut pulpit.

Leave time to wander that graveyard after the tour. Time has turned its tricks here. Some stones are all but buried in the grass. Others are listing at odd angles, their inscriptions obscured by swaths of lichen. Depending on how you regard cemeteries, it will seem either drop-dead gorgeous or spooky as all get out.

A Bridge to Freedom

Riverwalk begins in earnest at a modest bit of green space called Tubman-Garrett Park that sits along the Christina between King and Market streets. Wilmington began life near here as itty-bitty Willington, named for landowner Thomas Willing. The town didn't really take off until Quaker merchant William Shipley of Ridley, Pa. played the role of good husband and heeded his wife's intuition.

> In about 1728, ... Elizabeth Shipley had a strange dream. She dreamed that she was traveling through countryside she had never seen before. She rode to the top of a hill [and] saw beautiful country below her. A wide river was glistening in the sun. Two other rivers flowed into it. The land in the valley around those rivers was filled with green meadows and tall forests. A voice told her that she and her family would live in that valley someday.

Seven years later, Elizabeth made a pilgrimage to visit some distant Quaker communities. She took one look at Willington and decided it was that old dream come true. The Shipleys moved shortly thereafter, then set about transforming Willington into a haven for fellow Quakers, quite a few of whom followed them south from Pennsylvania.

The ever-so-slight change in the town's name was a clever affair. In the aftermath of a civic-affairs argument that left Shipley and Willing at odds, the Quaker decided to rechristen Willington in sound-alike fashion after Spencer Compton, the

British Earl of Wilmington. Compton never set foot in the city that bears his title.

By the mid-1700s, Wilmington ranked as a rising colonial star, passing nearby New Castle as Delaware's biggest town. During the Revolutionary War, the city saw bits of action that amount to footnotes in today's history books. An early naval battle took place off the mouth of the Christina in 1776. The following year, George Washington visited, parking his army in the nearby countryside while getting ready for the Battle of Brandywine. That disastrous affair led first to the fall of both Wilmington and Philadelphia and then to the grueling winter the Continental Army passed at Valley Forge, Pa.

Washington's army triumphed in the end, of course, but the liberties that victory secured didn't apply to all of his countrymen in the nation's early years. Slavery remained legal in Delaware through the Civil War, though it was always relatively rare here in Wilmington, with its sizeable population of abolitionist Quakers.

The name of Tubman-Garrett Park honors two of the most courageous activists along the Underground Railroad, Thomas Garrett and Harriet Tubman. Born on Maryland's Eastern Shore, Tubman escaped slavery as a young woman, then returned south time and again to lead others to freedom in the north, often along routes that passed through Wilmington.

My book, *Tubman Travels: 32 Underground Railroad Journeys on Delmarva*, tells many true-life tales of Tubman's heroics. Stories about Garrett are in those pages, too. Like William Shipley before him, the Quaker Garrett found his way to Wilmington from Pennsylvania as a young man. He then devoted most of the rest of his life to helping runaways.

No one knows for sure how many slaves Garrett helped on the way to freedom, but it was certainly in the hundreds. When slavery was abolished in Delaware in 1865, the black community of Wilmington made an impromptu procession of gratitude to Garrett's house, placing him in an open carriage and throwing a wreath of flowers over his shoulders.

Tubman and Garrett worked together on several occasions. The Christina River was a sort of tipping point for runaways on the journey to freedom, as it was the final big geographic hurdle on the way into the free state of Pennsylvania. Runaways reached that hurdle right here at this park—the modern-day incarnation of the Market Street bridge is on the right when you're facing the river.

An earlier version of that structure looms large in the story of Tubman's run for freedom with a group that included Josiah Bailey. Bailey's master had put an enormous price on his head, $1,500. By the time his group arrived in Wilmington, bounty hunters had gathered at this bridge like a flock of vultures.

Tubman sent out a call for help through the Underground Railroad grapevine, and Garrett answered that call by devising a clever plan. On a November morning, a team of bricklayers made their way in a wagon across the bridge from north to south. They made a raucous display of themselves, singing and shouting all the way, seemingly en route to just another day of labor. That evening, this same group returned, crossing the bridge from south to north and repeating the same raucous display. No one thought to search the wagon where Josiah Bailey and his fellow runaways lay hidden under stacks of bricks.

The centerpiece of Tubman-Garrett Park is a sculpture of these two champions of freedom. A marker nearby introduces another interesting twist of African-American history—this park is the modern-day home of the "Big Quarterly," the nation's oldest continuous celebration of black culture.

Now held in August, that event dates to the first decade of the 1800s, back before Harriet Tubman was even born. After the free black Methodist minister Peter Spencer grew disenchanted with the segregationist ways of his congregation, he broke away and founded the African Union Methodist Church. Starting in 1814, Spencer's congregation hosted one of the quarterly annual meetings of black Methodists from all over the Mid-Atlantic. Here is a taste of what that event was like in the 1930s:

> The feasting starts ... early in the morning, and the menu consists in part of fried chicken, chicken potpie, ham and cabbage, hot corn pone, greens, and side meat, frankfurters, watermelons, and drinks, vari-colored "ades," pig's feet, and dishes of unknown origin. ... [The] Big Quarterly presents a kaleidoscopic mass of humanity, vari-colored in dress and hue of skin—sleek, slender, buxom, and fat. Milling throngs of primitive folk are gathered to worship their God, shouting, singing, praying and giving vent to unbounded enthusiasms. ... This is a day of joy, gladness, and freedom.

Industrial Powerhouse

Riverwalk kicks into gear just across Market Street at the Riverfront Market, where you will be able to sample from an eclectic mix of dining stalls and do some shopping as well. My wife, Jill, and I made our most recent Riverwalk journey on foot, but you could opt for the river taxi instead during the warmer months. There are six different stops along the way where you can hop on or off, or you can sign on for a themed tour geared toward history buffs, families, or wine lovers.

You will find a bevy of cultural stalwarts in gleaming new buildings along the route, including the Delaware Theatre

Company, the Delaware Contemporary art museum, the Delaware Children's Museum, and the Delaware Sports Museum and Hall of Fame. Restaurants abound, with several offering expansive outdoor seating areas that overlook the river. The minor-league Wilmington Blue Rocks play baseball within walking distance.

The Riverwalk powers that be have done a good job honoring the history of the Christina riverfront amid all of these modern amenities. Historic markers dot the walkway. A clever Constitution Yards beer garden is full of old freight cars, which Wilmington manufacturers built in great numbers back in the day. The dramatic Dravo Plaza is named for a shipbuilding firm that did yeoman's duty during World War II.

An estimated 10,000 ships were built here between the age of schooners and those World War II years. Among the biggest firms on the Christina River in those decades were Harlan & Hollingsworth; Pusey and Jones; and Jackson & Sharp. The shipyards here were at the vanguard of the industry, pioneering the development of ironclad ships around the time of the Civil War. Many branched out into other product lines in time, such as the aforementioned railroad and trolley cars.

The jobs that opened up in these facilities drew hordes of newcomers to town—the city's population went from 8,500 in 1840 to 30,000 in 1870 to 76,000 in 1900 to 110,000 in 1920. The jobs those firms offered were dirty and demanding, by modern-day standards. In 1860, workers at Harlan & Hollingsworth toiled 60 hours over a six-day week. Shifts ran 7am to 6pm on five of those days, with one 45-minute lunch break. The company let workers leave at 4:30pm on Saturdays.

Back to the Future

When the manufacturing sector went into decline after World War II, the Christina waterfront was left littered with abandoned and deteriorating facilities. The Riverfront Wilmington project that created Riverwalk began back in the 1990s. From the get-go, it was a back-to-the-future affair, designed to return the Christina River to its rightful place as a hub of the city's economic activity.

The success of that endeavor will be obvious to anyone who takes the walk outlined here. At the southern end of that journey, you will find an extra layer to that back-to-the-future business in a pair of nature-oriented attractions, the DuPont Environmental Education Center and the 212-acre Russell W. Peterson Urban Wildlife Refuge. Both facilities offer visitors a glimpse into the more distant past, before the arrival of Swedish and Dutch and English colonists.

The Delaware Indians lived here then, hunting, fishing, and farming the vast bank of marshlands that spread inland from the Delaware River. They called this area *Maax-waas Unk*, "Bear Place," because it was near the *Maax-waas Hanna*, the "Bear River," which got its name because it flowed west into the land of the Susquehannock Indians, aka the "Bear People."

The DuPont education center is housed up in an observation tower overlooking the wildlife refuge and offering lovely views of the city. Here, you can also connect with the Jack A. Markell Bike Trail, which runs for seven miles to New Castle, a history-laden town on the banks of the Delaware River that's well worth a visit, too.

CONNECTIONS
• Riverfront Wilmington and Riverwalk
riverfrontwilm.com; 302.425.4890
• New Castle County Tourism
dscc.com/newcastlecounty.html; 302.655.7221
• Tubman-Garrett Riverfront Park
riverfrontwilm.com/directory/tubman-garrett-riverfront-park;
302.425.4890
Between King and Market streets on the Christina River,
Wilmington, Del.
• River Taxi Wilmington
wilmwaterattractions.com/river-taxi; 302.425.4890
• DuPont Environmental Education Center
delawarenaturesociety.org/centers/dupont-environmental-
education-center; 302.656.1490
1400 Delmarva Ln., Wilmington, Del.
• Russell W. Peterson Urban Wildlife Refuge
visitdelaware.com/listings/russell-w-peterson-urban-wildlife-
refuge/365; 302.656.1490
1400 Delmarva Ln., Wilmington, Del.

NEARBY TRIPS: A list of other trips on the upper Delmarva
Peninsula is on page 7.

Way Back Machine
Whaling Days in Wilmington
When thinking about the whaling ships of yore, your mind
probably runs up to New England. But the Mid-Atlantic region
had its whaling moments as well, with operations based up in
New York along the Hudson River and down here in Delaware,
too, where the Wilmington Whaling Company was launched in
the 1830s.

Whaling was a high-risk, high-reward proposition built on the success of risky, round-the-world voyages that could take two or three years. Alas, the Wilmington operation never really hit the jackpot. The company lasted about a decade, done in by an economic depression that set in across the country during the 1840s.

The [whaling] adventure ... gave [Wilmington] one of its most picturesque aspects in the ... [celebrations that greeted the] return of vessels [that had been] away to the Pacific around Cape Horn. ... A shot was fired from Whalers' Wharf when a returning vessel was sighted. With the sound, most of the town stopped work and went to greet the fishermen and sailors. If the voyage had been successful, the captain was "chaired." Husky sailors secured a chair at a tavern, seated the captain, and raised the chair on poles across their shoulders. Thus they bore him up one street, down another, and back to the inn, while he received congratulations of the inhabitants who lined the streets or joined the procession.

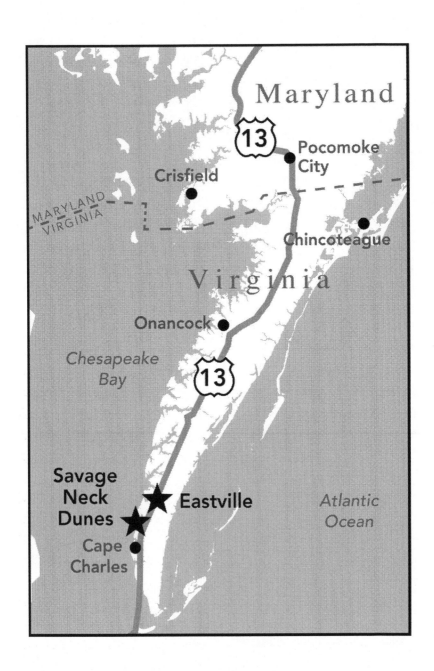

Maryland

13

Pocomoke City

Crisfield

MARYLAND
VIRGINIA

Chincoteague

Virginia

Onancock

Chesapeake Bay

13

Savage
Neck
Dunes

Eastville

Atlantic
Ocean

Cape
Charles

Road Trip #8

Eastville, Va. & Savage Neck

No one knows the back story on Thomas Savage. Which town in England did he call home? What sort of family was he born into? Why did that family ship him off, all alone, to the New World? All we know for sure is that he was about 13 years old on Jan. 2, 1608 when he stepped off of a boat that brought supplies and a fresh batch of settlers to the fledgling colony of Jamestown, Va.

Young Thomas walked down that plank into a colony teetering on the brink of destruction. Some 100 of the nearly 150 settlers who had landed at Jamestown the previous year were dead. Many fell to disease and starvation. Others were killed by Indians.

What happened to Thomas in this strange New World strikes me as something better fit for a Hollywood coming-of-age movie than the dry history books where I learned about his incredible adventure. The boy was soon assigned to join

Captain John Smith and a party of 30 on a diplomatic mission to the village of the most important Indian chief around, Powhatan.

The older white men in that party cut a crazy-sounding deal with the chief. They handed young Thomas Savage over to the Indians, while receiving in return a young Indian boy to take back to Jamestown. It was the first of several such exchanges between natives and newcomers in those years, with the idea apparently being that it would be good if a handful of individuals on each side had a grasp of the language and culture of the other.

That's food for thought on a three-plus mile drive down the winding, two-lane Savage Neck Road (Route 634) as it runs through the countryside outside of historic Eastville, Va. to a peninsula with the same name as the road. Out here, you will be able to follow a footpath out to a glorious run of sand dunes and beach overlooking the broad Chesapeake Bay.

Across the Great Divide

What went through 13-year-old Thomas Savage's mind when those older white men walked away, leaving him behind? How wide were his eyes in those first hours, surveying his exotic new surroundings? Did he have any sense for the big picture here, how he might well be the very first white man to live among these natives in this New World? Think about this, too: When is some Hollywood director going to latch onto this concept?

You've probably guessed by now that Savage Neck gets its name from the fact that Thomas Savage ended up on the Eastern Shore some years after his teenage adventures. We will see soon enough how that happened, and why. Back in that Indian village, though, the teenager probably got to know the famous Indian princess Pocahontas quite well—she was Powhatan's daughter, after all.

Another young boy who got sent off to live with the Indians a little bit later in this period reported that he and his compadres were treated reasonably well. They even got to dine with regularity at the chief's "oune Table mess." But there were tensions, too. At one point in Thomas's first year with the Indians, Powhatan exiled the teenager after some negotiations with white men at Jamestown failed to lead to the release of Indian prisoners.

Powhatan soon changed his mind, however. He sent Pocahontas herself off to find Thomas and bring him back into the tribal fold. Later in life, Pocahontas would recall Thomas as someone her father "loved exceedingly."

Things got dicey again for Savage in 1610, with the outbreak of an Anglo-Powhatan War. That was the first of the innumerable conflicts that unfolded in the centuries that followed, pitting Native American nations against European settlers in the lands that would become the United States. Powhatan nearly wiped out the Jamestown colony in that first conflict, by cutting off all trade and closing off hunting grounds in the midst of drought conditions that had the settlers scrounging for food.

The war was a brutal affair on both sides. Soldiers from Jamestown burned down whole villages and went out of their way to desecrate the sacred graves of dead chiefs. Meanwhile, the Indians tortured prisoners in horrific fashion, including an incident in which the women of one village used mussel shells to slowly skin an English soldier alive.

Unnerved by such atrocities, Thomas Savage decided to skedaddle. He invented a white lie for Powhatan about an errand that needed doing in Jamestown, then took off and didn't look back. As things turned out, he picked the winning side. Before Powhatan managed to finish off the colony, ships from Europe arrived at Jamestown carrying critical supplies and another fresh batch of settlers.

Back with the Europeans, Thomas Savage built a new life for himself. It's not clear what he did for a living at first, but he got called into duty with some regularity as a translator in talks with various Indian leaders. One such case came in 1621, when he accompanied a Jamestown official on a trading expedition across the Chesapeake Bay to the Eastern Shore.

By all indications, Savage got along famously with an Indian chief there. In some books and on some historical signage, this chief is identified as Debedeavon, but that seems to be a case of mistaken identity—Debedeavon didn't come along until many years later. Historians now think this chief was named Esmy Shichans, though he is more famously known by a nickname, "The Laughing King." No one knows for sure how he got this moniker, but it's fun to imagine the look of his face in any case.

The Laughing King made a gift to Savage of the large tract of land now known as Savage Neck. Thomas and his wife, Hannah, were probably living here full time with their infant son, John, by 1625. Savage did pretty well for himself in the fur-trading business. He did a lot of farming as well—an early census record says he had a house, a barn, a boat, and two servants at "Savages Choice."

Alas, Savage died young, in 1633. His demise is shrouded in the same sort of mystery that surrounds his earliest years back in England, but what we do know is that the Savage family survived and thrived through the centuries, leading right up to the present. Some of Savage's descendants still live in this area. Historians regard them as the oldest colonial family whose descendants can be traced fully through the historical record.

Today, most people who make the ride out through Savage's old stomping grounds do so to visit the 300-acre Savage Neck Dunes Natural Area Preserve. A small, well-marked parking area is where you can set off on a sweet walk of about a mile through forests and alongside a stream. Nature-oriented markers serve up a good introduction to the succession of ecological zones that unfold at the edge of the bay here.

In the end, the dirt underfoot turns to sand, and the trail rises up and over the dunes, ending in a glorious stretch of beach that's often quite isolated. The last time I visited, I wandered that beach for a couple of hours and enjoyed a lunch I'd brought along while perched atop a piece of driftwood. As I looked out over the bay, my mind kept picturing the vessel that brought Thomas Savage across from Jamestown in 1621 for his meeting with jovial Esmy Shichans.

A Birth of Freedom in Eastville

When you manage to tear yourself away from the beach at Savage Neck, head into Eastville and find your way to the pretty Courthouse Green, which has been at the center of life in the seat of Northampton County since about 1715. Court cases were being heard near here even before that—starting in 1677, sessions were held at the long-gone home of a man named Henry Matthews.

The Green is chock full of interesting old buildings. The older of the two courthouses here went up in the 1730s. After a second courthouse went up, that old one morphed for a while into a tavern. The "new" courthouse on the Green dates to 1899. Inside, the clerk's office houses the longest continuous set of court records anywhere in the country, dating back to the 1630s. One reason those records remain is that local officials in Civil War times studiously ignored an order from the state that all important paperwork be transported to the state capital of Richmond, which would soon be burned by Union troops.

As a result, visitors today can review records that include the marks of Indian chiefs and a document sealing the deal on a property transfer involving none other than Daniel Boone. Back outside, you'll also find an Old Clerk's Office (1830s), a Debtor's Prison (1814), and a Confederate monument (1914) on the Green.

Freedom is a word worth thinking about while wandering around here. Take a minute to imagine the scene that unfolded on Aug. 3, 1776 when a messenger arrived in town after a month-long ride from Philadelphia. The copy of the Declaration of Independence he had in his saddlebag was read aloud to the populace from the courthouse steps.

But Eastville has another, earlier claim to revolutionary fame. The context of that claim is a complicated affair, tied up in a messy bit of regime change back in England as well as contentious local debates over dealing with Indians. Here's the quick version: Virginia began life as a private enterprise ruled by soldiers in military fashion, then morphed into something more traditionally colonial as the royal powers that be in England asserted control. Virginians had a measure of autonomy in that arrangement through the so-called House of Burgesses.

Formed in 1619, the first democratically elected legislative body in the American colonies was set up to include members from various geographic regions, including Northampton County. But colonial leaders on the western shore ignored this little detail in the late 1640s, when the House of Burgesses went right ahead passing laws and imposing taxes despite the fact that no one had been elected or appointed during those years to represent the people of Northampton.

Eventually, the locals decided they'd had enough. The last straw came with the imposition of a stiff new tax on tobacco. On March 30, 1652, county leaders penned what is in retrospect an incredible letter:

> Forasmuch as wee had neither summons for Ellecton of Burgesses nor voyce in their Assemblie ... wee conceive that wee may Lawfullie ptest agt the pceedings in the Act of Assemlie for public Taxacons ...

Fight through that old language and those odd spellings, and you will get to the bottom line: No taxation without representation, please. This "Northampton Protest" was the first time anyone went public with such a complaint in the colonies—remarkably, it happened 124 years before the Declaration of Independence and nearly four decades before the same concept was spelled out across the Atlantic in the landmark English Bill of Rights of 1689. The protest was a success, by the way—those western shore leaders waved a white flag and agreed to most of Northampton's demands.

There is one last site to see here at the Courthouse Green—a stone monument that honors the memory of the "The Laughing King" who gave Thomas Savage all the land now known as Savage Neck. This is one of those markers where that king, Esmy Shichans, is confused with a later figure, Debedeavon.

Wander into the town proper and two interesting old buildings will grab your attention straight away. The lovely Eastville Inn (16422 Courthouse Rd.), with its long porch, started life in 1780 as the Taylor House tavern. Several chefs have tried to make a go of it in the old place in recent decades, but it housed a catering-only affair as of this writing. Nearby, the two-story Old Brick Store (1820) was built with two front doors, one perched right atop the other. Goods reached that upstairs door by way of a pulley system—the space was used for storage.

Eastville wasn't always as quiet as it is today. Right around the time that Old Brick Store was going up, the town boasted a coach maker, a harness maker, four stores, two taverns, a shoemaker, a tailor, a house painter, a hatter, a cabinetmaker, a blacksmith, and several offices for attorneys and doctors. Back then, Eastville was the southernmost stop on an old stagecoach route. Carriages departed daily at 6:30am; at the end of a 12-hour-long day of traveling, passengers would overnight in Horntown, 55 miles away. They hadn't even reached the Maryland line.

Three "caster oil manufacturies" are also listed in the old records. A vegetable oil squeezed out of the poisonous castor bean plant, this stuff was used in colonial times to make soap, paint, and lubricants. Physicians used it, too, in horrifying fashion. These were the days when bloodletting and leeches were believed to be reliable ways to suck diseases out of the body. Castor oil was used in a similar manner, as historians David and Elizabeth Armstrong point out in *The Great American Medicine Show*:

Calomel remained in favor, usually combined with medicinal wine, laxative salts, opium, and castor oil. Used to cleanse the system of foul, bilious liquids, this poison caused patients to salivate uncontrollably, bleed from the gums, and evacuate the bowels without restraint. Patients suffered horribly, losing teeth, developing sores on tongue and cheeks, dreading the doctor's call. A popular verse went: "Doctor comes with free good will, but ne'er forgets his calomel."

Stroll around town some more and you will see a number of lovely old homes representing architectural styles that run from Greek Revival to Gothic Revival and Italianate to Victorian. Be sure to find your way to old Christ Church (16304 Courthouse Rd.) on the north end of the downtown—it's the fourth oldest still-standing church on Virginia's Eastern Shore. Back in 1828, construction costs ran all of $2,960.

A couple of worthwhile side trips are a short drive away, if you're in the mood for more exploring. To the south is Cheriton, a town that grew up around the railroad line that came through in the late 1800s. The downtown there is small, but has its share of interesting old churches and small-town businesses. To the north, in the countryside outside of Machipongo, is the first-rate Barrier Islands Center, which tells incredible stories about the communities that once occupied the islands off of the Eastern Shore's Atlantic coast.

CONNECTIONS
• Eastern Shore of Virginia Tourism
visitesva.com; 757.331.1660
• Northampton County Chamber of Commerce
northamptoncountychamber.com/our-area.html; 757-678-0010
• Savage Neck Dunes Natural Area Preserve
dcr.virginia.gov/natural-heritage/natural-area-preserves/savage; 757.787.5989

NEARBY TRIPS: A list of other trips on the lower Delmarva Peninsula is on page 7.

Way Back Machine
'One Shall Not Call the Other Any Vile Names'

If you have a collection of court records going back nearly four centuries—as they do in Eastville—you are bound to have a few doozies in the bunch. In 2007, a team at the Northampton County clerk's office put together a 30-page booklet of highlights, *Exploring the Oldest Continuous Court Records of America*. One involves a matrimonial dispute from November 1714.

> When John Custis courted Frances Parke, many ardent and love-filled letters passed between them. After their marriage, discord began, and marital bliss was at an end. Their disputes and quarrels became so strident that the couple was forced to seek redress in the form of Articles of Agreement in Northampton County Court.

These articles cover five sides of a legal-size sheet of paper and list a dozen marital issues that needed to be resolved. The bottom line:

> It is mutually agreed between both parties that one shall not call the other any vile names or use any language of oath but behave themselves to each other as becomes a good husband and wife. Frances will not interfere with John's management of his business, John will not intermeddle with Frances' domestic affairs.

There are more fun oddities in that collection, including the will of one Mary Scott. Most wills filed in the courts of Northampton back in the 1700s begin with a common phrase, "In the name of God Amen," and proceed from there into the details of estate distribution. But when Scott fell ill in 1789, she filed a document that started like this: "In the name of God *a woman* ..."

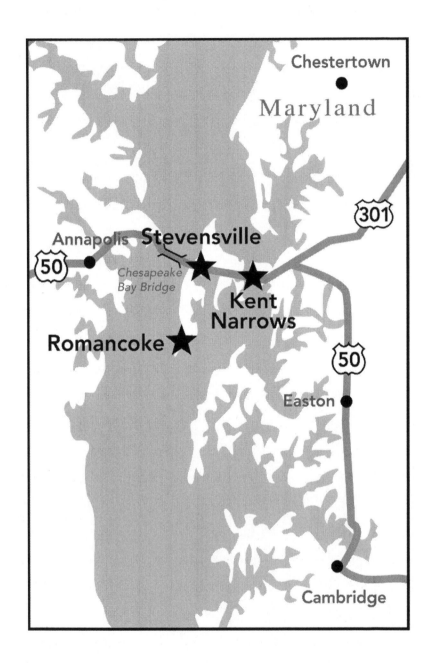

Chestertown

Maryland

301

Annapolis Stevensville

50

Chesapeake
Bay Bridge

Kent
Narrows

Romancoke

50

Easton

Cambridge

ROAD TRIP #9

KENT ISLAND, MD.

Every year, millions of travelers looking to get away from their busy big-city lives catch their first glimpse of the Delmarva Peninsula in the shoreline of Kent Island. That view from the Chesapeake Bay Bridge can be quite the powerful experience, judging by how many times over the years I've heard folks marvel at the way their stress levels ease the moment that Eastern Shore comes into view.

Kent Island is indeed a sweet, scenic destination, but there is a bit of irony in this, considering how much stress and contention the people of the place have endured over the centuries while trying to defend their turf against one set of invaders after another. The identity of those enemy hordes is interesting: First came Marylanders; then came the federal government; and then came all those tourists across that bridge.

In the Bitter Beginning
Kent Islanders have every right to have a chip on their collective shoulder. Across the Chesapeake Bay in Southern Maryland,

historic St. Mary's City sucks up all the tourism and media attention that goes with being the founding settlement of the Free State. They have the living history park. They have the replica sailing ships.

In point of fact, however, the first permanent settlement in what would become Maryland went up here on Kent Island, on the horizon that comes into view to the south while crossing that bridge from the western shore. William Claiborne explored the waters out that way in the 1620s, armed with a license from the British crown to trade with Indians under the auspices of Jamestown and its Virginia overlords.

He used that authority to buy Kent Island from local Indians. Then, in 1631, three years before the famed *Ark* and *Dove* sailed into St. Mary's City, Claiborne brought some 100 men onto Kent Island, where they put up a fort. The island has been home to Europeans and their descendants ever since.

Everything looked quite promising for Claiborne's venture until folks back in England changed the rules in the middle of the game. In 1632, King Charles I signed a charter awarding all Chesapeake lands north of the Potomac River to George Calvert, aka Lord Baltimore. This development pushed Claiborne's Kent Island out of Virginia and into the new *Terra Maria*, named in honor of Queen Henrietta Maria.

Claiborne raised quite a ruckus. The first skirmishes were legal affairs, fought by way of petitions arguing over this clause in Claiborne's license versus that one in Lord Baltimore's charter. Things got physical soon enough, however, with battles breaking out between newbie Marylanders and Claiborne's Virginians. In the midst of this, Claiborne sailed back to England to confer with business partners and file more legal claims. Alas, the guy he put in charge in his absence waved a white flag, surrendering the island to Maryland.

Next came the crazy days that historians refer to as "The Plundering Time." A furious Claiborne sailed back and re-conquered Kent Island. Meanwhile, a cantankerous bunch of Puritans who couldn't stomach life under the Catholic Calverts took the whole Maryland colony by force. Back in England, Charles I was losing his head, quite literally, on charges of treason.

Three often bloody years later, things got sorted out with Maryland back in the hands of the Calvert family. Claiborne remained bitter about this turn of events for the rest of his days. Just before his death in 1677 — three decades after "The Plundering Time" — he was still filing paperwork with the king, claiming that Kent Island rightfully belonged to him.

No physical remnants of those Claiborne days remain today on Kent Island. In all probability, the settlement he built was on land that is now under water. The best way to get a feel for the landscape in that general area is by heading south on pretty Romancoke Road, where you can take time to stop at little Matapeake Beach and stroll or bike along the South Island Trail that runs parallel to the road for six or so miles.

The closest you can get to the old fort is along Kent Point Road, which angles off to the right. There is no place to stop or markers to see that way, so take that drive only to enjoy a pretty run of farmland and waterfront mansions that ends in a little watermen's enclave. If you stick with (or return to) southbound Romancoke Road, it will end at a pretty fishing pier that looks out onto Eastern Bay. Ferryboats running from Annapolis used to stop here in the early 1900s on their way to a Talbot County town called, quite appropriately, Claiborne.

The 20th-Century Invaders

That view of Claiborne presents a sideways route into one of the two more recent invasions that have rolled onto Kent Island. For three centuries after Claiborne put up his fort, this remained a thoroughly isolated outpost accessible mainly by boat, with overland traffic from the western shore relegated to a ridiculously roundabout route that involved circling the top of the Chesapeake Bay at Elkton.

That all changed in July 1952, when the Chesapeake Bay Bridge opened for business. That project had quite a bit of support here on Kent Island and all around the Eastern Shore. Many folks liked the prospect of quicker trips to the big cities. They liked, too, that new jobs might arise to serve the throngs of people expected to use the bridge. Business leaders at the beach resorts loved the idea for obvious reasons.

But strong opposition arose as well. Shipping companies thought the span might present a navigation hazard during storms and fog. Ferryboat companies fought the project tooth and nail. Lots of locals feared that the bridge would bring an end to those old and isolated ways of life. Some local musicians penned a ditty that became an anthem for this anti-bridge crowd (it remains pretty popular today, actually).

> [A] dance band … got a rise from local partygoers when it played "The Old Gray Mare" to new lyrics. The chorus ended, "We don't give a damn for the whole state of Maryland/We're from the Eastern Shore."

The most public face of the opposition belonged to state Sen. Henry Balch, who hailed from Talbot County. A lawyer and a World War I veteran, Balch was rightly famous for his colorful way with words:

The proposal to build the Bay Bridge is extravagance to the nth power. The spending necessary would exceed the aggregate spending of every drunken sailor since John Paul Jones.

Balch and his compatriots lost this war, of course, though he did fight to the bitter end, filibustering away in a last-minute speech that delayed a final vote in favor of the bridge by a few hours.

You will see for yourself how things played out. The main drag of Route 50 is mostly a sea of gas stations, fast food joints, and strip shopping centers. Expansive housing developments cover many nearby properties, especially those where the waterfront is within sniffing distance. This is why, when I first moved to the Eastern Shore, I didn't have much use for Kent Island—my knowledge of the place just didn't go beyond that highway yet.

Eventually, I got off the main drag and discovered a fun, idiosyncratic destination. As road trips go, Kent Island is a mix-and-match affair. There is no real must-see attraction at the top of the agenda. Instead, you'll need to sort through a bunch of options and tailor an itinerary to your preferences.

If you are in a nature-loving mood, for instance, you should stay on Romancoke Road and cross over to the north side of Route 50. Turn left at a light onto Skipjack Drive into an industrial park, then go left again at Log Canoe Circle to find the parking area with access to Terrapin Park and the Cross Island Trail.

A short, easy footpath through the park leads out to a little beach with a cool view of the Chesapeake Bay Bridge. There, you can think about whether the TV show "Inside Edition" was right to name this the "scariest" bridge in the country. Back in the parking lot area, you can hop on the Cross Island Trail, which runs through nearby woods and across little streams for 6.5 miles to Kent Narrows, with a project in the works to extend the trail farther east.

After that, find your way into tiny downtown Stevensville, which is quite nearby, but tucked away at the intersection of Main Street and Love Point Road. Several antiques shops, a couple galleries, a restaurant, and a bakery were up and running on my last visit. You'll also find several interesting remnants of times gone by—an old post office here, the old bank there, and an old train station in the back corner of a little park. These are among the host of historic sites in Queen Anne's County that open their doors for inside tours one Saturday a month—you can check on that schedule through the Kent Island Heritage Society.

Two other buildings here in Stevensville are well worth pausing over. The first, on Love Point Road, is the old Lowery Hotel. Now privately owned, the building dates back to the Civil War. When overnight guests started arriving in 1883, a livery stable was part of the deal. By the early 1900s, facilities like the Lowery were becoming a big deal on Kent Island. At the height of the steamboat era, this was quite the convenient getaway from Baltimore.

The most famous of Kent Island's resorts was the Love Point Hotel, set on the northernmost tip of the island along Love Point Road. It was romantic as all get out, with sandy beaches, elegant porches, and long, lovely lanes perfect for strolling hand in hand. A poem from those days by Folger McKinsey sums things up:

Here comes the steamer, the lovers are here,
Jack with his daisy and John with his dear;
Soft crabs for dinner and oh, what a dream,

Peachcake for supper, and then the ice-cream!
Red roses fair on her cheeks of rose-red,
And these are the words that her true lover said:
"Good-by to the city,
To Love Point away;
The wind's on the water,
The boat's on the bay!
From toil and from trouble
Lighthearted we'll glide,
With lunch in a basket,
A girl at my side!"

The hotel closed in 1947, just as the state legislature was getting ready to approve construction of the Bay Bridge. You can take the pretty drive from Stevensville up to Love Point today, but the hotel building is gone—it burned in the 1960s—and there is no little park or other place to stop up that way.

A second building worth pausing over while in Stevensville is the former Christ Episcopal Church on Main Street. The congregation that worshipped here after the building went up in 1880 ranks among the nation's oldest Episcopal parishes, tracing its lineage clear back to the days of William Claiborne. The gorgeous Queen Anne-style affair has an unusual "lancet" chimney built with wooden pegs instead of nails.

The churchyard here is where Kent Islanders first marshaled their forces to fight off yet another threatened invasion. With World War I looming in 1917, the federal government decided to buy up the entire island and evict all of its residents. They were going to turn the place into a military "proving ground," where weapons are tested.

On the Monday evening of July 9, 1917, local civic leaders convened a meeting at Christ Episcopal that drew an overflow crowd ready to defend its turf. A Kent Island Home Preservation Committee took shape that night, and they soon headed off en masse to Washington, D.C. to press the issue. This is one battle the islanders won in the end. The bombing experiments the feds had in mind eventually found a home at Aberdeen Proving Ground, over on the western shore.

The Narrows and Beyond

The hero of that 1917 fight was James E. Kirwan, who by the time of his death in 1938 was known far and wide as "The Grand Old Man of Kent Island." You can get in touch with his story by finding your way to nearby Chester, where Kirwan's old house in the countryside at 641 Dominion Rd. is now a little museum.

Born in 1848, Kirwan was working aboard ships as a cabin boy and a cook by the age of 10. By 16, he was the owner of the *William Baynes*, the first of three schooners he would captain before age 25, at which point he gave up sailing and switched over to farming and shopkeeping.

His old general store was right here in the house, and its shelves are still full of goods from his day, most of them keepsakes that remained in family hands until they were donated to the heritage society. Kirwan's farm covered 300 acres—it had a lumber mill, a turtle farm, a cooper's mill, a blacksmith's shop, and much more. He served in the state senate and as a commander in the "oyster navy," but he remained most famous for his leadership of that march on Washington by the Kent Island Home Preservation Committee.

Offered over $3,000,000 for Kent Island, Mr. Kirwan was among the many who felt that there was not enough money in the mint to justify moving off the native heath.

Another sweet view of that native heath awaits at Kent Narrows, named for the waterway that runs right up through the island at the western edge of Chester. On the north side of the highway there, you can walk out to Ferry Point Park, a wishbone-shaped strip of land that extends out into the Chester River, serving up glorious views. The nearby Chesapeake Heritage & Visitors Center has brochures, exhibits, and restrooms. The Cross Island Trail is accessible from here as well.

Both sides of Kent Narrows offer an abundance of seafood options, ranging from simple outdoor tiki huts to fine-dining affairs. Kent Narrows might well have more outdoor tables than any other place on the Shore outside of the beach resorts. Be sure to check out the Maryland Watermen's Monument on the south side of the Narrows—it stands down near the base of Watermen's Memorial Bridge.

Last but not least, wander through Grasonville on the eastern side of the Narrows to find your way to the Chesapeake Bay Environmental Center, which offers a network of trails that wander through marshland and along shorelines, providing some great birdwatching opportunities. You can rent kayaks there in the warmer months as well.

CONNECTIONS
• Queen Anne's County Tourism
qac.org/151/tourism; 410.604.2100
Trails Guide: qac.org/1013/hiker-biker-trails
• Matapeake Beach
qac.org/1021/matapeake-clubhouse-beach; 410.758.0835
2010 Sonny Schulz Blvd., Stevensville, Md.
• Romancoke Pier

qac.org/facilities/facility/details/romancoke-pier-128;
410.758.0835
9700 Romancoke Rd., Stevensville, Md.
• Terrapin Nature Area
qac.org/facilities/facility/details/terrapin-nature-area-97;
410.758.0835
191 Log Canoe Circle, Stevensville, Md.
• Kent Island Heritage Society
kentislandheritagesociety.org
Kirwan House: 641 Dominion Rd., Chester, Md.
• Chesapeake Bay Environmental Center
bayrestoration.org; 410.827.6694
600 Discovery Ln., Grasonville, Md.

NEARBY TRIPS: A list of other trips on the upper Delmarva Peninsula is on page 7.

Way Back Machine
The Best Laid Plans

History is a funny thing. Once a big event is in the books, everything about the way it unfolded starts to look inevitable, like it was always bound to happen in just the way it did. So it goes here on Kent Island with the Chesapeake Bay Bridge.

But sometimes it's fun to play a game of "What if?" For instance: What if one of the various *other* bridge plans put forward over the years had been realized instead?

The 1907 Trolley Crossing: The earliest plan for a Chesapeake Bay crossing dates to 1907. At the time, business leaders in Baltimore were nervous, as railroad lines had begun making it easier and cheaper for Eastern Shore goods to get to Wilmington and Philadelphia. They got behind a proposal to build an electric trolley line between Baltimore and Chestertown.

The engineering firm Westinghouse, Church, Kerr & Co, Inc. delivered a plan that not only had the trolley crossing the Bay but also envisioned a 235-mile network of trolley tracks connecting all the major towns on the Shore. The price tag came in at $13 million, a number that seems to have scared everyone off.

The 1918 Double Decker: In the World War I era, Gov. Emerson C. Harrington got behind a plan to build a double-deck bridge linking the western shore town of Bay Shore with Tolchester Beach, on the Upper Eastern Shore in Kent County. One deck would have been for freight trains, and the second deck for passenger trolleys. The plan lost out to the launch of a new ferry service between Annapolis, Matapeake, and Claiborne.

The 1929 Tolchester Crossing: This is the one that came closest to actually happening. Both the Maryland legislature and the U.S. Congress signed off on the plan to build a bridge from the Baltimore suburb of Edgemere, near Hart-Miller Island, to Tolchester Beach. The politicians even went so far as to appropriate $500,000 to get the show on the road—then the stock market crashed.

Try, Try Again in the 1930s: Various bridge plans came and went during the 1930s. For the most part, these plans fell by the wayside because no federal funding ever materialized. The year 1937 seems to have been the first time that a crossing from Sandy Point in Annapolis to Kent Island entered the mix. That plan was still on the table when World War II broke out and put all bridge discussions on the back burner.

The Bridge at Last: Gubernatorial candidate William Preston Lane campaigned on a promise to get a bridge built at last, and the project was dubbed "Lane's Folly" by his opponents. But Lane actually delivered, and the first shovel went into the ground in January 1949. Three years later, the now ex-Governor Lane was a guest of honor in the first motorcade across the Chesapeake Bay Bridge. Between all the glad-handing and backslapping along the way, that motorcade took more than two hours to make the crossing, so that first ride across the span qualifies as the very first Bay Bridge traffic fiasco, too.

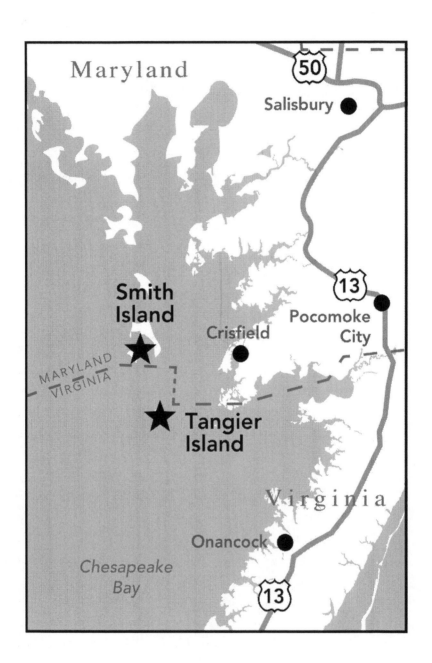

Maryland

Salisbury

Smith
Island

Crisfield

Pocomoke
City

MARYLAND
VIRGINIA

Tangier
Island

Virginia

Onancock

Chesapeake
Bay

ROAD TRIP #10

SMITH ISLAND, MD. &
TANGIER ISLAND, VA.

If we had any doubts that Smith Island, Md. would be a different sort of travel experience, they disappeared when we checked into our B&B, the Smith Island Inn, in the early afternoon and the owner told us we'd better start thinking about dinner. We hadn't had lunch yet. Both restaurants in Ewell close by 4pm.

That overnight trip marked 20 years of wedded bliss in my life. I decided to take my wife Jill to "the islands" to celebrate. Laugh if you like, but the trip was sweet as could be—endless hours of strolling and snapping pictures, a leisurely paddle along Levering Creek, and an early-morning crabbing excursion with a kindly local waterman.

Along with nearby Tangier Island, Va., Smith is the real island deal in the Chesapeake Bay. You don't get there by crossing a bridge. This trip involves a 40-minute boat ride that ıll leave you with a whole new notion of what it means to live out in the middle of nowhere.

'God Would Fight for the Good People'

Our journey began at the dock in Crisfield, Md., where big boats and small ones make regular runs out to both Smith and Tangier. You can also get to Tangier Island from the dock in Onancock, Va. If you are on the western shore, boats leave for Smith from Point Lookout, Md. and for Tangier from Reedville, Va.

We went with one of the smaller boats at Crisfield, the *Capt. Jason II*, whose captain is named Larry. There are benches in a little cabin for passengers feeling a need for shelter from the elements, but Jill and I chose to sit outside on this steamy day and watch the bay go by. The first mate, Hoss, came out now and again to check in on us. He showed us where the old Somers Cove Light used to stand. He pointed to a 50-foot-tall chimney towering in the distance, all that remains of the L.E.P. Dennis menhaden-processing plant that once operated to the south, on Old Island.

In the late 1800s, a whole community of workers lived out there in a sort of company town. The plant closed in the early 1900s, then burned in 1932. The place had a brief afterlife as a popular beach resort, but erosion took care of that in pretty short order. Old Island is now part of nearby Janes Island State Park, which is definitely worth a visit for paddling, hiking, and sightseeing while in the area.

We peppered Hoss with questions. One of our more pressing concerns was how bad the bugs might be in early August on Smith Island.

"Oh, I think they sprayed recently," he said, then paused a beat. "Usually, that's just enough to piss 'em off."

Once clear of Crisfield, the ride is mostly open water. Jill took a nap. I watched sunlight play on the waves. Workboats popped up now and again. I thought about how Indians would come out this way in big canoes to hunt and fish, perhaps as far back as 10,000 years ago. The experts don't think they had any permanent settlements on Smith or Tangier.

Eventually, a few spits of green grassland popped up. The *Capt. Jason II* powered down and then puttered into the harbor at Ewell, which is lined on both sides with eye-catching workboats and crab shacks. Ewell is one of three towns on Smith Island that have a combined population of fewer than 300, a number that has been shrinking steadily as more and more young people choose life on the mainland.

Legends abound here in the middle of the bay—some are true, some are false, and some are both. Capt. John Smith did not give Tangier its name because it reminded him of a place in the Mediterranean. And while he did, in fact, name an island after himself, it wasn't *this* Smith Island, but another one, much farther south. Smith's name for all the islands out this way was Russells Isles, after a doctor in his crew.

Then there is the matter of linguistics. Smith and Tangier residents talk with one-of-a-kind accents that sound strange and archaic to mainland ears, but linguists don't really buy into the story that this represents a miraculous surviving relic from the Elizabethan days of William Shakespeare. The accent is fascinating, to be sure, its uniqueness a measure of just how isolated these places have been for centuries. But in the end it's just an accent.

When Europeans first arrived in the Chesapeake Bay, there were other big islands out this way—Queens Ridge, Watts, and Shanks Fox among them. Those islands are now either barely visible or fully drowned. At first, white people weren't interested in all these islands, but that changed as the European population grew and land got a little harder to find. Still, the first few people to hold title to island lands didn't move to Smith or Tangier—they brought livestock out instead, then left the animals on their own to fatten themselves up.

Full-time residents finally moved in around the time of the Revolutionary War, when both Smith and Tangier had notorious reputations as nests of British loyalists, or "picaroons," who behaved more like thieves and pirates than soldiers. Real British soldiers came calling during the War of 1812—and the events that followed their arrival are the most famous in the annals of these two islands.

Joshua Thomas was in his mid-20s when he moved to Tangier in 1799. Six years later, he took a job shuttling some passengers to Pungoteague, Va. for a Methodist camp meeting. The Spirit grabbed hold of him there and never let go. By the time British warships arrived off Tangier in 1814, he was on his way to earning a place in history books as the "Parson of the Islands."

The British occupied Tangier with a force of 1,500 men, a mix of regular soldiers and escaped slaves who had signed up to fight in exchange for promises of freedom. They stayed for a while, then left to go burn Washington, D.C. When they returned, they had their sights set on Baltimore. Hearing this, Thomas tried to warn British officers off that destination, telling them that "God would fight for the good people in that city."

Before departing on Sunday, Sept. 11, a British commander asked Thomas to preach to his troops, explaining that this might be the last chance for some of his men to hear the word of God before they died in battle.

As I looked around on my congregation, I never had such feelings in my life; but I felt determined to give them a faithful warning, even if those officers with their keen glittering swords would cut me in pieces for speaking the truth.

Thomas preached some about sin, then moved onto the commandments, paying particular attention to "Thou shalt not kill." Then:

I told them it was given me from the Almighty that they could not take Baltimore, and would not succeed in their expedition.

No one cut Thomas in pieces that day — he would live to age 77. As for the Battle of Baltimore, that, of course, is where our National Anthem was born. When the British returned to Tangier in defeat — they would soon leave the Chesapeake Bay altogether — some soldiers pulled Thomas aside, telling him:

All the time we were fighting we thought of you, and what you told us. You seemed to be standing right before us, still, warning us against our attempt to take Baltimore.

A Perfect Day on the Water

Some folks visit Smith or Tangier island for an afternoon, enough time to walk around a bit and enjoy a traditional meal. Jill and I spent two overnights, and that time passed in the blink of an eye. We wandered the figure-eight-shaped streetscape of Ewell, admiring old houses and dawdling with our cameras near crab shacks and tied-up workboats. We paid a visit to Smith Island United Methodist Church. A sprawling, screened-in outdoor tabernacle stands nearby—they still hold an annual camp meeting here every July.

We stopped in the Smith Island Cultural Center and took in the well-done exhibits there. (Tangier has a similar place—the Tangier History Museum.) We grabbed bikes out back of our B&B and pedaled out to an even smaller town, Rhodes Point, which was called Rogues Point back when pirates and privateers used it as a hideout. On the way there, we passed a worried-looking family gathered near the island helipad, waiting, we assumed, for an airborne trip to a mainland emergency room.

We snuck into the Bayside Inn Restaurant for takeout just ahead of that 4pm deadline, then stored it in the fridge. There were bugs around, but they didn't seem all that pissed off.

The best hours of our trip were spent out on the water the next day. A number of watermen on Smith and Tangier islands take tourists out for a fee—the owner of our B&B had helped make arrangements so that we could do just that with Barry Bruce. We met Bruce in the predawn darkness, then hopped onto his workboat and crossed to the other side of the harbor, where the shack that serves as his "peeler pen" stands atop a pier.

Bruce was working the soft-crab market during those late summer days. Bare light bulbs hung over the trays full of water and scuttling crabs. Bruce checks on his peelers at least three times a day. When a crab reaches the culinary delight stage of molting, it ends up on ice in a corrugated cardboard box where four tidy rows number nine crabs each.

The inspection done, Bruce led us back out to the boat. Here in Ewell, most everyone is up and at it during the predawn darkness. One workboat after another was getting underway while we headed out.

Bruce grew up in the third of the Smith Island burgs, Tylerton. He started working the water with his father at age 12 and "fell in love with the job" immediately. By 16, he was running his own boat. A married father of two, he's a gracious host. Seeing Jill's fancy photo gear, he went out of his way to give her extra time and different angles to play with as distant workboats motored in front of a rising sun. Then he took a detour to show off the sprawling colony of brown pelicans that has found its way to Smith Island in recent years—the scene was beautiful beyond words, and I'm not exaggerating when I say that I expect to treasure forever the memory of that moment.

Bruce started the crabbing portion of his workday in a stretch of water known locally as the "Notches." Unhappy with the results there, he soon moved over to "Barn Cove." He crabs by scraping, dropping a metal cage into the water and using his motor to drag it along the bottom. He raises that cage at the end of every run by way of hydraulics, then pulls out any keepers that show up amid the grass and muck.

"A couple of years ago we weren't picking up any little crabs," Bruce said. On this day, he was tossing one juvenile after another back into the water, giving him a hopeful feeling about future harvests. He explained some about the economics of working the water—suffice it to say that the costs of his boat and his gear make for a pretty slim profit margin.

Bruce played the gracious host again on the way back. He took us past the pelican colony again, then fired up his engine to give us a high-speed joyride through a broad channel lined on both sides with tall marsh grasses. His count for a morning's work was 27 soft crabs and 118 peelers—the latter would end up spending a day or two or three in his pen before heading to market. He'd also caught a dozen or so hard crabs—a "lucky day" catch, he called it. He was planning to bring those home to steam, but the bottom literally fell out of his bushel basket while we were saying our goodbyes.

At this point, Jill and I badly needed a nap. Bruce's day didn't allow for such a luxury, of course. He was taking another couple out that afternoon to show them his native Tylerton. He had to inspect his peeler pen a couple more times. I'm sure there were a good number of maintenance and clean-up tasks on his hit list as well.

Thinking about his workday, I remembered another local legend, this one recorded by the folklorist George Gibson Carey in his 1977 book, *A Faraway Time & Place: Lore of the Eastern Shore*. This tale centers on a God-fearing waterman whose long, arduous days leave him so exhausted every evening that he falls asleep the second his head hits the pillow, before he gets a chance to say his nightly prayers.

This failing weighed on the waterman's mind, until one day when he got out a piece of paper and jotted some thoughts down about loving God and being thankful and perhaps making a couple of humble requests. He taped that piece of paper to the headboard on his bed. And every night as his head dropped toward the pillow, he'd point to that note and mutter:

Lord, them's my intentions.

Refreshed after a nap, Jill and I grabbed a couple of kayaks and headed out along Levering Creek. We hung out for a bit off of an island full of wild goats. We gawked at scores of raptors and shorebirds. We took a run through the harbor, where Jill clicked her shutter a few hundred times. It was quite the leisurely paddle, until we found ourselves on the wrong side of a strong tidal flow. We stepped back on land just in time for that 4pm takeout deadline, then dawdled and wandered some more, all the way up through sunset.

Back to the Mainland

We played the role of lazy tourists the next morning and lollygagged in bed until nearly 5am. As always, Smith Island was up and at it by then. Jill went chasing after the sweet morning light with her camera, while I made one last stroll along the Ewell waterfront. Watermen shuffled this way and that under bare bulbs in their peeler pens. A pickup truck stopped at one home after another, loading up on cardboard boxes full of soft crabs on ice, bound for early-morning transport to the mainland.

I found myself lamenting that it had taken me too long to make this trip. I thought, too, about the many writers, painters, and photographers who've been drawn out here in recent decades, trying to get a sense for the ways of a place that seems destined to disappear someday off in the future. The islands are fertile territory for armchair travelers. If you want to take deep dives into the people and culture of these places, spend some quality time with Tom Horton's *An Island Out of Time: A Memoir of Smith Island in the Chesapeake* and Earl Swift's *Chesapeake Requiem: A Year with the Watermen of Vanishing Tangier Island.*

When the *Capt. Jason II* departed for the mainland at 7:30am, she was chock full of crab boxes and passengers. Barry Bruce was aboard, headed into Crisfield for a doctor's appointment. A cheery young waitress we'd met at the Bayside Inn was very excited about the fact that she'd just rented an apartment on the mainland. She'd soon be moving away.

Back in Crisfield, we tried to hang on to the magic of the trip for a little while longer. Having breakfast in a roomful of watermen at the classic old Gordon's Confectionary (831 W.

Main St.) helped in that regard. So, too, did a visit to the J. Millard Tawes Museum (3 9th St.), which has an exceptional collection of old photos of Somerset County. In the wake of our visit to Smith Island, those pictures left us thinking a little less about the way things have changed and a little more about the ways they've stayed the same.

CONNECTIONS
• Smith Island
visitsmithisland.com
• Somerset County Tourism
visitsomerset.com; 800.521.9189
• Smith Island Cultural Center & Museum
smithisland.org; 410.425.3351
20846 Caleb Jones Rd., Ewell, Md.
• Tangier Island
tangierisland-va.com
• Eastern Shore of Virginia Tourism
visitesva.com; 757.331.1660
• Accomack County Tourism
co.accomack.va.us/visitors; 757.787.5700

NEARBY TRIPS: A list of other trips on the lower Delmarva Peninsula is on page 7.

Way Back Machine
'A Mirror of the Almighty'
The modern-day tourism trade on Smith and Tangier islands dates to the 1960s, when tour boats first started shuttling daytrippers out into the middle of the bay. But visitors have actually been flocking to these islands for centuries. In 1821, one observer reported seeing more than 400 boats anchored around

Tangier. He estimated the crowd attending that year's Methodist camp meeting at more than 5,000.

In 1828, a young Eastern Shore of Virginia lawyer named Henry Wise—he would go on to become the state's governor—was on his way up to Baltimore when the boat he was aboard approached Tangier to drop off passengers at that year's camp meeting.

We had started in a sail vessel from a beautiful creek late in the evening and when within about two miles of the beach [on Tangier where the camp meeting was under way], the breeze died away and we were helplessly becalmed. The sun set clear o'er the bay, smooth and rippleless like a mirror of the Almighty; in a few moments the island was not to be seen until the moon effulgent rose o'er the eastern land and lighted up the glassy waters, and she had not risen high when suddenly the light-wood flambeaux of the camp shot forth their beams, and the rows and avenues of hundreds of broad and high blazes were like supernatural lamps of the heavens; and soon the hymns of the multitude came softly stealing by moonlight o'er the mirrored bay, mellowed by distance, as if angel voices were in choirs of melody coming from an island cloud! Oh it was sweet beyond fancy's dreams! ... Tears both of joy and grief were wept!

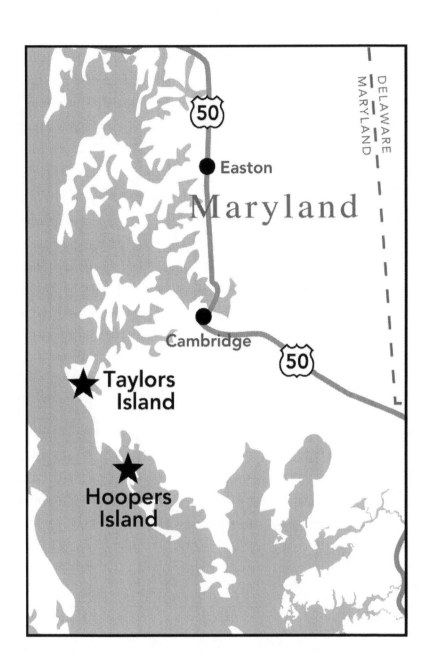

ROAD TRIP #11

TAYLORS & HOOPERS ISLANDS, MD.

A few years back I was wandering the back roads of south Dorchester County, Md. when I felt a need to check my cell phone reception. I punched one application or another to see if it would load, and it did, offering one and only one nearby location: "The Middle of F#&!@*! Nowhere!"

The wiseacre who created that check-in gave me a good laugh that morning. What made his or her joke even better, of course, is the kernel of truth behind it. One thing that makes south Dorchester so interesting is the fact that it has remained relatively isolated from the rest of the world for such a long time.

It's true, of course, that people here have been involved for centuries with maritime trade and the seafood industry. It's true, too, that automobiles and steamboats showed up in these parts just as surely as they showed up everywhere else in

America. We're not talking on the level of some long-lost Indian tribe in the midst of the Amazon rainforest.

But here on the Delmarva Peninsula, south Dorchester ranks right up there when it comes to hanging on to highly local traditions and bloodlines. The biggest annual communal celebration here is the National Outdoor Show, which famously involves both a beauty pageant for teenage girls and a world-championship competition in muskrat skinning.

In the introduction to her book of historic photos, *Hoopers Island*, island native Jacqueline Simmons Hedberg lists the surnames that appeared in the 1930 census of Hoopers Island and then points out that the same list in the 1800 census was nearly identical. After wading through a few more data points, Hedberg concludes:

> [Just] ten families, with all their branches, were almost the entire population of Hoopers Island for 300 years.

The Road 'Down Below'

When you head out of Cambridge on Route 16 bound for the vast expanse of marshland locals refer to as "Down Below," you are heading into one of the best places on the Eastern Shore to get a sense for the way those relatively isolated centuries have piled up, one on top of the next. First up is Taylors Island, a 20-minute ride along a two-lane affair known first as Church Creek Road and then as Taylors Island Road.

There are a couple of places to watch for along the way. The big red tomato that pops up on the roadside a little way after the endearingly named Pig Neck Road marks Emily's Produce, 2214 Church Creek Rd., a first-rate farm stand operated by Kelly and Paul Jackson, members of a family that has been working the land hereabouts for seven generations. You can pick up a snack or a meal here to enjoy at a picnic bench. If you have kids (or kids at heart) in tow, they will be able to feed chickens and ogle goats.

A little farther down the road is Woolford Store, 1614 Taylors Island Rd., where you will find grocery staples, a sandwich grill, and other essentials amid of a bevy of hunting supplies. Here is a little something extra to put in your mind's eye: In the dead of winter, big-city dealers in the fur-coat business set up shop at the Woolford store, waiting for local muskrat trappers to bring in their bounty.

Just past the store, Route 16 intersects with Harrisville Road, which winds south through farmland for a bit before shrinking into a one-lane dirt path with forestland on both sides. Most historians believe Underground Railroad heroine Harriet Tubman was born during the 1820s in a long-gone cabin that stood near where this road dead ends. If you venture that way to commune with her spirit, please be respectful of the fact that the land on both sides is privately owned. (There's a hunting camp here, too; you might want to wear some blaze orange in season.)

Next, you will come into the sleepy burg of Madison, where a handful of local watermen keep workboats at postcard-pretty Caper's Wharf. The scene here would have been anything but sleepy in Harriet Tubman's time, however — back then, Madison was filled with the noise, traffic, and dust of big timbering and shipbuilding operations.

Tubman made her escape from slavery in 1849. That same year, 17-year-old Joseph W. Brooks began an apprenticeship with his uncle, a local shipbuilder. The yard that Brooks would open in Madison a few years later became the stuff of legend, churning out more than 150 schooners, pungies, sloops, and bugeyes before his death in 1915. In the estimation of maritime historian M.V. Brewington,

> Few shipyards in the world have in one man's lifetime launched as many vessels.

The rest of the drive to Taylors Island is quiet and gorgeous. One last scenic reminder of those busy days gone by comes at the bridge over little Parsons Creek, which began life as Stewart's Canal. Enslaved and free blacks dug this waterway out by hand in the 1830s to facilitate the transport of logs to local shipyards and sawmills. I always find myself imagining here how oppressive the heat and bugs must have been for those workers on summer days.

Cross the next bridge over Slaughter Creek and you'll be on an island whose first European residents gave their new abode a tongue-in-cheek name, "Taylor's Folly," back in the 1600s. There are no museums to visit here—no tours to take, plans to make, tickets to buy, or directions to follow.

What you do on Taylors Island is wander around a bit and see what catches your fancy. One day the wildlife might be front and center, as hawks, herons, eagles, and sika deer are here in abundance. Another time, the if-walls-could-talk beauty of abandoned houses and old churches might strike your imagination.

Just over that Slaughter Creek bridge is a pull-off where you can admire a 12-pound cannon mounted atop a hunk of stone. It was captured from the British in an obscure, unimportant War of 1812 skirmish, the Battle of the Ice Mound.

Three churches here are on the National Register of Historic Places. Grace Episcopal, 4401 Hoopers Neck Rd., is a Victorian Gothic affair with a small Chapel of Ease on its grounds that dates back to the 1700s. On a recent walk through the gorgeous cemetery there, the grave of Medford Shenton made me do a double take. Medford has one of the biggest gravestones around, but he lived for just a couple of months in the late 1800s, when infant mortality was a much bigger scourge than it is today. His stone left me with a visceral feel for the joys, challenges, and, in this case, heartbreaks that visited families in places like this during times gone by.

Nearby Bethlehem Methodist Episcopal, 4519 Hoopers Neck Rd., is a Gothic Revival building that dates to 1857. Graced with a photogenic belfry that's adorned with a dome-and-spire combo, it has the look of an upside-down ice cream cone. Some of the graves in the cemetery across the road date to the 1700s. Nearby at 4511 Hoopers Neck Rd. is Lane Methodist Episcopal, which dates to 1897 and served the island's once-sizable black community. Summertime camp meetings here drew overflow crowds into the mid-20th century.

On the south end of the island, along Robinson Neck Road, look for another little pull-off at the entrance to the Robinson Neck Nature Preserve, a 920-acre tract owned by the Nature Conservancy. The sweet hiking trail that runs through the preserve is worth your time, especially in non-buggy months. Pack boots if this stroll is up your alley—the trail is frequently dotted with wet spots.

To Hoopers and Beyond
Next up is storied Hoopers Island. But first, a brief detour through the long lens of geologic time: Back in the mists of the distant past, the islands we know as Taylors and Hoopers (along with another one, James) were all connected into one big land mass. Their breakup over the years was the result of natural phenomena going back many centuries in the

Chesapeake Bay, where the water is slowly rising, the land is slowly sinking, and waves are always nibbling away at the shoreline.

To get on the road to Hoopers, head back to the mainland from Taylors and then turn southbound on Smithville Road, another sweet stretch of Down Below driving. For much of the way, this road will be sandwiched between Blackwater National Wildlife Refuge and the Taylors Island Wildlife Management Area. The spots of water that pop in and out of view carry evocative names like Hog Marsh Gut and Scallop Point Gut.

Keep an eye out early on here for pretty New Revived Methodist Church, 4350 Smithville Rd., still known among locals by its original name of Jefferson Methodist Episcopal. Its congregation is still active, the last one standing among the several churches that used to serve that once-sizeable African-American population. Most of those families moved to Cambridge or other towns in search of work once the timbering, seafood, and packing industries went into decline as the 20th century unfolded.

Oak Grove Church, 3647 Smithville Rd., is another beauty along this route, with tall, skinny windows and a high-pitched roof. The church, which dates to the late 1800s and served a white congregation, takes its name from the gorgeous stand of trees there. If the sunlight is falling right, you won't be able to resist the temptation to stop and snap some pictures.

Turn west on Hoopers Island Road and you will soon come to one more pretty little church, the Catholic St. Mary's Star of the Sea, 917 Hoopers Island Rd. Actually, two churches stand across the street from each other here. This is the kind of place where when people talk about the "new" building, they're referring to a structure that went up in 1872.

The older chapel predates the Revolutionary War by a decade. In his diary, one of the circuit-riding priests who visited this congregation on horseback in 1801 referred to his Eastern Shore road trip in charming fashion, as a visit to "ye islands of Dorset." His itinerary, like yours, included Hoopers and Taylors. Back then, James and Barren islands were on his hit list as well.

Today, Hoopers Island is a string of three different little spits of land, with only two still inhabited and the third mostly washed away. Like Taylors, the place got its name from the first European family to arrive back in the 1600s. Astounding scenery marks the ride down Hoopers Island Road, especially in spots that serve up views of the open Chesapeake Bay on the west and the broad Honga River on the east. The island is thick with raptors, herons, egrets, and other birds. You will find churches and graveyards to explore as well.

Places to grab a bite to eat are few and far between on this trip. The most iconic of your options here is Old Salty's Restaurant, 2560 Hoopers Island Rd., housed in a former high school. It's a local institution when it comes to Eastern Shore comfort food.

A healthy smattering of "come heres" and "weekenders" have homes on Hoopers Island nowadays, but many families still have deep roots in the place and still live in ways closely connected to the water, whether that means working as crabbers and oystermen, running charter fishing boats, or doing shifts in one of the island's seafood-packing houses.

The first village you'll come to is Fishing Creek, a postcard-pretty scene filled with bobbing workboats tied up on Back Creek. The scenery gets even better as you cross the tall, swooping bridge from Upper Hoopers to Middle Hoopers and come into the town of Hoopersville. Look out into the bay from that bridge on a clear day and you might catch a glimpse of the 63-foot-tall Hooper Island Lighthouse, which dates to 1902. Keepers lived out there up until 1961.

Among the half dozen or so seafood houses on the island, one in particular stands out for its history. A.E. Phillips & Son started doing business here in 1914. Half a century later, the Phillips family opened a small crab house in the resort town of Ocean City, Md. and that arm of the business has since grown into Phillips Seafood, a chain of restaurants stretching from Myrtle Beach to Washington, D.C. Phillips is probably the best-known crab company in the world. (Last I checked, tours of the old packing house here at 2423 Hoopers Island Rd. were available by appointment.)

Not everything you'll see on Hoopers Island is about looking back in time. The island is home to several firms striving to make a go of it in the thoroughly modern venture of oyster aquaculture, raising hopes that a new and sustainable way of working the water can help grow the local economy as the 21st century progresses.

With both islands down, it's possible that you'll be in the mood to head straight back to civilization. To take a different way back to Cambridge, continue past Smithville Road, staying on Route 335, and then following that route number when it turns left (north) to wander through more spectacular forest and marshland. This will take you right past the first-rate Harriet Tubman Underground Railroad Visitor Center and Blackwater National Wildlife Refuge, with its popular Wildlife Drive nature loop.

If you are in the mood to keep wandering, however, don't make that turn toward Cambridge with Route 335. Instead, stay straight on what now becomes Route 334 and continue meandering through one tiny south Dorchester town after another — Crapo, Wingate, Bishops Head, and Crocheron among them.

On the way back from that run of wandering, keep an eye out for Andrews Road. If you turn right there, the road will eventually become Maple Dam Road and cross the Blackwater River at Shorter's Wharf. That will drop you into one of my all-time favorite runs of marshland scenery. (If you stick with Maple Dam Road, it will take you all the way back into Cambridge. Or you could turn left at Key Wallace Drive to find the aforementioned Blackwater refuge and Tubman visitor center.)

CONNECTIONS
• Dorchester County Tourism
visitdorchester.org; 410.228.1000
• Blackwater National Wildlife Refuge
www.fws.gov/refuge/blackwater; 410.228.2677
2145 Key Wallace Dr., Cambridge, Md.
• Harriet Tubman Underground Railroad Visitor Center
nps.gov/hatu/planyourvisit/index.htm; 410.221.2290
4068 Golden Hill Rd., Church Creek, Md.

NEARBY TRIPS: A list of other trips on the middle Delmarva Peninsula is on page 7.

Way Back Machine
'A Monument to Man's Stupidity'
The story of how the modern Hoopers Island bridge came into existence is a tale of politics and bureaucracy. Before 1980, the crossing from Upper Hoopers to Middle Hoopers was a one-lane affair on a low wooden bridge with a draw in the middle so boats could get by and an itty-bitty pull-off area so vehicles

coming in opposite directions could pass each other. This is how the writer Tom Horton describes that earlier bridge in his book, *Bay Country*.

[It is] the longest, narrowest, clatteringest old wooden bridge in Maryland, and no matter how far you've come, crossing it is the most memorable part of your trip.

Horton recalls making that crossing himself as a newly licensed young driver. The nerve-racking ordeal involved navigating through a gauntlet of

... summer crabbers who bend unconcernedly over both railings, giving no quarter as they lean to dip crustaceans flippering on the tide. Somehow, no hind ends ever were fractured there, although a couple of windshields were sharded by the long, wooden handles of crab nets.

This may sound problematic, but with a population of less than 500 and a daily travel volume of 250 vehicles, it's not like the old Hoopers Island bridge was causing traffic jams. Then, in the 1970s, the possibility of progress came calling in the form of an opportunity to have federal funds cover most of the cost of replacing the "clatteringest" bridge.

To be fair, it was time for a new bridge. One commenter on the Secrets of the Eastern Shore website recalled how the old bridge was sometimes under water at high tide. There were worries about the stability of its aging wooden timbers, too–it got to a point where school buses no longer made the crossing. Instead, children from Middle Hoopers Island were taken across in small groups, where a full bus would be waiting for them on the Lower Hoopers side.

Initial estimates on that new bridge came in at $500,000, which meant that just $125,00 would be due from local coffers in Dorchester County. That original concept involved building a bridge not so different from the one that was already there, just more stable, more reliable at high tide, and perhaps even paved.

But in taking the deal for that federal grant money, the county also ceded design control over the project to federal engineers. They were the ones who insisted on an over-the-top design that tried to account for every possible future risk. The feds wanted the bridge to soar to a peak of 35 feet above the water. They brushed aside pleas to leave the old wooden bridge standing out there so local folks could keep on using it for fishing and crabbing.

A slew of other technical bells and whistles got added in by those federal engineers, too, sending the price tag soaring from $500,000 to more than $3.5 million, seven times higher than the original estimate. In the end, the county was on the hook not for $125,000, but for $900,000. They could have saved a bundle by never taking that federal grant money at all.

All of which brings us to Tom Flowers, a Hoopers Island native who enjoyed a distinguished career as a local educator and politician. Flowers was also renowned as a great Eastern Shore storyteller. He dubbed himself "The Old Honker" while spinning yarns at public appearances and in newspaper columns.

On Sept. 6, 1980, County Commissioner Flowers was invited to give the invocation at a ceremony marking the completion of the new Hoopers Island bridge. What he said before the crowd of local politicians, big-wig state bureaucrats, and other VIPs that day ended up getting attention from newspapers and TV stations all over the country. Here is the blessing he offered up:

> Father, today we are gathered here to dedicate a bridge that is a monument to man's stupidity, a monument to man's waste, a monument to government interference and inefficiency. For there is no need for such an elaborate structure as this is and which is so out of keeping in the peaceful and lovely environment of south Dorchester.
>
> We, the County Commissioners, State and Local officials, and other guests should this day learn a lesson and be aware of the great waste of taxpayers' money–over $3 million; we should this day be aware of the loss of resources that our own children and grandchildren will suffer ... but we can, however, rejoice that our community's need for a safe bridge has been admirably and efficiently completed through the dedication and hard work of the McLean Construction Company personnel.
>
> We ask our great Creator and Father to bless this bridge [and] our families, our friends, and our visitors who will use this structure to meet their needs, knowing that wind and wave and tide are daily at work destroying that which has been built. In the name of Jesus, Our Father, Amen.

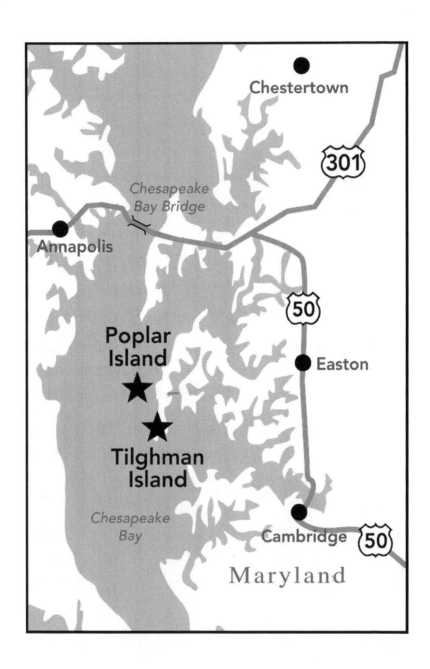

Chestertown

301

Chesapeake
Bay Bridge

Annapolis

50

Poplar
Island

★

Easton

★

Tilghman
Island

Chesapeake
Bay

Cambridge

50

Maryland

ROAD TRIP #12

TILGHMAN & POPLAR ISLANDS, MD.

The road to Tilghman Island follows a fitting pattern. Outside St. Michaels, Route 33 runs northwest through swaths of sweet farmland and then makes a big shepherd's crook turn to the south just as the broad Eastern Bay pops up on the western horizon. The scenery is lush and productive all the way out to this skinny little spit of land where life has been tied for centuries to the bounties of soil and bay.

A while back, one islander famously described Tilghman as "a place that gets up and goes to work." Those words may not be quite as true today, given the recent arrival of increasing numbers of retirees and second-home owners, but it's still the right thought to put in mind as you cross a drawbridge and ogle all the workboats tied up along Knapps Narrows.

Exploring the Old Ways on Tilghman Island

Your first order of business should be a leisurely drive along the three-mile length of the island. Lots of old Indian artifacts have turned up on Tilghman over the years, so human activity is a pretty ancient affair here. The first European name linked to the place is that of Seth Foster, who was given a grant of ownership by the royal powers that be in 1659, but most likely never visited his property.

The family that gave the island its name arrived in the first part of the 1700s and stuck around for more a century. The key figure in this stretch was Matthew Tilghman, a prominent Maryland politician whose property holdings stretched to more than 7,000 acres on various parts of the Eastern Shore. He lived just across the way on the mainland, in the town of Claiborne. (If you take a side trip through that pretty little burg, the house he built still stands just north of town along Rich Neck Road.)

A staunch advocate for American independence, Tilghman had a leadership hand in all manner of colony-wide projects advancing the revolutionary cause. He would have been a signer of the Declaration of Independence except for a scheduling snafu that forced him to leave that famous session of the Continental Congress early so as to chair a meeting back on his home turf. Historians often refer to him as the "father of the American revolution in Maryland."

Quite a few neighbors were none too fond of Tilghman's politics. Threats lodged against him by British loyalists drove the Maryland Navy to station an armed barge at Tilghman Island once the war began. Nothing much happened during the Revolutionary War, but the British had a fleeting moment of glory here during the War of 1812, when the bad guys seized 43 cattle, 15 calves, 50 sheep, 12 barrels of corn, and three tons of hay from the island while rampaging through the Chesapeake in preparation for their attack on Washington, D.C.

The island served as one big piece of farmland during most years of Tilghman family control. In the 1830s, the family began breaking the island up into small lots, launching its transformation into more of a small-town community. That process really took off after the Civil War, when the market for Chesapeake Bay oysters went into the stratosphere and set off the closest thing to a gold rush that would ever strike on Delmarva.

During those boom times, oyster shells were discarded off of Tilghman Island in such volume that they soon congealed into an island that would grow large enough to house a store, a post office, and, eventually, the storied Tilghman Packing Company. You can catch of glimpse of that island today if you wind your way through a residential housing development called Tilghman on Chesapeake, and keep an eye out for the community's clubhouse, which sits at 21610 Island Club Rd., out past a marina at the end of a skinny road snaking out from the island.

Founded in 1877, the Tilghman Packing Company ranked for a while among the biggest companies in Talbot County, with 600-plus workers. Four post offices and three schools dotted the island at one point. There was even a full-fledged department store. The historian Dickson Preston had some fun describing the heyday of Tilghman in *Talbot County: A History*:

There was more excitement in 1890 when Hode Taylor set up a merry-go-round in a field, for which the charge was five cents a ride. It was powered by a white horse which often got dizzy from continually going round and round, and had to be spelled by a substitute. A second merry-go-round, imported by Ira Harrison about 1909, took a dunking when the boat bringing it to the island sank in a storm. Fished out of the water, it ran as good as new. Its gasoline motor was considered a great improvement over the horse; at least it didn't get dizzy on the job.

By 1908 Tilghman even had a movie theater of sorts. Ira Harrison, the merry-go-round entrepreneur, set it up in a tent in front of the firehouse. It had coal-oil lighting and a hand-turned projector. The films were of the nickelodeon type, with handsome heroes, damsels in distress, and leering villains. Since the hero always won, the films soon got to be boring. Therefore, Harrison varied his fare by running them upside down or backward, to great applause from the audience. Admission was ten cents for children, fifteen cents for adults.

The best place to get in touch with these and other great stories from days gone by is the wonderful little Tilghman Watermen's Museum, which is on the main drag between Mission and Coopertown roads. Speaking of roads, most of the driving you'll do on this island will be atop surfaces that were originally "paved" with oyster shells.

The first thing to take note of at the museum is the exterior, which is designed in an odd shape that mimics the letter W. Local lore has islanders believing that this design delivered better air flow on hot summer days. Thirteen of these W houses were built back in the 1890s: As far as anyone has been able to tell so far, the design is unique to Tilghman and nearby Sherwood. Seven W houses are still standing, but only this and one other are in near-original condition.

Inside, the museum tells the story of that famous Tilghman Packing Company. Other sections explore the history of boatbuilders, watermen, artists, big storms, and more. If you find yourself hooked on these Tilghman tales, ask about the series of oral-history videos the museum has produced — they're quite well done.

Now that you have the lay of the (is)land, find your way to Dogwood Harbor Road, a couple blocks south of the museum. The marina there is home to the oldest of the surviving skipjacks, those storied only-in-the-Chesapeake sailing workboats of days gone by. Built in 1886 a little way south of here on remote Taylors Island, the *Rebecca T. Ruark* now occupies a place on the National Register of Historic Places. In the warmer months, you can reserve a spot on sails with Captain Wade Murphy or his son, Wade Jr. (The elder Murphy is a central and memorable character in a well-done book by Christopher White, *Skipjack: The Story of America's Last Sailing Oystermen.*)

The Phillips Wharf Environmental Center is located back near the drawbridge that carried you onto the island. It's a worthwhile stop for everyone with an interest in nature, but especially so if you have kids in tow. They will love the "estuarium," which is full of little aquariums and pools showcasing live critters — fish, amphibians, reptiles, and crustaceans among them. Another building at Phillips Wharf houses a working oyster aquaculture facility that doubles as an educational experience for visitors. You can launch your kayaks from here if you want to do a bit of paddling. (Rentals should be available through the Tilghman Island Marina.)

Quite a few other interesting stops deserve a spot on your Tilghman hit list. The Tilghman Island Country Store at 5949 Tilghman Island Rd. is just that, only with a good wine selection and tasty carry-out. The island has several sit-down dining options as well. If idiosyncratic bookstores are your thing,

Crawford's Nautical Books at 5782 Tilghman Island Rd. will seem a slice of heaven on earth. It's housed in the classic old Tilghman Island Bank building. Two big outdoor parties dominate the annual calendar—a seafood festival in the summer and Tilghman Island Day in the fall.

Resurrection Stories on Poplar Island

Have you read James Michener's *Chesapeake*? If so, you'll recall the fate of Devon Island, where much of the action in the novel unfolds over the course of many centuries. Every now and again, Michener has one character or another pause during the action to take note of the way the island is shrinking over time. In the end, Devon succumbs altogether:

> At dawn the storm abated and in full light they all went out to survey the wreckage and find what consolation they could. ... They were starting to inspect the opposite shore when Amos Turlock, using his binoculars, uttered a loud cry, "Look at Devon!"
>
> Everyone turned toward the island that guarded the river, and Caveny said, "I don't see anything wrong." He grabbed the glasses, stared westward and said in a low voice, "Jee-sus!"
>
> ... The island had vanished. Above the crashing waves, where splendid fields had once prospered, there was nothing. On the spot where the finest mansion on the Eastern Shore had offered its stately silhouette, nothing was visible. The final storm which overtakes all existence had struck.

The phenomenon behind this fictional plot development isn't something Michener made up. Islands have been disappearing in slow-but-sure fashion under the waters of the Chesapeake Bay for many centuries now. Three villains are to blame: erosion caused by storms and waves; rising sea levels; and subsidence, or the gradual sinking of land. Most experts believe the modern-day phenomenon of global warming is accelerating this process.

Tour boats depart Tilghman Island regularly between March and October, bound for boomerang-shaped Poplar Island. When Europeans first arrived in the 1600s, the island covered nearly 1,500 acres. Originally known as Popeley's after an early European visitor, the island was home to a pig farm in the 1630s. Later that same decade, a man named Richard Thompson moved out here with his wife, their child, and seven indentured servants. That adventure ended in unspeakable tragedy, with the woman, her child, and those servants all slaughtered by a band of Nanticoke Indians while Thompson was away on a fur-trading trip.

By the Civil War years, Poplar was down to 1,000 acres. Around 100 people had homes out here in the 1880s. Their community boasted a post office, a church, and a sawmill, among other businesses. By 1900, only four houses remained. By 1920, even those stragglers had given up and moved to the mainland.

Eventually, Poplar Island split into three separate dollops of land with separate names—Poplar, Coaches, and Jefferson islands. The isolation of the place made it a perfect base for bootleggers during Prohibition times. In 1929, authorities arrested five moonshiners out here and dumped more than 20,000 gallons of their whiskey.

That same year, some political bigwigs with the Democratic Party bought Poplar and Jefferson, turning the two islands into a VIP retreat destination where party leaders could both work and play.

[The idea was to have] a quiet, undisturbed and attractive spot where [we] might mix the travail of political conferences with the pleasantries of clubhouse fraternity and where the humdrum of party politics might be broken now and then by communion with the great outdoors.

A bevy of bigwigs came calling in the years that followed, including presidents Franklin Roosevelt and Harry Truman. With Secret Service boats prowling nearby waters, presidential parties enjoyed skeet shooting, hunting, fishing, and crabbing. One famous anecdote here has a local little girl, Mary Jane Haddaway, spilling a plate of peas down Truman's back. Seeing the look of horror on the girl's face, the president said:

Aw, hell, honey, don't worry about it. You'll have a story to tell your grandchildren.

Alas, that Jefferson Islands Club burned to the ground in 1946 (though the organization behind it is still going today, with a mission of "promoting congenial bipartisan discourse for a better America"). In the 1960s, the Smithsonian Institution purchased Poplar Island and used it to conduct research into the ways of herons and ospreys. By the 1990s Poplar seemed ready to share the final fate of Michener's Devon Island — it had dwindled down to just five acres.

But the tour boats that depart from Tilghman Island these days showcase a miracle of modern environmental engineering — the island is in the midst of a dramatic rebirth into a 1,700-acre nature preserve. That resurrection has been in process for two decades as of this writing. Another two decades of work still lie on the horizon. Several state and federal agencies are partnering on the project, which involves building new landmass out of materials dug out from the bottom of the bay in order to maintain a proper depth along the shipping channel that leads into the Port of Baltimore.

Such materials once got discarded into open water outside the channel. This project puts them to a more positive purpose, restoring island habitat that can be quite important in the life span of birds, turtles, and other creatures. More than 200 bird species have already been spotted on reborn Poplar Island—it now boasts the only colony of common terns in the state of Maryland. Students at nearly 50 schools have been helping researchers track the growth and behavior patterns of diamondback terrapins.

The island tours begin with an indoor orientation session. After that, everyone boards a bus to ride around with an expert guide and check out sections, or "cells," of the new land mass that are in various stages of development, from freshly laid muck to well-established marshland and full-fledged island habitat. The work on bringing Poplar Island back to life is expected to run deep into the 2040s.

CONNECTIONS
• Tilghman Island Tourism
tilghmanisland.com
• Talbot County Tourism
tourtalbot.org; 410.770.8000
• Tilghman Watermen's Museum
tilghmanmuseum.org; 410.886.1025
6031 Tilghman Island Rd., Tilghman, Md.
• Phillips Wharf Environmental Center
phillipswharf.org; 410.886.9200
6129 Tilghman Island Rd., Tilghman, Md.
• Poplar Island Tours

poplarislandrestoration.com; 410.770.6503

NEARBY TRIPS: A list of other trips on the middle Delmarva Peninsula is on page 7.

Way Back Machine
The Fur Flies on Poplar Island
One of the strangest chapters in the history of Poplar Island opened in 1847 when ads appeared in area newspapers promising 25 cents apiece for up to 1,000 female black cats. The man behind those ads, R.O. Ridgeway, told customers that the felines should be "delivered at Poplar Island or my store."

Ridgeway was the front man for the entrepreneurial dreams of one Charles Carroll, who hailed from a Maryland family so prominent that his grandfather had signed the Declaration of Independence. Carroll had heard there was a big market for black cat fur in China, and he figured that he could tap into that trade market by turning Poplar Island into a cat farm.

He got a good number of male cats settled on the island, then started importing ladies at 25 cents apiece. He even hired a waterman to spread his daily catch of fish and crabs around to keep the cats well fed.

All went well, especially for the tomcats, until the weather turned severely cold late that winter. Ice soon formed a natural bridge between the island and the mainland. "As soon as the cats found this out," one account said, "they took off for their former homes without waiting for another meal of fish. Probably the Shore has never seen such a migration of felines."

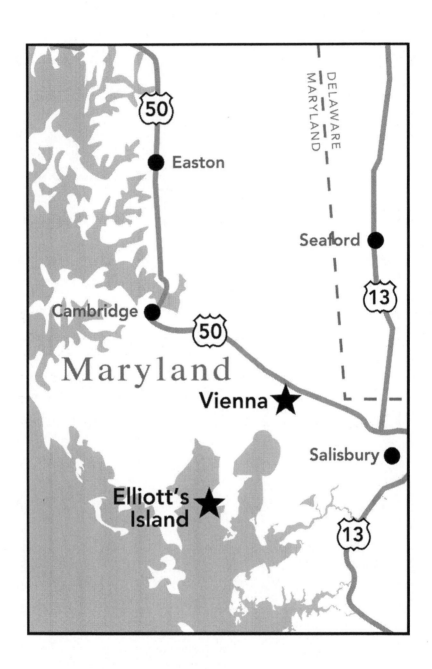

Road Trip #13

Elliott's Island, Md.

L et us count the natural reasons why you might want to hop off the highway and wander down to Elliott's Island. The drive is gorgeous. The birding can be amazing. Cycling, paddling, hunting. fishing — this isolated stretch draws outdoorsmen and women of all stripes. A bigwig with the Nature Conservancy once had this to say about this stretch of two-lane road:

> It is one of the great natural areas on the East Coast. Those marshes are some of the great coastal wilderness we have left.

Interesting human stories abound as well. One of my favorites gets at how isolated life could be in days gone by in the most remote corners of Maryland's Eastern Shore. In their wonderful book *Elliott's Island: The Land That Time Forgot*, writers Ann Foley and Freddie T. Waller tell a story about a woman named Bethania Smith Gray. Born on the island in the 1870s, Bethania made it into her 20s without ever leaving the island. She and a friend named Rebecca ventured out to the tip of the island one day in the 1890s to watch the arrival of the very first steamboat to ever land here.

The young Bethania was so stricken at the sight she exclaimed, "Stand back, Beck! Here she comes and she's big as a drugstore!" All the Islanders in the crowd knew she had no better notion of a drugstore than she had of a steamboat and it became a catchphrase on the Island that something was "big as a drugstore."

Starting Point: Vienna

By comparison with the community on Elliott's Island, Vienna ranks as a little metropolis. Home to about 300 souls, it's situated on a beautiful bend in the broad Nanticoke River that's chock full of history. Captain John Smith came calling on the Chicone Indians who lived nearby in 1608. A good swath of land near here served as an Indian reservation during much of the 1700s.

In recent decades, the town has transformed its gently sloping waterfront into a lovely park where you can stroll a wooden walkway overlooking the river, then turn around to admire the beautiful homes on Water Street. An old 1768 custom house still stands here. Visiting tall ships used to have to check in with colonial authorities there. Feel free to wander a few inland streets as well if you are in the mood for a bit more small-town bliss.

Our starting point for the ride to Elliott's Island is the big water tower on Market Street. Make sure you have some gas in the tank and snacks on hand before setting out. You've got a 40-

mile round trip ahead that offers nothing in the way of shops, gas stations, or restrooms.

Market Street quickly turns into Elliott's Island Road and runs through a mix of farmland and forest here that hints at the classic Delmarva industries, such as vegetable canning and shipbuilding, that have come and gone over the centuries. Six miles into the ride, that landscape starts shifting to marsh-scape as you enter the Fishing Bay Wildlife Management Area.

The wetlands that follow will seem to stretch on to infinity. In summer and fall, marsh grasses sway in glorious expanses of green. In winter and spring, they unfold in shades of tan and brown that are no less magnificent for their muted tones. Keep an eye out for herons, egrets, and other wading birds as you pass Savannah Lake and Little Savannah Lake on the left. After that, Island Creek will start winding in and out of view on the right.

High tides creep up onto the roadway here with some frequency. The last time I drove down this way, those puddles started appearing about 10 miles into the ride. A boat ramp and popular fishing spot pops up at 12 miles. Wide open Fishing Bay comes into view a little way after that, fed by a trio of rivers, the Chicamacomico, the Transquaking, and the Blackwater.

Everything is flat as can be, of course, but you will see if you pay attention what a difference even itty bitty changes in elevation can make, as little stands of tall pine trees come back into view. Keep your eyes open for bald eagles in those trees.

Destination: The Island

The first houses in forever pop up at mile 17. Then comes a tiny bridge, followed by a view of the gorgeous Elliott's Island Methodist Church. The island, which is a mile and a half long, takes its name from a family that arrived in the 1690s. Descendants of those first Elliotts were still living here as recently as 1967.

If you wander around the church graveyard, you will come to the final resting place of waterman and hunting guide Wylie Abbott Sr., a legendary Dorchester County character who won the world championship of muskrat skinning 13 times between the 1970s and the 1990s. You might stop and pay respects to Job T. Langrell as well. He died in 1858, and his tombstone details the length of his life with heartbreaking specificity: "Aged 7 years, 3 months, and 1 day."

There used to be a measure of commercial activity on Elliott's Island—a couple of stores, as well as vegetable canneries and oyster-packing houses. But those things are no more. Just past the church comes the only real intersection on the island. Keep straight and you will soon pass a road sign sure to raise a smile: "Mosquito Crossing." This way leads to a dead end of a roundabout where there is no place to get out and stretch your legs.

The other way from that intersection leads into a marina where, if you are lucky, the porta-pot will be in an acceptable state of cleanliness. Here, you can stretch your legs, walk along the docks, admire the workboats, and take your time with the extraordinary views of Fishing Bay, imagining all the sails that used to dot the horizon here when local watermen did their work aboard old bugeyes and skipjacks.

Another scene from days gone by pops into my mind here, again thanks to that book, *Elliott's Island: The Land That Time Forgot.* Back in the years when there was a one-room schoolhouse on the island, a teacher named Brady Todd commuted to his job daily from across this stretch of water in a town called Crocheron. His regular mode of transport was by boat, of course, but every once in a while in those years, this whole stretch of Fishing Bay would freeze over, and Mr. Todd would glide his way into work on ice skates.

If 40 miles of marshland wandering isn't enough for you, take the scenic route over to Blackwater National Wildlife Refuge by turning left at Henry's Cross Road, left at Griffiths Neck Road, left at Bestpitch Ferry Road, and then left again at Greenbrier Road. That runs into Maple Dam Road, where you continue straight for a bit before turning right onto Key Wallace Drive, crossing over the Little Blackwater River, and finding your way to the refuge. The Harriet Tubman Underground Railroad Visitors Center is nearby, too.

If you are in more of a history mood, come back through Vienna to check out Handsell House, a beautiful old building on a site thick with black, white, and Indian history dating back to the 1600s. The interior is only open occasionally, but you are free to wander the grounds, which features a Native American longhouse in addition to an array of signs detailing some interesting history about the property and its residents. A narrated cell phone tour is on option here, too. To get there, head back into Vienna, then take Rhodesdale Vienna Road (Route 331) out of town, continuing past Route 50 and turning right on Indiantown Road.

CONNECTIONS
• Dorchester County Tourism
visitdorchester.org; 410.228.1000
• Town of Vienna
viennamd.org; 410.376.3442
• Blackwater National Wildlife Refuge
www.fws.gov/blackwater; 410.228.2677
2145 Key Wallace Dr., Cambridge, Md.

• Harriet Tubman Underground Railroad Visitor Center
nps.gov/hatu/planyourvisit/index.htm; 410.221.2290
4068 Golden Hill Rd., Church Creek, Md.
• Handsell House
restorehandsell.org; 410.228.7458
4837 Indiantown Rd., Vienna, Md.

NEARBY TRIPS: A list of other trips on the middle Delmarva Peninsula is on page 7.

Way Back Machine
'The People Were Filled with Astonishment and Alarm'
Vienna ranked as a busy little trading post in the late 1700s, with commercial vessels pulling in regularly to buy and sell goods. Maryland did not yet have a significant population of free blacks in those years, so the white people in Vienna had probably never seen the likes of Paul Cuffee.

A free black man from Massachusetts, Cuffee had signed on with a whaling ship as a teenager in 1776. He was barely 20 when he somehow built a small boat for himself and launched an unlikely career as a freelance merchant sea captain. By the 1790s, he owned a 69-ton schooner, *Ranger*. That vessel was docked in Norfolk, Va. when Cuffee heard a rumor that a town on Maryland's Eastern Shore was enjoying an Indian corn harvest for the ages. Cuffee recounted what happened next in his *Memoir of Captain Paul Cuffee: A Man of Color.* (Though it's an autobiography, Cuffee wrote about himself in the third person.)

> Thither he sailed, but on his arrival the people [of Vienna] were filled with astonishment and alarm. A vessel owned and commanded by a black man, and manned with a crew of the same complexion, was unprecedented and

surprising. The white inhabitants were struck with apprehensions of the injurious effects which such circumstances would have on the minds of their slaves, suspecting that he wished secretly to kindle the spirit of rebellion and excite a destructive revolt among them.

Under these notions several persons associated themselves for the purpose of preventing Paul from entering [the town] or remaining among them. [But] on examination, his papers proved to be correct, and the Custom-house officers could not legally refuse the entry of his vessel.

Paul combined prudence with resolution, and on this occasion conducted himself with candor, modesty, and firmness; his crew behaved, not only inoffensively, but with a conciliating propriety. In a few days the inimical association vanished, and the inhabitants treated him and his crew with respect and even kindness.

Many of the principal people [of Vienna] visited his vessel, and in consequence of the pressing invitation of one of them, Paul dined with his family in the town. In three weeks Paul sold his cargo and received into his schooner 5,000 bushels of Indian corn. With this he returned to [Massachusetts], where that article was in great demand; his cargo sold rapidly, and yielded him a profit of 1,000 dollars.

ROAD TRIP #14

CHESAPEAKE
& DELAWARE CANAL

The journeys that bring giant civic projects from vision to reality can be long, winding affairs that end in unpredictable ways. So it goes with an idea that first surfaced back in 1661, when an immigrant from Prague named Augustine Herman floated the concept of slicing a manmade sailing route across upper Delmarva so as to cut 300 miles off the trip between Baltimore and Philadelphia. Back then, that voyage involved a long run down to the mouth of the Chesapeake Bay followed by another run back up the Atlantic Ocean and into the Delaware River.

A century passed before the first detailed plan appeared for what would become the Chesapeake & Delaware Canal, but the investors behind that plan ran out of money. Things didn't get serious again until 1799, when a new company came on the scene with a plan for charging tolls to make such a waterway profitable.

The route they chose ran for 14 miles, from the upper reaches of the Elk River in Maryland to the bottom of a C-shaped bend in the Delaware River, well below New Castle. When construction began in the 1820s, some 2,600 men—many of them Irish immigrants, many others free black laborers—earned 75 cents a day toiling with picks and shovels to cut a ditch 10 feet deep and 36 feet wide.

The job took five long years and cost $2.25 million, making it one of the largest and most expensive canal projects of its day. The Chesapeake & Delaware Canal finally opened in 1829, 168 years after Augustine Herman had floated the concept. Nearly two centuries later, the C&D has proved itself a keeper—it's the country's only manmade waterway from the 1800s still functioning as a full-fledged shipping route.

This storied canal is at the heart of this trip, which runs between Chesapeake City and Delaware City, two towns that grew up in very different ways at either end of the waterway. While exploring, you'll get to cruise out to an island that houses an old Civil War prison, wander through the expansive Lums Pond State Park, and stroll or cycle a sweet trail that runs along the canal's northern bank.

Big Dreams in Delaware City

I'll start here on the eastern end, but you could just as easily reverse that if you want. On the shores of the Delaware River, quaint Delaware City is home to fewer than 2,000 souls. The historic buildings that line the northern side of Clinton Street, the main downtown drag, house a modest mix of shops and restaurants. The southern side belongs to Battery Park, a stretch of green space that offers commanding views of Pea Patch Island out in the river, the home of spooky-looking Fort Delaware.

Battery Park has the feel of an open-air museum, thanks to a run of first-rate signage telling stories about the roots of Delaware City. Be sure to give a look to the old "diving bell" on display, so you can imagine how men crawled inside that metal box and descended into the depths of the canal to clear debris from locks in the years before modern diving suits.

The men who founded the town chose a grand-sounding name, didn't they? They did so in confidence that their brainchild was destined to become a major metropolis. You can still sense the scope of their dreams today from the way the streets are cut; they're a good bit wider than in other towns of this size.

Such dreams of civic boom times seem to come and go like the wind here in Delaware City. The first of those dreams centered on the canal, of course. Brothers Daniel and William Newbold started the work of transforming family farmland into a future big city while the canal was under construction. Their project ended up in the hands of a Philadelphia businessman, Manuel Eyre, who threw a grand promotional dinner party on July 4, 1827 on an outdoor table that stretched the length of a full downtown block. Scads of speechifying that night focused on the pot of gold that was sure to turn up at the end of the canal rainbow.

When the canal opened two years later, it ran into the Delaware River right where Battery Park is today, but that pot of gold never really materialized. Most commercial activity along the canal was just a pass-through affair, shuttling from one big city to another without dropping much in the way of real money in smaller towns along the way.

Instead of becoming a big metropolis, Delaware City settled into life as a little wharf town with wide streets. Those wharves were often busy as all get out, thanks to an up-by-the-bootstraps entrepreneur named Philip Reybold. The son of a Philadelphia butcher, Reybold was orphaned at the age of 10 and somehow found his way to Delaware as a young man. He bought a farm, but it went belly up. Not one to give up easily, he rented the same farm back from its new owners and made the finances work the second time around by raising livestock and manufacturing castor oil out of beans.

Reybold's fortunes headed into the stratosphere after he got involved with the C&D Canal. He made a lot of money supplying meat and bread to those 2,600 construction workers. Then he set about buying one little farm after another in the countryside around town. He recharged the tired soils on those farms by covering the fields with "marl," a rich fertilizing mix chock full of old shells.

Where did that marl come from? It was in the dirt dug up by canal workers.

Somewhere in here, Reybold started experimenting with peach trees. By 1845, that experiment had grown into an array of orchards filled with more than 100,000 trees—his operation helped launch an agricultural boom that spread across the whole state. On the Delaware City wharf in those days, peach baskets were "stacked three tiers high and a hundred yards long to be loaded on three steamboats at one time." By the time Reybold died in 1854, he was known far and wide as "The Peach King." (Alas, the boom he launched went bust starting in the late 1800s, thanks to a devastating and contagious peach-tree disease.)

Countless other classic Delmarva scenes unfolded here at Battery Park. Steamboats came on the scene in the mid-1800s, a time when road trips like the ones in this book involved boarding a steamer in Philadelphia in the early morning, having breakfast on the boat, and dancing to a live orchestra in between stops here in Delaware City and a number of other towns on the river.

Hunters and fishermen kept the wharves hopping, too. In the late 1800s, local anglers worked waters that comprised the largest sturgeon fishery in the country. Sturgeon are ugly, prehistoric-looking creatures that can weigh in at 500 pounds, or more. Their bellies were full of roe that got shipped up to Philadelphia and New York to be packed as caviar.

Greed brought those sturgeon glory days to a premature end. When the price of roe skyrocketed in the early 1900s, anglers overfished their meal ticket right out of existence.

Duck hunters made a financial killing, too. The late 1800s and early 1900s were the days of "market gunners," who employed oversized firearms akin to small cannons, dropping scads of waterfowl in a single shot. They packed those dead ducks up in humongous barrels that lined the wharves here, awaiting shipment up to big-city markets and restaurants.

In late February when the ice was coming down the river, [these market gunners] dressed in white clothes, rowed out through the floes in white "ice-boats," and sculled down on rafts of sleeping black ducks which they slaughtered with huge white-painted swivel guns mounted in the bow.

When the waterfowl population started to crash—not just here, but everywhere market gunners were doing their thing—the federal government responded by outlawing the big guns through the Migratory Bird Treaty Act of 1918. Yet another route to quick riches in Delaware City had fallen by the wayside.

But the powers that be in town soon latched onto another dream. In 1919, the federal government bought out the private C&D Canal Company and announced plans to widen the canal to accommodate the bigger vessels that were coming into vogue. News of these plans led to yet another big civic event on Clinton Street, during which another bevy of dignitaries filled the air with promises of another pot of gold. In the end, the feds shifted the terminus of the canal out of downtown Delaware City in favor of a wider spot two miles south of town.

Still, Delaware City's dreamers kept at it. In 1929, a businessman proposed the construction of a giant residential project on 9,000 acres outside of town. Dubbed "The Ideal City," the project went belly up almost immediately, thanks to the Great Depression. Interestingly, there is now a 21st-century echo of that Ideal City in the works. As of this writing, construction is under way on the Canal District, a fancy residential complex just south of town, where the new homes will be constructed amid refurbished historic structures that were once part of old Fort DuPont, which dates to 1898.

Turn east from Route 9 onto New Castle Avenue to drive through that project and see the old parade ground, as well as buildings that served as officers' quarters, a hospital, barracks, stables, and even an old movie theater. Some 3,000 German soldiers were held prisoner here during World War II. The southern end of the site features smallish Fort DuPont State Park, where you can stroll past some fort ruins and take in more sweet Delaware River views while contemplating the stories of all the get-rich-quick dreamers who've chased their fortunes in Delaware City through the centuries.

From Prison to Promenade to Pond

If you visit Delaware City in the warmer months, you'll want to plan things so that you can take the ferry from Battery Park out to Fort Delaware State Park. The origins of the island where that fort stands are shrouded in folklore. Supposedly, this spit of land started life as a minuscule mud flat. By one account, it was "the size of a man's hat" in the 1770s.

When a vessel loaded with peas got mired out there, some peas spilled out and took root. As the plants grew, more mud and debris got caught up around them. Things eventually reached a point where the story ends in a 300-acre acre island that's 1.6 miles long.

Once it became a full-fledged island, this Pea Patch got the attention of military planners looking for ways to protect the shipping channel that leads to Wilmington and Philadelphia. Their worries were understandable: The British had attacked the nearby town of Lewes during the War of 1812. The first fort that went up here, in 1831, lasted just 15 years before getting wiped out by bad weather. The fort you'll visit see today opened up just in time for the Civil War. Planners didn't take any chances with the weather the second time around. The walls of Fort Delaware are 32 feet high and 30 feet thick. Construction workers sank some 5,000 tree-trunk piles into the river in order to stabilize things under the island.

But all that work turned out to be sort of pointless since Confederate forces never came close to threatening the Delaware River. Instead, the fort was turned into a prison camp where some 33,000 Confederate soldiers were locked up. The fort has a gray, forlorn aspect to it, which is fitting considering the voluminous stories of ghosts and hauntings that have sprung up around it in modern times. While walking around and taking in exhibits, it will be easy to imagine what a cacophony of noise must have filled these walls when prisoners were here, living under the watchful eye of a garrison that totaled nearly 300 Union soldiers and officers.

> Sleeping in three tiers on rough planks, they were tortured by mosquitoes in summer and half frozen in winter; mortality from cholera was as high as 331 in one month.

The ground on Pea Patch Island was too marshy for burials. Dead prisoners were taken instead to the New Jersey side of the river, where an 85-foot-tall Confederate Monument stands today in their memory at Finn's Point National Cemetery, which is about a half-mile walk from Fort Mott, in Pennsville. (Some of the ferry rides from Delaware City include a stop at Fort Mott as well.)

Back on Pea Patch, nature lovers and photographers will want to find their way to the hiking trail that leads to an observation platform overlooking the marshlands that spread out beyond the fort. Pea Patch ranks as one of the largest wading bird nesting areas on the East Coast, with nine different species of herons, egrets, and ibis spending summers here.

Upon returning to Delaware City, follow that main drag of Clinton Street to the west and out of town, where its name changes to Cox Neck Road. Soon enough, you will come to the Biddle Point Parking Area, which leads down to the C&D Canal and the multipurpose trail that runs along its shores. That trail is also accessible from the nearby little town of St. Georges, which you can find your way to by veering left, or southwest, when you come to Clark's Corner Road.

The trail is a flat and easy affair. If you're lucky, one of those 21st-century megaships will roll through the canal while you stroll or pedal the path, officially known in Delaware is the Michael N. Castle Trail. (On the Maryland side, it's the Ben Cardin Trail.)

The way west out of St. Georges is Kirkwood-St. Georges Road, which will take you right up to 1,800-acre Lums Pond State Park, which once housed Native American hunting camps. Today, it features zip lines and elevated treetop rope walks in addition to the more traditional array of hiking trails, picnic areas, and campsites. Boating and fishing are popular here, too, thanks to the 200-acre pond that gives the park its name.

Like everything else in this trip, that pond is connected to the C&D Canal. A man-made affair, it was constructed in the early 1800s to gather up a generous supply of water from St. Georges Creek that could then be used to fill up the nearby canal lock where vessels stopped to make a change in elevation and continue on their way.

Staying the Course in Chesapeake City

With its sweet waterfront and interesting shops and restaurants, downtown Chesapeake City might look at first like just another small-town gem on the Delmarva Peninsula. But no other town in the region has a bridge like the one that towers over this downtown. With a steep, horseshoe-like shape, it reaches up 140 feet so as to accommodate the thousands of cargo ships that pass under it along the C&D Canal every year. This is the midpoint of the journey those behemoths — some are 700 feet long — take across the peninsula. The Chesapeake Bay lies 15 miles to the west; the Delaware Bay is 15 miles to the east.

Like Delaware City, Chesapeake City took shape in the earliest days of the canal. Unlike Delaware City, no one here made grand plans for future stardom as a major metropolis. When the canal opened on Oct. 17, 1829, just two buildings stood on the south bank of the waterway. One was a tavern. The other was the new lock house where schooners and other vessels paid tolls. The place was known as Bohemia Village then.

The canal had four locks, which operate like watertight boxes where vessels park while canal engineers add in or take out enough water to adjust for the elevation changes that occur between the Chesapeake and Delaware bays. Two of those locks were here, so folks had to wait around for a while—and it soon became clear that they needed more amenities than that one tavern. Within a decade, Chesapeake City had grown into a town of 300.

Schooners dominated canal traffic early on. Steamboats came along a little bit later. A chapter in my book, *Tubman Travels: 32 Underground Railroad Journeys on Delmarva*, tells the story of teenager Lear Green, who escaped from slavery by spending 18 hours stuffed inside an old sailor's chest on one of those steamships. Other enslaved men and women made their runs to freedom through this canal aboard schooners whose captains hid runaway slaves in secret compartments.

The post-Civil-War years were relatively prosperous ones in Chesapeake City. So-called "showboats" stopped to put on theatrical shows. Floating stores rolled through as well. Many of the beautiful buildings that stand downtown today went up in this period.

But the 20th century wasn't so kind, as the town endured a one-two-three-four series of punches to the civic gut. The first of those came in 1927, when an improvement project turned the canal into a lock-free affair. No longer did passengers and crew have to disembark and wait around in town.

Newfangled automobiles provided a measure of compensation. Cars then crossed the canal on a vertical-lift bridge that led traffic straight through the heart of town, connecting Lock Street on the north with George Street on the south. Chesapeake City became a popular way station where folks stopped for gas, food, and shopping.

The second punch came on a July afternoon in 1942. A 10-year-old boy named R. Harper Hazel was playing outside on his family's nearby farm when:

> I heard a sort of dull clanking sound coming from town. … Back then, I could always see the black lift bridge looming in the distance, outlined against the sky. My grandmother came outside and I pointed and yelled. She said, "My word, where's the bridge?"

A passing tanker, *Frans Klassen*, had crashed into the vertical lift bridge. The canal reopened to ship traffic one week later, but the bridge wasn't replaced for seven long years. In the interim, a ferry was the only way across—and that drove many of the passersby who had loved stopping here to choose other ways to get where they needed to go.

Punch #3: When the new bridge finally opened in 1949, it had that steep horseshoe silhouette that hovers over the town today. It works like a highway bypass, giving everyone a high-speed opportunity to roll right past Chesapeake City, no stopping. The fourth and final 20th-century punch landed during the 1960s, when another canal-improvement project resulted in the demolition of 39 waterfront homes that once counted as prime real estate.

By the time the 21st century dawned, Chesapeake City had settled into a quiet sort of normal. The population is a smidge under 700. In addition to browsing shops and having a meal, you'll want to visit the C&D Canal Museum, where you can get a look at a massive waterwheel that once operated at the old locks, as well as old steam engines that powered the wheel. Lots of other interesting exhibits are up as well.

When you leave the museum, take a look back up at that big bridge. Guess who the stretch of road up there is named after? That would be Augustine Herman, the 17th-century immigrant who first came up with the notion of digging a sailing shortcut across the heart of Delmarva.

CONNECTIONS
• New Castle County Tourism (Delaware City area)
dscc.com/newcastlecounty.html; 302.655.7221
• Delaware City, Del.
delawarecity.delaware.gov; 302.834.4573
• Fort Delaware State Park (and Pea Patch Island ferry)
destateparks.com/history/fortdelaware; 302.834.7941
• Fort DuPont State Park
destateparks.com/history/fortdupont; 302.834.7941
• Michael N. Castle C&D Canal Trail
delawaregreenways.org/portfolio_page/c-d-canal-trail; 302.655.7275
• Cecil County Tourism (Chesapeake City Area)
seececil.org; 800.232.4595
• Chesapeake City, Md.
chesapeakecity.com; 800.757.6030
• C&D Canal Museum
chesapeakecity.com/cd-canal-museum; 410.885.5621
• Ben Cardin Trail
chesapeakecity.com/cd-canal-recreational-trail; 800.757.6030

NEARBY TRIPS: A list of other trips on the upper Delmarva Peninsula is on page 7.

Way Back Machine
Steamboat Jumpin'

In 2012, *Cecil Soil Magazine* published an article titled, "Steamboat Days on the C&D Canal." In it, a man named Walter Cooling offers this fun bit of oral history about his childhood in Chesapeake City:

> I recall the steamboats that used to come through here. As a kid I used to jump off them into Back Creek. You see, we kids used to swim off the V, which was a wharf area at the entrance to the Chesapeake City Lock. The lock was next to Schaefer's old store. Well, if we saw the *Penn* or the *Lord Baltimore* in the lock, ready to drop into Back Creek, we would run up there, climb aboard, ride it a short distance, and then dive off into the water. Nobody on the boats ever objected.

Road Trip #15

Baseball Greatness Tour

No one knows where William Julius Johnson was born. Not much is known about his earliest years, either, aside from the fact that he was born in 1899 either in little Snow Hill, Md., or in the countryside nearby. According to family legend, his mother, "Miss Annie," had been abandoned and left on a doorstep as an infant. His father was some sort of waterman or sailor.

In his later years, Johnson shared a cherished memory from his hardscrabble younger years, recalling how he and his sister, Mary Emma, would climb up a ladder at bedtime to sleep in a chilly loft. Come morning, they would wake to the smell of a country breakfast wafting up from the main floor.

This simple memory illustrates the humble beginnings typical of the men who rose from traditional Delmarva roots to the heights of stardom in major-league baseball. Frank "Home Run" Baker, was the son of a farmer. Vic "The Delaware Peach" Willis was the son of a carpenter. You can follow in their footsteps by visiting small towns, little museums, statues, and parks where their accomplishments are celebrated.

Halls of Fame, Delmarva Style

Small-town baseball was once a huge deal on the Delmarva Peninsula. Pretty much every little town had its own team—not for Little Leaguers, but for grown men. That tradition lives on today through two area minor-league teams, the Wilmington (Del.) Blue Rocks and the Salisbury (Md.) Shorebirds.

You should definitely take in a game if you get the chance—both teams serve up affordable, family-friendly, game-day experiences. Plus, both teams' stadiums have something to offer history buffs. In Wilmington, Frawley Stadium is adjacent to the Delaware Sports Museum and Hall of Fame. (The end of this tour in Newark, Del. will leave you a short distance away.)

At Perdue Stadium in Salisbury, Md., the Eastern Shore Baseball Hall of Fame is open for an hour before every home game, as well as on Mondays during the baseball season and other times by appointment. Founded in 1997, this hall has an eclectic mix of old photos, uniforms, bats, balls, gloves, letters, programs, tickets, trophies, and more. A writer with the *Washington Post* once said:

> It is the way a baseball museum should feel, like digging through your grandparents' attic.

One wall has photos of all of the 28 big-league players through the years who hailed from Delmarva. You will find William Julius Johnson's photo up there. *Clutch* is the word that pops up over and over again when baseball people talk about how "Judy" Johnson earned his place among the game's all-time greats. He wasn't particularly strong, or fast, or powerful. He stood less than 6 feet tall and weighed less than 150 pounds. There was nothing flashy about his style, but, as fellow Negro League star James "Cool Papa" Bell put it:

> No one would drive in as many clutch runs as he would. No matter how much the pressure, ... Judy could do it when it counted.

Johnson was less than 10 years old when his family moved to Wilmington, Del. His father, William Henry, worked in the shipyards there for a while, then became a boxing instructor. In fact, William Henry wanted his son to become a boxer so badly that in the absence of a proper sparring partner, he forced Johnson to practice fighting against his sister. Johnson could never bring himself to hit her back.

Instead, he fell in love with baseball. He never forgot the first time he got to put on a real uniform:

> I was strutting around at 5 a.m., even though we didn't play until two in the afternoon.

Johnson dropped out of Howard High School, following at first in his father's footsteps by working in the shipyards. He played some for local teams, including the Rosedale Blues and the Madison Stars. His big break came in part because of his skills, but also because of World War I. With so many older men serving overseas, the semi-pro Bacharach Giants in Atlantic City, N.J. needed fresh blood and signed Johnson to a contract that paid $5 a game.

By the early 1920s, he was making $125 a month with the big-league Hilldale Daisies, who played near Philadelphia. Johnson's teammates on the Daisies gave him the nickname

"Judy" because of his resemblance to another Negro League star, Judy Gans. In the 1924 Negro World Series against the Kansas City Monarchs, Johnson hit a dramatic three-run, inside-the-park home run in the ninth inning to win game five of a 10-game series. The Daisies eventually lost that series, but they would go on to win a rematch the following year.

Johnson hit for a .392 average in that championship season. The following winter, he joined a number of other black baseball stars in Palm Beach, Fla., where two rival hotels hired their own "teams" of athletes to wait on tables by day and then play games by night for the entertainment of white guests.

The Great Depression wreaked havoc on many Negro League teams. The Hilldale Daisies folded altogether, and Johnson joined the Pittsburgh-based Homestead Grays as player/manager. Later, he played with a Pittsburgh Crawfords team that is often described as the Negro League version of the powerhouse 1927 New York Yankees.

After retiring in 1937, Johnson ran a general store and worked for the Continental Cab Company in Wilmington. In 1954, while working as a scout for the Philadelphia Athletics, he recommended that the team sign a talented young man named Henry Aaron.

> I got my boss out of bed and told him I had a good prospect and he would not cost too much. My boss cussed me out and said $3,500 was too much money.

In 1975, Judy Johnson became just the sixth black player inducted into the Baseball Hall of Fame. His renowned calmness under pressure deserted him on the day of his induction ceremony, as he broke down in tears and walked off the stage unable to deliver a proper acceptance speech beyond muttering, "God bless you all."

Johnson died on June 15, 1989. In addition to the two Delmarva halls of fame, there are three other places you can go to get in touch with Johnson's legacy. In 2019, a marker went up outside the library in Snow Hill (307 N. Washington St.), honoring that town's native son—the movement to put it up was inspired by an essay written by a local high school student. A statue of Johnson, poised in fielder's crouch, stands outside of Frawley Stadium in Wilmington, home of the minor league Blue Rocks. And Judy Johnson Memorial Park is in Wilmington, at West 3rd and North Dupont streets.

A Baker in Trappe

The little leaguers of Trappe, Md. play their games on fields with a Hall of Fame name. Home Run Baker Park, at 4200 Main St., honors a man whose roots on the Eastern Shore ran about as deep as those roots can go. Frank Baker's family had been working the land in Talbot County, Md. for six generations by the time he was born in 1886.

Legend has it that Baker decided to pursue a baseball career by age 10. As a teenager, he played with minor-league teams in the nearby towns of Ridgely and Cambridge. He also played briefly for the then-minor-league Baltimore Orioles, whose manager, Jack Dunn infamously cut Baker loose because he "could not hit."

Baker made his big-league debut with the Philadelphia Athletics in 1908, at age 22. This was the height of the so-called "dead ball era" when home runs were few and far between. Baker led the American League in home runs four times, but the most he ever hit in a single season was 12.

His most famous long balls came against the New York Giants in the 1911 World Series. In Game 2, he hit the go-ahead home run off of the famous Rube Marquard. In Game 3, he hit one off of the even more famous Christy Mathewson to tie the game in the ninth inning. The A's would win that game in 11 innings—and the series in six games. Baker and the A's went to four World Series between 1910 and 1914, winning three of them. This was the team that had the so-called "$100,000 Infield," which historian Bill James has rated as the greatest of all time. The A's later sold Baker's contract to the New York Yankees, where he played in two more World Series—both losing efforts.

The dead ball era came to a close with the rise of Babe Ruth in the 1920s. Baker's theory about the sudden surge in home runs was that the league had engineered a switch to a new type of "rabbit" ball. After his retirement, Baker returned home. He managed the minor-league Easton Farmers for a while—it was in that job that he discovered Jimmie Foxx, another Hall of Famer on our agenda here.

Eventually, Baker settled back into the family trade, farming. He was a member of the Trappe town board for a while, as well as a volunteer firefighter. Baker was inducted into the Baseball Hall of Fame in 1955. He died in 1963 and is buried at Spring Hill Cemetery in nearby Easton.

A little way west of Easton is the town of St. Michaels, of course. That is the hometown (and current residence) of Harold Baines, who was elected to the Hall of Fame in 2019 in honor of his hitting exploits with the Baltimore Orioles, Chicago White Sox, Texas Rangers, Oakland Athletics, and Cleveland Indians during the 1980s and 1990s. If you're lucky, you might catch a glimpse of Harold out shopping or dining in that Easton/St. Michaels area.

A Statue to Swish

The next stop on this Delmarva baseball tour is Chestertown, Md., the hometown of William "Swish" Nicholson. Another product of a farm family, Nicholson might never have reached baseball stardom had it not been for his color-blindness, as that's what caused the Naval Academy to reject his application. Instead, he enrolled at Washington College in Chestertown and tried out for the baseball team.

Nicholson made his big-league debut with the Philadelphia Athletics in 1936, but it was with the Chicago Cubs between 1939 and 1948 that he made a lasting name for himself. Cubs' fans used to do a whispered chant of his "Swish" nickname when he came up to bat. He twice led the National League in home runs and runs batted in. He was the star of the team in 1945, when the Cubs made it to the World Series, but lost.

Physical problems associated with diabetes led to Nicholson's retirement. He came back to Chestertown and lived the rest of his life on the family farm. In 1991, the town held a big dinner in his honor. Lots of big leaguers showed up to sing Nicholson's praises, and the event led to a local fundraising drive that rounded up $35,000 in private money to put a statue of Nicholson up in front of City Hall (118 N. Cross St.), where it still stands today.

Nicholson died in 1996—he is buried outside of town in the Old St. Paul's Churchyard. My favorite bit of trivia about him dates to a July 23, 1944 doubleheader against the New York Giants. Nicholson hit home runs in four consecutive at-bats that day. When he came up again in the eighth inning of the second game, the bases were loaded. But the Giants had seen enough. They walked him intentionally to force in a run. No one else in baseball would receive a bases-loaded intentional walk for more than 50 years after that, until Barry Bonds got the same treatment in a 1998 game.

'The Beast' of Sudlersville

Fourteen miles east of Chestertown is itty-bitty Sudlersville, Md., with a population of just 500. There, at the corner of Main and Church streets, you will find a statue of Jimmie Foxx, aka "Double X" and "The Beast." The town's old train station is of interest here, too—it houses a museum with an array of Foxx memorabilia on display. (The station is open only once a month or so, so you'll want to plan accordingly or perhaps call to ask about scheduling a tour.)

Foxx dropped out of high school to join a minor-league team in nearby Easton that was managed by Frank Baker, who quickly identified the youngster as a star in the making and sold his contract to the big-league Philadelphia A's. Foxx made his major-league debut in 1925 at the tender age of 17. The career that followed spanned 20 years, some with the A's and some with the Boston Red Sox.

Here is the hit parade that places Foxx among the game's all-time great sluggers: He hit 30 or more home runs in a dozen straight seasons. He had 100 or more RBI in 13 straight seasons. In 1932, he hit 58 home runs. (He actually hit 60 that year—enough to tie Babe Ruth's then-record total—but he lost two homers to rainouts.) He won three MVP awards. Yankees pitcher Lefty Gomez famously said of Foxx: "He has muscles in his hair."

The most amazing Foxx factoid of them all is this: He held the record for being the youngest player to reach 500 career home runs for an astounding 68 years—until Alex Rodriguez got there at a slightly younger age. Foxx was inducted into the Hall of Fame in 1951.

His relationship with his middle-of-nowhere hometown over the years was, well, complicated. Sudlersville held big banquets in his honor in both 1929 and 1933. At the first one, everyone got up to sing a ditty titled "Jimmie Boy! Our Jimmie Boy!" to the tune of "Maryland My Maryland." At the second one, the tune was "Jingle Bells" and the lyrics began:

Jimmie Foxx, Jimmie Foxx is our hometown boy,
He can hit the ball so hard it fills our hearts with joy ...

After his career ended, Foxx lived in Ohio, mostly. He came back home with some frequency, but managed somewhere along the line to lose hold of the affection that Sudlersville had previously displayed toward him. There are rumors of hard drinking. Foxx also had financial woes later in life, and there is a story out there about how on one visit back home no one in town would cash a check for him.

On the other hand there was Gil Dunn. A lifelong fan, Dunn put up a makeshift wall of tribute to Foxx in the pharmacy he ran on Kent Island. Once he built up a sizable collection of memorabilia, Dunn started promoting this little corner of tribute as the Jimmie Foxx Museum. One day in 1967, "The Beast" himself showed up at the pharmacy and led Dunn out to his car, opening the trunk.

Here is some stuff you may have. ... Nobody else wants it.

The treasure trove included MVP awards, gloves, uniforms, baseballs, and more. That's the heart of the Foxx collection that is now in the Sudlersville train station. Foxx passed away shortly after his visit to Dunn's pharmacy, choking to death on a piece of food while visiting his brother in Florida in 1959. Since his death, Sudlersville has come back around and re-embraced its native son. The statue went up on Main Street in 1997.

'The Delaware Peach'

Victor Gazaway Willis was born in Cecil County, Md., 11 short years after the Civil War ended. His father, a carpenter, moved the family across the border to Newark, Del. while Vic was still quite young. He starred on the diamond during his school years at Newark Academy and Delaware College, finding his way from there onto semi-pro teams in Pennsylvania and New York.

He made it to the big leagues at age 19, joining the Boston Beaneaters. Nerves got the best of him on his first outing, as he allowed eight runs in an 18–2 loss to the Baltimore Orioles. But he settled in quite nicely after that, finishing his first season with 25 wins, 13 losses, and a 2.84 ERA. The *Boston Sunday Journal* marveled:

> Willis has speed and the most elusive curves. His "drop" is so wonderful that, if anyone hits it, it is generally considered a fluke.

Known as "The Delaware Peach," Willis had his share of big-league triumphs. He had a four-year run with the Pittsburgh Pirates in which he compiled a record of 88–46 and had an ERA of 2.08. Those Pirates won the 1909 World Series against Ty Cobb and the Detroit Tigers.

But he had lots of bad luck, too, especially in Boston, where he compiled a miserable record of 42-72 between 1903 and 1905. In fact, Willis still holds the post-1900 record for losses in a season — 29, in 1905. But the Beaneaters couldn't hit a lick. Willis actually pitched pretty well in those years, only to lose one low-scoring game after another.

What's most interesting about Willis is his innings count. A modern-day pitcher is considered a workhorse if he throws 200 innings in a year. At the age of 23 in 1899, Willis pitched 342 innings. In 1902, he pitched 410 innings and threw an unthinkable 45 complete games.

His career ended in 1909, at which point he returned home to Newark, where two years later he sunk his baseball savings into the Washington Hotel on Main Street, where he advertised such extravagances as electric lights and steam heat as highlights of his "first-class accommodations to the traveling public." Willis and his wife, Mary Jane, ran the place for more than three decades.

Willis died in 1947, nearly five decades before his 1995 election into the Baseball Hall of Fame. The Newark Historical Society has Willis's hall of fame plaque in its collection, along with other memorabilia. They also erected a marker in his honor a few years back at the intersection of Elkton Road and West Park Place.

There is one other claim to fame in Vic Willis's life that will warm the hearts of several generations of University of Delaware alumni—it was Willis who installed the faux-stone exterior in front of the bar at the old Washington Hotel. Starting in the 1970s, that bar became the Stone Balloon Tavern, a legendary nightclub where scads of young up-and-coming rockers—from Bruce Springsteen to Metallica—appeared in the years before they went on to earn fame and fortune. Alas, the Washington Hotel was torn down in the early 2000s, though a new version of the Stone Balloon is up and running on that site today.

CONNECTIONS

• Wicomico County Tourism (for Salisbury, Md. area)
wicomicotourism.org; 800.332.8687

• Perdue Stadium/Delmarva Shorebirds
milb.com/delmarva; 410.219.3112
6400 Hobbs Rd., Salisbury, Md.

• Eastern Shore Baseball Hall of Fame
esbhalloffame.org; 410.546.4444
6400 Hobbs Rd., Salisbury, Md.

• Worcester County Tourism (Snow Hill, Md.)
visitworcester.org; 800.852.0335

• Talbot County Tourism (Trappe, Easton, and St. Michaels, Md.)
tourtalbot.org; 410.770.8000

• Kent County Tourism (Chestertown, Md.)
kentcounty.com/visitors; 410.778.0416

• Queen Anne's County Tourism (Sudlersville, Md.)
qac.org/151/Tourism-Office; 410.604.2100

• The Sudlersville Train Station Museum
sudlersvillemuseum.org; 410.438.3501
101 S. Linden St., Sudlersville, Md.

• The Newark Historical Society
newarkdehistoricalsociety.org; 302.224.2408
429 S, College Ave., Newark, Del.

• Wilmington (Del.) Tourism
visitwilmingtonde.com; 800.489.6664

• Frawley Stadium
milb.com/wilmington; 302.888.2015
801 Shipyard Dr., Wilmington, Del.

• Delaware Sports Hall of Fame
desports.org; 302.425.3263
801 Shipyard Dr., Wilmington, Del.

NEARBY TRIPS: "The Baseball Tour" includes stops on the upper, middle, and lower Delmarva Peninsula. The other trips in this book are broken out by region on page 7.

Way Back Machine
A Tantrum for the Ages

If your past travels in Delaware ever took you to the Mr. Donut franchise in the Milford Plaza Shopping Center, then you had a brush with baseball fame. Forrest "Spook" Jacobs owned that shop for fortysome years, up until his death in 2011. Jacobs was not a hall of famer — he spent most of his 17 baseball seasons in the minor leagues.

One day while playing in the old Pacific Coast League, Jacobs got hit by a pitch and went after the pitcher, throwing punches furiously. Not satisfied with taking out one opponent, he went after the second baseman. The former was Tommy Lasorda, and the latter was Sparky Anderson. I'm betting that no one will ever equal Jacobs's record of clocking two future hall-of-fame managers in the same tantrum.

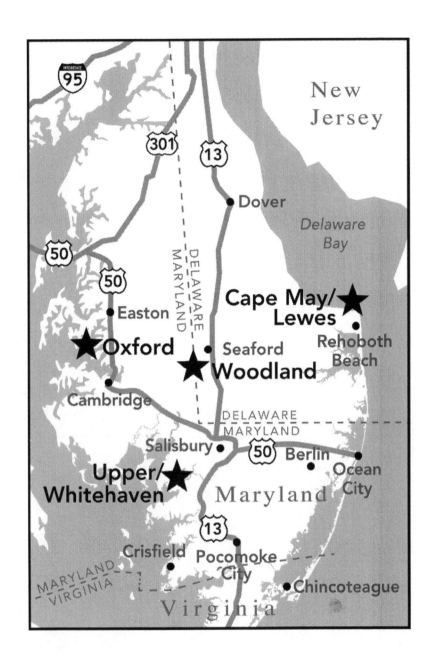

Road Trip #16

Five Ferry Tales

Oftentimes, we look back toward the past through rose-colored glasses. If we hear, for instance, about a ferry dating clear back to the 1600s that still runs today across the Tred Avon River in Talbot County, Md., our minds tend to conjure up images that have a straight-out-of-Hollywood quality, with distinguished colonial characters perched atop noble-looking steeds and set against a backdrop of gorgeous clouds and golden light.

In reality, these crossings were less than idyllic affairs. The travelers who arrived at ferry landings back then were likely filthy, exhausted, and short-tempered. Overland roads in colonial times were in dreadful shape, full of hazardous ruts and mud-soaked stream crossings. It took two or three days to make the trips we knock out in two or three hours.

I'm happy to report, however, that no such unpleasantries surround the five ferry rides in this road trip. These crossings all rank as scenic, serene experiences, even if the stories they have to tell occasionally touch on unsavory matters—think murder, forgery, ghosts, and kidnappings.

Not one of these trips is an essential element in getting from one specific Point A to another Point B. They rank more as optional diversions along roads less traveled. I like the way the writer Casey N. Sep put it a few years back in a magazine article about the first crossing on our agenda here, the Oxford-Bellevue Ferry:

> I have taken that same ferry … many times. Not because it is useful—for the crossing is less than one mile—but precisely because it is useless.

'Notoriously Scandalous' on the Tred Avon

The ride across the Tred Avon River between the towns of Oxford and Bellevue runs just 20 minutes or so and ranks as quite the popular side trip with wanderers on their way from one to another of the voluminous tourist attractions in St. Michaels (see Chapter 1), Easton, and Tilghman Island (see Chapter 12).

The local government first authorized this crossing in 1683, promising to pay 2,500 pounds of tobacco per year to the man who ran it. First up on that list was Richard Royston, who ranked as a leading citizen in the founding days of Oxford. He had family connections to the prominent Fosters who then owned all of what we know now as Tilghman Island. When the town of Oxford was first laid out, Royston got prestigious "Lot #1" on the map.

But his status took a tumble after he was convicted of forgery. The details of that case seem to be lost in the mists of history. Royston was sentenced to receive a severe public whipping, but it's not clear whether that actually happened. We do know that he left town shortly thereafter and eventually died at sea in 1694.

His old friends in Maryland had not forgotten him by that point. The state's General Assembly greeted the news of his demise by passing a formal resolution in condemnation of the dead man, charging that his "life and actions" were "notoriously scandalous in this province."

Flash forward two centuries, to the late 1800s. Before then, muscle power fueled this ferry's trips across the river, by way of a 14-foot-long sweep oar at the stern, which by all reports required near super-human strength with heavy loads aboard. Later, a sail and more traditional oars came into play. The era of those oars finally passed in 1886 with the arrival of a steam-powered tug, *William H. Fisher.*

Here, too, our mind's eye tends to roam into rose-colored territory. The steam-engine era is often romanticized in modern-day books and exhibits, but the reality of those vessels involved deafening noise, filthy smoke, and the ever-present risk of explosion. The *Fisher* was the ferry equivalent of a ramshackle old pickup truck you get stuck behind in a traffic jam—it constantly belched black soot and frequently conked out mid-river. A crew member recalled:

> She had a habit of sinking during the night, and a good many mornings we had to pump her out. A couple of times she went down to her gunnels and when we got her up we had to get the crabs and the hardheads out of her.

Interestingly, quite a few women served as ferry keepers over the centuries here on the Tred Avon. The first, Amy Jensen, did so back in the 1690s. Another, Judith Bennett, had help from three different husbands during her tenure in the early 1700s, but she also ran solo for more than 10 years, "when between spouses." At least two other women ran the show here during the 1700s as well. I have not seen any report on whether they had hired help or perhaps just flexed their own biceps when in need of that super-human strength with heavy loads.

As of this writing, the Oxford-Bellevue Ferry has been owned and operated by Tom and Judy Bixler for nearly two decades. Be sure to leave some extra time so you can wander around Oxford, whose streets are lined with gorgeous old homes, mast-filled marinas, and scenic river views. Old-time log canoes still race out on the Tred Avon River several times a year.

The little Oxford Museum has items of interest about the rich history of the town. Tench Tilghman, who famously served as right-hand man to George Washington during the Revolutionary War, was born nearby and is buried here. A man named Robert Morris made a small fortune here as a merchant in early colonial times—that's his name on the famous Robert Morris Inn. His son, also Robert Morris, grew up to become even more famous than his father, doling out such big wads of patriotic cash during the 1770s and 1780s that history books often refer to him as the "financier of the American revolution."

If you feel like splurging on a meal, that Robert Morris Inn has quite a longstanding reputation for high-end culinary excellence. But you could also opt for a simpler approach, grabbing sandwiches from the deli counter at the Oxford Market and carrying them to the waterfront park across the street. Either way, you should probably save room for a scoop of ice cream from the Scottish Highland Creamery.

Double Cross on the Wicomico River
The second and third entries in this collection of ferry tales are a back-and-forth affair on the Eastern Shore backroads. Two old-

school ferries operate within eight miles of each other along the pretty Wicomico River as it winds its way toward the Chesapeake Bay from up in Salisbury, Md.

You can cross one way at Upper Ferry and come back the other way at Whitehaven. In between, there will be a good number of back-country towns and sites to see. The first thing you'll need to do is look over a map and make some choices: Will you be approaching the river from the south or the north? Which crossing would you like to make first?

Once known as Lower Ferry, the three-car-maximum Whitehaven operation dates back to the same colonial period as Oxford-Bellevue. In fact, various competing claims to fame get tossed around in this little subculture—this one is the oldest *continuously operating* ferry in the country, while that one is the oldest *privately owned* ferry. Bottom line: They're all really old.

Whitehaven takes its modern-day name from the cute-as-a-button village on the north side of the river. That name honors the English birthplace of town founder George Gale, whose claim to brush-with-greatness fame involves being the second husband of one of George Washington's grandmothers.

The first time I made this crossing, I was headed from the south bank to the north, so the view up ahead was all about Whitehaven. The three-story Whitehaven Hotel, built in 1810, is a gorgeous remnant of times gone by. Accounts of travelers stopping at the hotel grace the pages of a couple famous old novels about the region, *The Entailed Hat* and *River of Rogues*. In the latter, guests gather beneath a tulip tree on the grounds to sip iced rum on a hot summer day.

Not every scene through the centuries was quite so genteel. During the 1800s, traveling salesmen who worked this route could stay overnight for the bargain rate of 25 cents apiece, but they slept *four* men to a bed. An oft-repeated bit of oral history has the writer Edna Ferber staying here while doing research for the 1926 novel that eventually became the Broadway musical *Show Boat*.

Early on, this ferry was part of a stagecoach route between the towns of Princess Anne and Vienna. Steamboats stopped regularly at Whitehaven in the late 1800s and early 1900s. The town was a bustling affair then, with shipyards, canneries, blacksmiths, and several types of stores. Those businesses slowly faded away as commerce on the Eastern Shore moved inland after first railroad lines and then trucks and highways came along.

The hotel fell into disrepair and nearly ended up demolished, but a local nonprofit saved the day in the 1990s. Among the tidbits that surfaced during the restoration work that followed was a hidden door that experts say was probably used to facilitate the arrival and departure of rumrunners during Prohibition times.

One batch of liquor smugglers working this area back then had a wonderfully colorful moniker, "The Whippoorwill Gang." They rigged up their small boats with airplane engines so as to outrun the revenue agents on their tail.

The streets of Whitehaven are definitely worth a stroll, especially for the sweet-steepled Whitehaven Methodist Church, which dates to 1892, and the old one-room Whitehaven School. Both buildings are now owned by the preservation-minded Whitehaven Heritage Association. The Whitehaven Hotel is a privately run bed & breakfast.

What happens after your Whitehaven crossing depends on which side of the river you end up on. If you land on the north shore, you could wander your way deeper onto the backroads, through the towns of Bivalve, Nanticoke, and Tyaskin (see Chapter 22). If you end up on the south bank, the way around to the Upper Ferry winds in a horseshoe shape down Whitehaven Ferry Road, along Folks Road, and back up along Allen and Upper Ferry roads. You might choose to extend that trip by wandering farther south and into Princess Anne, if you like— the old Teackle Mansion there is an interesting option.

The Upper Ferry vessel is even smaller than the one at Whitehaven, with a capacity of just two cars. This crossing started out geared toward a different 17th-century stagecoach route, between the towns of Westover and Sharptown. If you end up on the south bank, you will want to make the reverse of the horseshoe-shaped drive described above to reach the crossing at Whitehaven.

A landing on the north bank here will put you near Pemberton Road. If you head northeast on this, you will soon be at the edge of Salisbury, where the 262-acre Pemberton Park serves up sweet hiking trails and a fascinating old plantation house (again, see Chapter 22). One other possibility to look up here is Red Roost restaurant, which specializes in Eastern Shore comfort food (including steamed crabs) and is housed in a refurbished old chicken house. It gets rave reviews from friends of mine.

'Celtic Vindictiveness' at the Woodland Ferry

There is a touch of infamy about the fourth crossing on this ferry tour. Woodland Ferry is a cable-operated affair that runs across a thin stretch of the Nanticoke River near Seaford, in Southern Delaware. A man named James Cannon launched the service in the 1740s, and his family remained in charge for a hundred-plus years—the place was known as Cannon's Ferry for most of its history.

Rates in the early days were 5 cents per person, 5 cents per horse, 10 cents for a two-wheeled carriage, and 30 cents for a four-wheeled affair. There is no charge today. The ferry is operated by the state of Delaware.

If that Cannon name rings a bell, well, it should. The Cannons that ran the ferry were related to Patty Cannon, the mastermind in an infamous gang that worked this area in the mid-1800s, catching escaped slaves and kidnapping free blacks. She may well have used this ferry while transporting some of her victims, who often ended up sold off to plantations in the Deep South. Many wound up dead, too.

The Cannon in charge at the ferry during that pre-Civil War period was Jacob. He built Cannon Hall, the showpiece house at this crossing, in 1810. The accounts I've seen of its construction all agree that Jacob had the Georgian-style abode built for his fiancée. Most of those sources say that she jilted Jacob at the last minute, though one claims instead that she died tragically just before the wedding.

In either case, Jacob ended up distraught and decided not to move in—Cannon Hall stayed empty for decades after its completion. Jacob seems to have turned into a nasty piece of work along the way. He and a brother, Isaac, had a fleet of sailing vessels working trade routes to Baltimore. They owned thousands of acres of land hereabouts, many acquired in ruthless fashion via foreclosure and usury.

In 1843, Jacob sued a man named Owen Daw (some accounts have him as Owen O'Day) over a stolen beehive. Cannon won the suit, but lost his life. A "man of Celtic vindictiveness," Daw shot Jacob Cannon right on the wharf where the ferry lands today. The old *Works Progress Administration Guide to Delaware* says that the murder happened "under the eyes of condoning neighbors," who seemed to feel that Daw had done everyone a public service by killing Cannon. The killer ran off, headed on last report for the "wilds of Missouri." He was never caught.

Woodland Ferry is mainly a tourist attraction today, though some people still use it as a regular route between the towns of Seaford and Laurel. If you make this crossing, it will be aboard the *Tina Fallon*, which was built on the Delmarva Peninsula by Chesapeake Shipbuilding of Salisbury, Md.

Ghostly Crossing of the Delaware Bay

The final crossing here operates on a different scale altogether from the other ferries in this trip. Rather than a short journey across a calm stretch of river, the ride across Delaware Bay from Lewes, Del., to Cape May, N.J. covers 17 miles and takes nearly an hour and a half. The vessels involved are longer than a football field. This trip involves elevators, air conditioning, snack bars, and free wi-fi.

You will catch glimpses along the way of three historic lighthouses — Cape May Light, the Harbor of Refuge Light, and the Delaware Breakwater East End Light. In the summer months, you might see some dolphins as well.

This Cape May-Lewes Ferry dates only to 1964, though politicians in Delaware and New Jersey had been talking on and off for most of the prior century about getting such a service up and running. When they finally managed it, things got off to an ignominious start, as the opening-day festivities with skydivers, jet fighters, bagpipe bands, and thousands of spectators were marred by an incident involving a propeller caught in a steel cable that left hundreds of passengers stranded on the very first crossing.

After reading up on the history of this ferry, I couldn't help but wonder if ghosts might have been involved in that mishap. The accident happened at the Lewes terminal, which stands near historically dangerous waters where deadly shipwrecks have occurred with regularity over the centuries. Some of those shipwreck victims were supposedly buried here, in graves that lie under the parking lot at the terminal.

There have been several newspaper accounts in recent decades of strange goings-on at the terminal—doors slamming in empty rooms, hand dryers turning on in mysterious fashion, and a strange man in a cape with long white hair spending time in the women's restroom. One ferry manager told a reporter that it has been nearly impossible to keep overnight staff on board. He described the case of one woman who had only been on the job three or four nights when:

> She came running in, threw the keys at me and told me, "There's ghosts in here, nobody told me that. I'm not staying—I quit, I'm done."

The ghost stories add a fun element to a trip in which you can't really go wrong. The scenery on this voyage is outstanding, and the towns that lie on either end are full of interesting bits of history, as well as one-of-a-kind shops and restaurants (see Chapter 18 for Lewes). The Cape May-Lewes Ferry also offers a number of themed cruises during the year—think wine dinners, beer tastings, and fireworks-show trips.

CONNECTIONS
• The Oxford-Bellevue Ferry
oxfordbellevueferry.com; 410.745.9023
W. Strand Rd. and N. Morris St., Oxford, Md.
• Talbot County Tourism
tourtalbot.org; 410.770.8000
• Town of Oxford
oxfordmd.net; 410.226.5122
• The Oxford Museum

oxfordmuseummd.org; 410.226.0191

101 South Morris St., Oxford, Md.

• Whitehaven Ferry & Upper Ferry

www.wicomicocounty.org/301/Ferry-Schedule; 410.543.2765

Whitehaven: 23865 River St., Quantico, Md.

Upper: 5420 N. Upperferry Rd., Salisbury, Md.

• Wicomico County Tourism (Wicomico River north bank)

wicomicotourism.org; 800.332.8687

• Somerset County Tourism (Wicomico River south bank)

visitsomerset.com; 800.521.9189

• The Woodland Ferry

deldot.gov/programs/woodland_ferry/index.shtml;

302.629.7742

5426 Woodland Ferry Rd., Seaford, Del.

• Southern Delaware Tourism

visitsoutherndelaware.com; 800.357.1818

• The Cape May-Lewes Ferry

cmlf.com; 800.643.3779

43 Cape Henlopen Dr., Lewes, Del.

• Lewes Chamber of Commerce

leweschamber.com/visit; 302.645.8073

• Cape May Tourism

capemay.com; 609.463.6415

NEARBY TRIPS: A list of other trips on the middle and lower Delmarva Peninsula is on page 7.

Road Trip #17

Sailing the Tall Ships

At perhaps the lowest point in his life, long before he became a world-famous abolitionist, Frederick Douglass would sometimes gaze out toward the Chesapeake Bay from the farm in Talbot County, Md. where he was toiling as a slave under a sadistic master. The white sails of schooners on that horizon left him dreaming of a different life:

> You are loosed from your moorings, and are free; I am fast in my chains, and am a slave! You move merrily before the gentle gale, and I sadly before the bloody whip! You are freedom's swift-winged angels, that fly round the world; I am confined in bands of iron! O that I were free! O, that I were on one of your gallant decks, and under your protecting wing!

None of us live today in the depths of bondage that Douglass endured. But those tall ships of yore still have the power to spark our imagination, inspiring dreams of adventure and freedom. The Delmarva Peninsula is home today to a pair of replica tall ships that give you a chance to get in touch with those sails of freedom. Each ship has its own stories to tell about American history. You can climb aboard as these vessels set out for public cruises. Once under way, you can clamber below decks and feel the rolling of waves. Back on deck, the crew might even let you help hoist a sail or two.

Forgotten Chapter: 'New Sweden'

The older of these two ships, *Kalmar Nyckel*, is basically the *Mayflower* of Delaware. Emblazoned in the bright blue and gold of Sweden, this enormous replica stretches 140 feet from bow to stern. The vertical run from waterline to topmost flagstaff is 105 feet.

The original was built in a Dutch shipyard in 1625. A middling affair, this pinnace was small enough to serve as a large merchant ship and large enough to serve as a small warship. That flexibility is exactly what King Gustavus Adolphus of Sweden wanted when he urged his cities to stock up on commercial vessels that might also be able to serve the country when winds of war started blowing, as they did with great frequency in the 17th century.

The cities of Kalmar and Jonkoping went in together on *Kalmar Nyckel*. The ship did a brief stint in the Swedish navy before ending up in the hands of New Sweden Company, a private firm that operated through a special royal charter issued by the successor to Gustavus Adolphus, Queen Christina, who took the throne in 1632 at the tender age of six. (Her name now adorns the Christina River in Wilmington, Del.)

Kalmar Nyckel set off on her first trip across the Atlantic in 1637, trying to claim for Sweden a piece of the new North American pie. The leader of that mission was a fascinating character, Peter Minuit. Born in the land we know as Germany, Minuit had a wealth of experience. He had already explored the East Coast for the Dutch East India Company. He had served as governor of the New Netherland colony, too—he's the guy who famously bought Manhattan Island from the Lenape Indians for a batch of baubles and trinkets.

Minuit got fired from that Dutch gig over allegations that he looked the other way while some greedy settlers pocketed money that belonged to his employer. It's possible that he pursued a Swedish assignment in hopes of winning vindication for this stain on his reputation.

In any case, he seems to have done an admirable job in establishing New Sweden on the site of modern-day Wilmington, Del. Earlier European settlements along the East Coast had endured all manner of disasters, from starvation to deadly disease to battles with natives. One reason why things went smoothly in the early days of New Sweden is that Minuit knew how to time his arrival, crossing the ocean in the dangerous winter months so that his colonists might arrive in time for the spring planting season of 1638.

The *Mayflower*, by contrast, chose a safer sailing season and arrived off of Massachusetts in November, at which point its leaders decided it would be better to spend winter aboard the vessel. By springtime, half of those colonists and crew were dead from disease.

Expert planning is one of three things that make Minuit stand out among his fellow explorers. A second is the way he treated Indians with a level of respect and deference unusual among Europeans of his day. After sailing up the Delaware Bay, Minuit did nothing in the way of settling in until he arranged a meeting with the locals aboard the *Kalmar Nyckel* and completed the purchase of some land. The Swedes never ended up doing battle with the locals in the way the Dutch did at Lewes, or the English at Jamestown.

The third thing that makes Minuit interesting was his vision for the New World. In his native area along the Rhine River, the people known as "Walloons" had endured their share of war and religious persecution. Minuit had a Statue-of-Liberty notion in mind for his Swedish expedition. He hoped that once the new colony got established, it would become a much-needed haven for the poor huddled masses of Walloons.

Alas, he never got a chance to realize that dream. A few months after landing in Delaware, Minuit set out for a return trip to Sweden, where he planned to load up on supplies and round up new colonists. He detoured to the West Indies en route to make some side money picking up a load of tobacco. The weather got the best of him there. He was visiting aboard the vessel of a fellow captain in the port we now know as St. Kitt's when a hurricane rolled in, blowing that vessel out into open seas, where it sank, killing everyone aboard.

You can walk today in the footsteps of Minuit at the site of Fort Christina, which once stood atop "The Rocks" along a quiet stretch of the Christina River quite close to the plethora of museums, restaurants, and diversions along the Riverwalk in downtown Wilmington (see Chapter 7).

The park is lined with gorgeous shade trees and dotted with an informative array of signage about the events of the mid-1600s. Here, too, is a monument to the settlers of New Sweden that was erected in 1938 as a gift from the people of Sweden honoring the 300-year anniversary of *Kalmar Nyckel*'s landing. Nothing remains of the fort, of course, though it's easy enough to put the structure squarely in your mind's eye while visiting the site. A bit of trivia: That fort housed the first two log cabins ever built in what would become the United States.

Even without Minuit's expert leadership, the colony flourished for a bit, expanding its geographic reach along a string of forts running up the Delaware River toward modern-day Philadelphia. But things started to go south for New Sweden when Minuit's old employers at the Dutch East India Company built their own fort nearby, at the site of modern-day New Castle, Del.

One of Minuit's successors as governor of New Sweden, Johan Risingh, treated the Dutch presence as an unacceptable provocation, seizing the fort by force in 1654. This outraged the notoriously short-tempered governor of New Netherland, Peter Stuyvesant, who soon showed up with a stupendous array of seven tall ships and more than 300 soldiers. The Swedes surrendered their colony without a fight.

Might things have turned out differently if Minuit had survived? Would his mix of experience, diplomatic instincts, and legal acumen have led to a different outcome? There is no way of knowing.

What we do know is that the Dutch couldn't hold onto the place, either. In 1664, the British ousted them from both New York and Delaware. A long, complicated spat ensued over which rich Englishman would take control of the place. Quaker William Penn and his colony, Pennsylvania, eventually won that debate, setting the old Swedish outpost onto its way to becoming the biggest city of "The First State."

Just down 7th Street from Fort Christina is the shipyard where the modern-day replica of *Kalmar Nyckel* was constructed. At a visitors center there, you can learn more about how that job was done. The *Kalmar Nyckel* offers public cruises here in Wilmington. It frequently sails out of nearby New Castle as well, along with a seasonal schedule of other ports.

To me, the most striking aspect of the vessel is its myriad ornate carvings, including depictions of lions, griffins, angels, and wind gods. These sculptures were all crafted using mallets, scrapers, and other tools that would have been used by 17th-century artisans.

There was a bit of imagination involved in the *Kalmar Nyckel* reconstruction. With no detailed plans of this specific pinnace available in the historical record, the builders had to guesstimate how the vessel might have been put together based on what's known more generally about how things worked during the "golden age" of Dutch shipbuilding.

Those original builders constructed a real stalwart. After Minuit's death, *Kalmar Nyckel* made it back to Sweden to complete that first round trip. In the years that followed, the boat made three more such round trips, and those four crossings of the Atlantic are the most recorded for any European vessel in the 1600s.

Colonial Conflict: A Taxing Situation

Things worked differently with the construction of the *Sultana*, a replica schooner whose home port is Chestertown, Md. The modern-day reconstruction of this vessel is based on a meticulous survey conducted on the original in 1768 by the British Royal Navy, which bought the *Sultana* one short year after she launched from a shipyard in Boston.

Most *Sultana* cruises today are school field trips, but the vessel also offers public sails several times a month during spring, summer, and fall. It's also a star attraction at Downrigging Weekend, a wonderful annual event that brings a gaggle of tall ships to Chestertown at the end of October. (The *Kalmar Nyckel* is usually on hand for those festivities as well.)

Back when the original *Sultana* sailed, schooners still ranked as newfangled affairs. They were designed to be faster and more maneuverable than older square-rigged boats. For the man assigned to command this particular schooner, it was a case of love at first sight. In a letter written the day before he stepped aboard the ship as captain, John Inglis had this to say:

> I have seen her and think she is the best vessel employ'd that way, as she is strong and vastly pretty.

The *Sultana*'s speed and agility were exactly what the British navy was looking for in those momentous times. The stories the *Sultana* has to tell touch at every turn on the roots of the American revolution. The long Seven Years War had just ended, leaving the British government strapped for cash and desperate to get its finances in order.

The thinking in London was that American colonists should be happy to do their part, considering that one front of that Seven Years War was focused on the colonists' own security — in schoolbooks on this side of the Atlantic, that front is known as the French and Indian War. Thus came a series of taxes, including the Stamp Act, the Townshend Acts, and the Tea Act.

These laws imposed new levies on economic staples like paper, glass, paint, and, most famously, tea. The colonists were not at all happy about being forced to do their part for those British war debts — instead, they launched protests against "taxation without representation."

The *Sultana*'s mission was to help put the kibosh on these protests, as well as to nab the legion of smugglers trying to evade those taxes. The *Sultana*'s voyage from England to tackle this job was a perilous affair. A wicked storm nearly toppled the schooner, and desperate crew members had to throw all of their beer overboard to stay afloat. This wasn't a laughable turn of events, actually — beer was basically the only healthy liquid available to them, as it was impossible back then to keep water fresh during a months-long sail across the ocean.

Sultana arrived in Boston in October of 1768, then spent the next four years patrolling the Atlantic Coast, including long stretches in the Delaware and Chesapeake bays. Its crew boarded and searched hundreds of vessels during that time, often in circumstances that could get quite tense. They exchanged fire with one brig, the *Carolina*, on May 9, 1772. Later that year, the *Sultana* returned to England, where she sailed off into the mists of history. No one is quite sure what became of her.

Painted in stately swaths of gold and black, the *Sultana* replica is every bit as "vastly pretty" as the original must have been. Once you climb aboard, there are lots of interesting things to discuss with crew members. Why was the desertion rate aboard this ship so high? A total of 100 sailors were stationed aboard during its North American tour of duty, and 60 of them tried to skedaddle at one point or another.

You'll get a sense while wandering about for the frustration those sailors endured. The quarters were tight, the food was awful, the medical care was barbaric, and the work was dangerous. A bit of trivia: You've heard the phrase "three square meals?" One crew member told me that the term may come from the shape of the plates you'll see down in the dining area.

A wealth of other details are worth your attention while aboard the *Sultana*. But it's the big picture that I found myself thinking about the most. As the Sultana Foundation puts it in one of their school lesson plans:

The laws *Sultana* enforced drove the colonists to reassess fundamental assumptions about government and society that had shaped Europe for more than two thousand years. The egalitarian principles that took root in America during *Sultana*'s years have been the driving force behind much of American history ever since.

CONNECTIONS
• *Kalmar Nyckel*
kalmarnyckel.org; 302.429.7447
• Wilmington (Del.) Tourism
visitwilmingtonde.com; 800.489.6664
• Schooner *Sultana*
sultanaeducation.org; 410.778.5954
• Kent County (Md.) Tourism
kentcounty.com/visitors; 410.778.0416

NEARBY TRIPS: A list of other trips on the upper Delmarva Peninsula is on page 7.

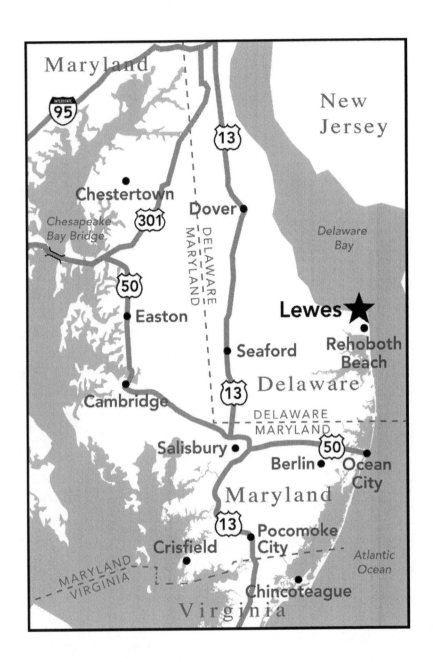

Road Trip #18

Lewes, Del.

The peninsula we know as Cape Henlopen would have looked like catnip to early European explorers, promising the possibility of sheltered harbors ahead after months on the open seas. And that broad opening beyond the cape, into what we know as Delaware Bay? It would have looked like a potential shortcut to China, a trade-route dream those early mariners were chasing.

It's possible the Vikings or some other early seafarers found their way to this cape, but the first European ship that sailed into the historical record arrived in 1609. That vessel made a pit stop, nothing more, as Englishman Henry Hudson soon headed back into the ocean, veering north and eventually sailing past the future site of New York City along the river that now bears his name.

A Hudsonesque pit stop won't cut it in modern-day Lewes — there is far too much to see and do. Lewes is the Goldilocks of Delmarva beach resorts, perfect for people worried on one hand that places like Rehoboth Beach and Ocean City will be too crowded, but afraid on the other that places like Assateague Island won't offer enough in the way of creature comforts.

There is one big stretch of beach right in town and another just outside in an expansive state park. If they get too crowded, you're a short drive from much more isolated stretches of sand. The downtown has a small-town scale, but you'll still be able to find a good vegan meal and a first-rate toy store. Even if it does turn out in the end that Lewes is too small for you, Rehoboth Beach is within pedaling distance, and storied Cape May on the New Jersey side is a sweet ferry ride away.

False Starts for the 'First Town'

What's in a name? That question will pop up time and again around Lewes. The second English adventurer to arrive here, Samuel Argall, christened the bay in honor of his sponsor, Sir Thomas West, aka Lord de la Warre (pronounced *del-uh-wear*—get it?). When Dutchman Cornelius Jacobsz Mey visited in 1614, he named both Cape Mey and Cape Cornelius (which has since washed away) in honor of himself. Cape Henlopen pays homage to Mey's business partner, Thijmen Jacobsz Hinlopen.

This last christening caused a bunch of confusion. Mey applied the "Hinlopen" name to a spit of land farther south, at Fenwick Island. Somehow or another the moniker migrated north over the centuries, creating a bevy of mix-ups over which cape was the site of this, that, or another event.

This Cape Henlopen is definitely where the Dutch put up a fort in 1631. This is how Lewes earned its nickname, "The First Town in the First State," though the story of that settlement amounts to a disastrous false start. Those pioneers decorated their fort in dramatic fashion, adorning its front gate with a patriotic image of the sword-wielding, tongue-wagging "red lion, rampant."

A seemingly minor incident early on ballooned into a catastrophe for the place these settlers called Zwaanendael, or "swan valley." A local Indian took away a piece of tin while visiting the fort, apparently wanting to use this exotic-to-him object as part of a homemade tobacco pipe. But the Dutch were attached to that particular piece of tin—it had the word "Holland" on it, apparently—and they let the Indians know of their displeasure.

The Indians responded by having the "thief" executed. There are a couple of versions of what happened next. In one, this thief turned out to be a bigwig whose family avenged his death by massacring every settler in sight. In another, the Indians returned to the fort carrying the severed head of the culprit. They may have meant this as a gesture of goodwill, but in a bit of cross-cultural miscommunication, it shocked and angered the Dutch, setting off a run of events that came to the same sad ending, with every Dutch settler dead, and Zwaanendael up in flames.

For understandable reasons, new colonists stayed away from Lewes in the years that followed, heading instead to New Amsterdam and laying the groundwork for the future New York City. A smattering of settlers finally decided to test the Zwaanendael jinx in the late 1650s. They didn't build a town or anything, but they rechristened the area "Hoerenkill," which translates from the Dutch as "Harlot's River." Some historians speculate that this unsavory moniker—later, when the English came along, it would actually turn into "Whorekill"—may have roots in a cultural tradition that had local Indian men sharing "their" women with settlers in rather freewheeling fashion.

No such unsavory activity surrounded the second full-fledged town that popped up in 1663, when the Dutch awarded a batch of land here to a ragtag group of Mennonites led by

Pieter Cornelis Plockhoy. Plockhoy was a 17th-century hippie, basically. His dream was to find a place where he and his followers could live in a blissful state of classless equality "separate from other men, where we may with less impediment or hindrance love one another, and mind the wonders of God."

The town worked like a commune: Every resident was required to put in six hours of common-good labor a day, with any and all proceeds from that work divided equally. One historian has described Plockhoy as the New World's first publicist. He churned out a couple of books worth of letters and essays trying to drum up recruits for his utopian adventure. Some of that writing comes off like laughably overdone travel brochures.

> New Netherland is the flower, the noblest of all lands … birds obscure the sky, so numerous in their flight, the animals roam wild … fish swarm in the waters and exclude the light…

Alas, happiness was not in the cards for Plockhoy and his fellow hippies. Just like Zwaanendael before it, Plockhoy's commune went up in smoke. It was barely a year old in 1664, when regime change came to Cape Henlopen in the form of English warships sailing into the Delaware Bay. The soldiers on those boats left some scattered Dutch settlers in the Whorekill area alone, but their commander reported that his men destroyed the "Colony of Plockhoy to a nail."

The "Saltiest" Metropolis

The third town was the charm for "The First Town." After the English put the land we know as Delaware in the new colony of Pennsylvania, Zwaanendael (or Whorekill, or Plockhoy) finally found a measure of longevity. William Penn himself dished out the rather boring names of Lewes and Sussex County in honor of places back home in England.

What grew up at Cape Henlopen in the centuries that followed is a town that the writers who put together *Delaware: A Guide to the First State* in the 1930s dubbed the "saltiest" in the state.

> Lewes ... has a tradition of the sea borne by every east wind that haunts its narrow streets and aged cypress-shingled houses. Its present is saturated with the drama of its past. ... Lewes has been plundered by privateers and has bargained with Captain Kidd for his loot; it has been bombarded in war, and knows all about shipwreck and sunken treasure. ... [It] is to Delaware what Plymouth is to Massachusetts and Jamestown is to Virginia.

A good place to start getting in touch with these stories is the Zwaanendael Museum, erected on the occasion of Lewes's 300th birthday in 1931. Skinny and tiered, the odd-looking building at 102 Kings Hwy. is the mirror image of the Stadhuis, or City Hall, in the Netherlands city of Hoorn. The town also celebrates its Dutch roots every spring with a two-week-long Tulip Festival.

If you miss out on the tulip show, no worries: You'll be able to enjoy plenty of other blooms in the green space that surrounds the museum, along with lots more such handiwork around town, courtesy of the first-rate Lewes in Bloom garden club. Stop in the visitors center outside the museum to get your bearings — and to soak in the atmosphere of a little building that dates back to 1730.

Make your way into the downtown next to get a sense for the modern-day incarnation of Lewes. The restaurants and shops along those few blocks are mostly housed in sweet historic buildings. At the Gothic-style St. Peter's Episcopal Church, the oldest stone in the graveyard belongs to the remains of a woman born in 1631, the first year of ill-fated Zwaanendael. Speaking of ill-fated, the captain of the *HMS DeBraak* is resting at St. Peter's as well—his story is a topic covered in Chapter 20.

Once you've had your fill of browsing and eating, meander your way to Front Street and Canalfront Park, a pretty patch of green that's exactly what its name says. The folks who built the Rehoboth-Lewes Canal in the years before World War 1 had dreams of drawing big commercial traffic, but that never materialized. From day one, the thin waterway has been used mostly by smaller workboats and recreational vessels.

The park presents a stroll through the maritime ages. The most prominent attraction is up on the northwest end of things, opposite Shipcarpenter Street. Lightship *Overfalls* is one of the nearly 200 floating lighthouses built by the United States Lighthouse Service (which eventually morphed into the Coast Guard) between 1820 and 1952. Only 17 of those lightships still exist—and just seven are, like this one, open to the public.

The *Overfalls* actually did its tour of duty up in New England. After it got pulled out of service in 1972, local history buffs arranged to bring it here to pay tribute to a different old lightship, which had helped guide vessels through the shipping channel at the mouth of the Delaware Bay starting in 1898. Now operated by the nonprofit Friends of Lightship *Overfalls*, it's quite the impressive affair—the light shines from 57 feet above the waterline and can be seen from 12 miles away. At midnight on New Year's Eve, townsfolk gather for a big "Anchor Drop" along the 57-foot height of that light tower.

One interesting story after another will pop up as you stroll southward through Canalfront Park. There's an old boathouse here that used to stand alongside the Lewes Life-Saving Station (the station was moved at some point to Rehoboth Beach, where it now serves as the home of a VFW chapter). A restored Monomoy lifeboat from the World War II years sits under a pavilion. A marker tells the story of the age of shipbuilding in Lewes, which ran from the 1680s up through the Civil War. One yard, Cato Lewis & Sons, was founded by a former slave in the late 1700s — and may rank as the first black-owned shipyard in the country.

Another marker describes how Lewes became a center of menhaden fishing. Those oily, underappreciated little herring have proven their value time and again in the centuries since an Indian named Squanto taught pilgrims up in Massachusetts to use it as a farm fertilizer. At various points since then, menhaden has been a key ingredient in lamp oils, paints, perfumes, and lubricants. It's still doing duty in the 21st century, in fish oil supplements.

The first menhaden processing plant in Lewes opened during the late 1800s. Interestingly, the fishing boats that chased this one-plus-inch-long creature went about their business in the same way earlier sailors had looked for whales in the time of *Moby Dick* — by stationing a spotter in a basket up top of the mast. That spotter knew the tell-tale signs of menhaden on the move in humongous schools numbering into the hundreds of thousands.

Later, that spotting work was done by airplane pilots. By 1953, the menhaden boats of Lewes were bringing in an annual catch of nearly 400 million pounds and employing 650 workers. In the end, the industry succeeded too well, fishing itself out of business.

A little farther south, beyond the Inn at Canal Square, is the War of 1812 Memorial Park. As those hostilities got under way, British warships formed a blockade around the mouth of Delaware Bay. But those ships couldn't sit out there forever without supplies — they tried to land troops and take what they needed, but local militia held off those assaults. They then tried to negotiate a deal for supplies, but locals refused to play along. In the end, the British commander sent this dark note into town:

Whatever sufferings may fall upon the inhabitants of Lewes may be attributed to yourselves.

The bombardment began on April 6, 1813 and lasted into the next day. Locals responded with cannon fire of their own, and the exchange ended in a standoff. Among the many buildings that took hits during that bombardment is the so-called Cannonball House, just across the street from the park. That is one of nine buildings operated by the Lewes Historical Society.

The society's lineup includes a country store, a ferry house, a doctor's office, a one-room school, and more. The new Lewes History Museum on Adams Avenue is a society project as well — the exhibit materials there are first rate. If all this is up your alley, be sure to check in advance on their busy schedule of events, walking tours, and history-by-boat excursions. If you are interested in blacksmithing, make your way over to Preservation Forge at 114 W. 3rd St. to check out the work of artisan John Ellsworth.

One last interesting historical detour is Shipcarpenter's Square, a nearby development of private residential homes. The project dates from the 1980s, but the homes inside this development are from the 1700s and 1800s — they were all at-risk-of-demolition properties that were jacked up and moved into town from the surrounding countryside in a project spearheaded by preservation buffs David Dunbar and Jack Vessels.

The Natural Options

That in-town beach I mentioned lies nestled in the crook below Cape Henlopen, just barely inside of Delaware Bay. Beyond that is the 5,000-acre Cape Henlopen State Park, where another long stretch of beach faces out into the Atlantic Ocean.

That "First Town" business isn't the only first of note in Lewes. The state park here may not have taken official shape until 1964, but the story of its status as open-to-the-public property dates clear back to the days of William Penn. In 1682, a man named Edmond Warner asked Penn for permission to set up a "coney," or rabbit warren, on the cape.

Penn said yes, but in doing so he specified in writing that the non-rabbit bounty of the Cape — its berries, marshland, fishing grounds, timberlands, etc. — should be "reserved for public use." The language of that "Warner Grant" is arguably the first time anyone in what would become the United States formalized the notion of setting aside something like a big piece of parkland.

The park has lots to offer in addition to that long stretch of beach. There are hiking trails, a fishing pier, and the Seaside Nature Center. The remains of the World War II-era Fort Miles are here as well, so you will be able to check out underground gun batteries, see old buildings, and photograph castle-like observation towers. Alas, the storied Cape Henlopen Lighthouse is no more — thanks to erosion and storms, it toppled over into the sea on April 13, 1926.

A pair of lighthouses are still standing relatively nearby. The best ways to get up-close looks at Harbor of Refuge Light and the Delaware Breakwater East End Light are from aboard the aforementioned Cape May-Lewes Ferry or through occasional tours organized by the Delaware River & Bay Lighthouse Foundation.

Back in town, you have a couple more worthwhile natural options. The Junction & Breakwater Trail is an easy six-mile pedaling route down to Rehoboth Beach. Pretty little Blockhouse Pond sits behind the big hospital in town—and smack dab in the middle of it is the green space of George H.P. Smith Park.

A more remote brand of natural goodness is just a few miles north of town. Prime Hook National Wildlife Refuge is a 10,000-acre mix of forests and marshland with a good number of hiking trails and observation decks. Access to remote stretches of beach can be found up this way at the ends of Broadkill Road (Route 16), Prime Hook Road (Route 39), Fowler Beach Road, and Slaughter Beach Road (Route 224).

That last bit of beach brings us back to our what's-in-a-name starting point. The macabre name of Slaughter Beach is probably a simple matter—there was, after all, a man named William Slaughter who served as postmaster here in the mid-1800s.

But other possibilities have arisen over the centuries, all steeped in local lore. One involves the wreck of a boat loaded with pigs, whose carcasses were then slaughtered right here on the beach. Another refers to the large number of horseshoe crabs who meet their maker on this beach during that prehistoric creature's incredible annual migration ritual every May and June. The last, grisliest option surrounds legends about a group of Indians who were massacred in cold-blooded fashion here after rumors spread that they were planning some sort of attack.

CONNECTIONS

• Southern Delaware Tourism
visitsoutherndelaware.com; 800.357.1818
• Lewes Chamber of Commerce
leweschamber.com; 302.645.8073
• Zwaanendael Museum
history.delaware.gov/museums/zm/zm_main.shtml;
302.645.1148
102 Kings Hwy., Lewes, Del.
• Lewes Historical Society
historiclewes.org; 302.645.7670
Lewes History Museum location: 101 Adams Ave., Lewes, Del.
• Lightship *Overfalls*
overfalls.org; 302.644.8050
219 Pilottown Rd., Lewes, Del.
• Cape Henlopen State Park
destateparks.com/beaches/capehenlopen; 302.645.8983
15099 Cape Henlopen Dr., Lewes, Del.
• Cape May-Lewes Ferry
cmlf.com; 800.643.3779
• Delaware River & Bay Lighthouse Foundation
delawarebaylights.org; 302.644.7046
• Prime Hook National Wildlife Refuge
www.fws.gov/refuge/prime_hook; 302.684.8419
11978 Turkle Pond Rd., Milton, Del.

NEARBY TRIPS: A list of other trips on the middle Delmarva Peninsula is on page 7.

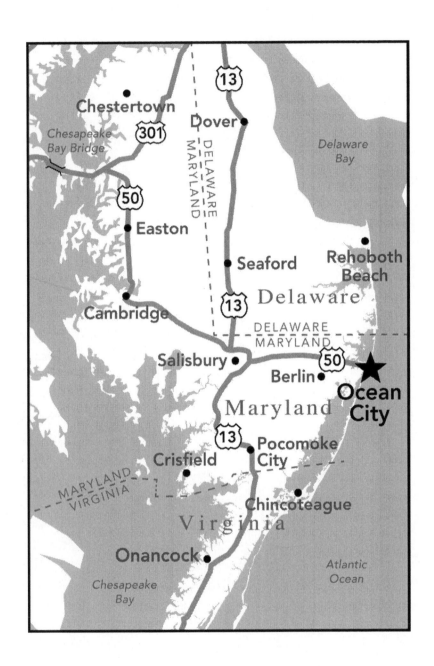

Chestertown

Chesapeake
Bay Bridge

301

Dover

13

DELAWARE
MARYLAND

Delaware
Bay

50

Easton

Seaford

Rehoboth
Beach

Delaware

13

Cambridge

DELAWARE
MARYLAND

Salisbury

50

Berlin

**Ocean
City**

Maryland

13

Crisfield

Pocomoke
City

MARYLAND
VIRGINIA

Chincoteague

Virginia

Onancock

Chesapeake
Bay

Atlantic
Ocean

ROAD TRIP #19

OCEAN CITY, MD.

One couple wants to share a bucket of Thrasher's fries on the boardwalk. Another makes a beeline for the old-school salt-water taffy at Dolle's. This family goes all-in on arcade games and mini-golf. That one keeps toes tucked in sand from early morning right through to sundown. One of the many interesting things about Ocean City is the way so many people make pilgrimages to a place full of high-rise hotels and six-lane streets in search of scenes that might as well fill fading Polaroid prints.

I'm in the same boat, though my treasure hunts tend to involve seeking out bits and pieces of the resort town's fascinating history. Time and again over the last century and a half, Ocean City has been transformed into something newer and bigger than it used to be. It's as if each new generation of entrepreneurs sets about producing a fresh episode of "Extreme Makeover."

The place doesn't look like the standard sort of "historic" travel destination. Think Savannah, say, or even nearby

Rehoboth Beach. In places like those, the past is presented to visitors by way of meticulously regulated preservation districts where the look of buildings and streetscapes is carefully managed to appear old and "authentic."

The stories Ocean City has to tell aren't manicured like that. Here, remnants of the past bubble up unexpectedly, hiding in the shadows of hypermodern high rises. A few years back some civic-minded folks asked the state of Maryland about possibly winning official designation for a historic district. The idea was a non-starter—too many buildings in the oldest part of town had been moved, altered, or obliterated.

This is as it should be, I think. In the many tales of entrepreneurship that have unfolded in Ocean City, the heroes tend to share a common trait. They're dreamers with eyes set on a big new future, not a quaint old past. I suspect most of those folks would have hated being reined in by backward-looking rules and regulations.

These men and women gambled everything they had on their notion of the next big thing. One such dreamer, the recently widowed Maud Laws, arrived in Ocean City in 1950 at age 70 and promptly launched a new career developing apartment complexes. She was still starting new projects in her 90s. One of those projects, the Coronet Apartments on 13th Street, is still going strong under new owners. An old saying Laws adopted as her life's marching orders might double as a fitting civic motto for Ocean City:

Bite off more than you can chew, and chew like hell.

Goin' Round and Round

So let's do a little treasure hunting in the oldest, southernmost end of town. For starters, take a ride on the merry-go-round that lies deep inside an old-school amusement park, Trimpers Rides. That business has been through several entrepreneurial transformations since the 1890s, when German immigrants Daniel and Margaret Trimper came to Ocean City on vacation and fell in love with the place. Only a few fledgling hotels were here then. There was no boardwalk yet. There wasn't even a significant stretch of sandy beach — the ocean waters flowed differently in those years, waves lapping pretty much all the way up to the hotels.

Back in Baltimore, Daniel Trimper Sr. closed down his Silver Dollar Bar, which, by the way, had real silver dollars embedded in the floorboards. The family's move was an arduous affair that started with a steamboat ride across the Chesapeake Bay. Family legend has it that the bay was so deeply frozen during that move that the steamship *Cambridge* couldn't get up to the dock in Claiborne, Md. The Trimpers trooped out on the ice, presumably with many of their life's belongings in tow, and walked to shore behind steamship staffers stepping gingerly to see how much weight the ice could handle.

Daniel Trimper Jr. was six years old that day. As he walked across that ice, he was carrying a box with a new puppy in it. He and his family then boarded a steam-powered train for Ocean City. Folks in those days used to joke that the initials of the Baltimore, Chesapeake & Annapolis line stood for Bugs, Cinders, & Ashes. When the frozen family finally reached Ocean City, Dan Jr. was not impressed:

None of us could see what father saw in Ocean City at that time. We had no street lighting. You had to carry a lantern to walk out at night. It was spooky in winter when the wind howled.

Dan Jr. would come around in the long run, serving as mayor between 1944 and 1959. His transformation from skeptical child to firm believer began with his father buying a pair of hotels. After one suffered damage in a storm, Dan Sr. rebuilt it with turrets up top, supposedly in an attempt to evoke Great Britain's Windsor Castle. A theater and an amusement park were soon added to the mix. By 1900, the whole shebang was known as Windsor's Resort.

Trimpers Rides is what remains. Still owned by Dan Sr.'s descendants, it ranks as the oldest family-owned carnival in the country. The merry-go-round I mentioned entered the Trimper story in 1912 when the family ordered it from the Herschell-Spillman Company in upstate New York, a famous firm in the so-called "golden age" of carousels.

This one is a giant of its type, 50 feet in diameter. Herschell-Spillman did a similarly big project in the same period for Coney Island, but that one is long gone, destroyed by fire. This survivor is a priceless time capsule from days when immigrant artisans used all manner of building-trades projects—even kiddie rides like this—as artistic canvases. Horses, dragons, frogs, and more are featured in the menagerie of wooden animals, many depicted with a frightening aspect that evokes the dark moments in classic fairy tales. Eyes are wild with fury, or is it fear? Necks are twisted, veins bulging, and mouths wide open, tearing at bridles.

There is a reason those horses were carved as if in the midst of a ferocious battle. The word *carousel* comes from the Spanish *carosella*, or "little war." Rides like this have their roots in military horsemanship training exercises that date back more than a millennium, to the time of the Crusades. Some 4,000 such carousels were built during that golden age in the early 1900s. Only about 150 remain. We are lucky to have one here on

Delmarva, especially one that the Trimpers have kept around long enough for children from four or even five generations in the same families to enjoy.

Laying the Foundation

A second carnival operates in this part of Ocean City as well. Jolly Roger at the Pier doesn't have as much history as Trimpers, but it, too, manages to evoke the joys of days gone by. That word *pier* here can be confusing, because it does not refer to the most obvious candidate for the word—the iconic Ocean City Fishing Pier, which stands quite nearby, jutting out into the ocean atop a maze of splayed legs. Here, *pier* refers to the foundation under Jolly Roger and its giant Ferris wheel.

The skinny-beach era in Ocean City lasted until 1933. In my first collection of *Eastern Shore Road Trips*, I told the story of how a hellacious hurricane that year tore a hole between the ocean and Sinepuxent Bay. That hole is now the strip of water known as the Inlet—its arrival changed the way the ocean waves flowed, causing sand to start piling up in front of the boardwalk.

The Jolly Roger *pier* was built out over ocean waters before that happened. The first incarnation went up in 1907, but it was destroyed by a fire in December 1925 that also leveled several blocks in the nearby downtown. Four years after that fire, a second pier went up. That's the foundation under Jolly Roger today.

In the early days, it boasted a skating rink, a bowling alley, a pool hall, and a second-floor ballroom. That dance hall served as the focal point of Ocean City nightlife starting back in the 1930s. The cream of the big-band crop played on its stage--

Glenn Miller, Duke Ellington, Benny Goodman, Cab Calloway, and Count Basie among them.

As joyous as those scenes might look in your mind's eye, we should remember that they had a sad aspect as well. For much of the 20th century, Ocean City was a highly segregated place. Black tourists weren't allowed in or around its premier attractions except on once-in-a-blue-moon "Colored Exclusion Days." Those segregation rules also meant that black performers like Ellington, Calloway, and Basie couldn't stay in the same hotels as their audiences. If you find your way to the nearby intersection of South Division Street and Baltimore Avenue, you will see a place that did take them as overnight guests — Henry's Colored Hotel, which dates to 1895.

The pier fell into a slow-but-sure decline after the big-band era passed. The last concert there happened in 1973. In fitting Ocean City fashion, a team of entrepreneurs soon leveled that ballroom and reinvented the pier. Jolly Roger came along in 1975. So, too, did Morbid Manor, a long-gone haunted house that was so over the horrifying top it ranks as an Ocean City legend. The Ripley's Believe It or Not museum, which is still there, first opened atop the pier during the 1980s.

The ride on that Jolly Roger Ferris Wheel will give you a glorious view of the skyline that Ocean City's various entrepreneurs have built over the past 150 years. Take the time afterward to stroll out that fishing pier, which stretches nearly 500 feet out into the ocean. If you're an early riser, this is the place to come to enjoy and photograph the sunrise.

More stories of old Ocean City are on display at the nearby Ocean City Life-Saving Station Museum, which has a glorious array of old photos. The town's tourism department has developed a pair of well-done walking-tour brochures that will help you find more hidden remnants of days gone by.

If you follow the "Lower Downtown" brochure over to St. Louis Avenue and check out the run of quaint old bungalows there that were originally built for the families of fishermen, you might as well grab a drink and some comfort seafood at the Angler Restaurant, which is tucked under the bayside bridge over Route 50. A fourth-generation affair, the eatery is the oldest family-owned restaurant in town.

The Story of Plimhimmon

Back on the boardwalk, you will find the Plim Plaza Hotel at 109 N. Atlantic Ave. The 1960s building is nothing special to my eyes, but the odd dome up on the roofline is a replica that pays tribute to another great story of Ocean City entrepreneurship. A century ago, this was the site of the Plimhimmon Hotel, which ranked as the then-fledgling town's most iconic structure, with elegant oceanfront porches, expansive decks, and the same kind of distinctive dome that's now on the Plim Plaza.

The woman who built the Plimhimmon in the 1890s, Rosalie Tilghman Shreve, grew up in plantation-era luxury in Talbot County, Md. She was the great-granddaughter of Col. Tench Tilghman, who famously served as an aide de camp to Gen. George Washington during the Revolutionary War. She was the daughter of Gen. Tench Tilghman, a West Point grad whose accomplishments in life were all over the map, but usually pointed in the direction of trying to bring prominence and commerce to the then-sleepy town of Oxford.

Home base for this branch of the Tilghman clan was Plimhimmon, a plantation outside of Oxford that hit on hard times after the Civil War, about the time Rosalie reached her teens. Her father sided quite publicly with the South during that war. One of Rosalie's brothers died fighting for the Confederacy. The postwar loss of slave labor put the profitability of the family's farmland in a precarious state. In addition, a railroad project led by Rosalie's father turned into a debt-ridden affair that went bankrupt. The famous Tilghmans found themselves in a state of near destitution.

> This family, … once very wealthy, are now reduced to that state which is even worse in my estimation than actual poverty, large debts, large pride, large wants: small income, and small helpfulness. … The young ladies on Wednesday and Thursday milked the cows, while their father the General held the umbrella over them to keep off the rain.

At age 17, Rosalie married Thomas Jefferson Shreve, a Confederate war veteran who had finished his military service as a prisoner of war on Pea Patch Island in the Delaware Bay (see Chapter 14). That's probably where he contracted tuberculosis, which soon became the death of him. At 19, Rosalie found herself a widowed mother of two. Her father died not long thereafter.

At some point in the midst of all this ill fortune, Rosalie made her way to Baltimore and started running a boarding house. According to family legend, there was one day in here when Rosalie went to a nearby market to stock up on food for her guests. She asked a young black boy at the market if he would carry her things home, and then she gave him a little tip—more about that boy in a moment.

After getting a taste of entrepreneurial success, Rosalie was hungry for more. She turned her attention to Ocean City in the 1890s, opening a summertime-only boarding house called Goldsborough Cottage. In 1894, she bought two lots on the ocean and set out to build the grandest hotel in town.

Named after the old plantation in Oxford, the 48-room Plimhimmon Hotel wowed guests with one shared modern bathroom on every floor and electricity powered by the hotel's own steam engine. That steam engine produced more power than the hotel needed, so Rosalie sold its spare output to nearby building owners.

Obviously, she was quite the businesswoman. But that wasn't as unusual as you might think: There were actually a large number of savvy businesswomen working in Ocean City back then. In fact, Rosalie was one of the key players in the so-called "Petticoat Regime" that ruled the town in the early part of the 20th century. In 1926, 30 of the 32 hotels in Ocean City were run by women. There is more about that in my first collection of *Eastern Shore Road Trips*, including this famous quote by "Regime" leader Ella Phillips Dennis:

Ocean City is 70 percent run by women, built by women, and the men are all henpecked.

For quite a long stretch during its six decades of operation, the Plimhimmon was the pinnacle of Ocean City society, with a parade of prominent Marylanders passing through its doors to enjoy parties, concerts, and, most of all, meals. A "light supper" there might include "broiled spring chicken, corn fritters, butterfish, cold ham, oysters poullette, hominy grits, peas, potatoes, grilled apples, rolls, corn-pone cake and peaches."

The topic of that menu brings us to a final twist to this story. Do you remember that little boy who carried Rosalie's groceries home from the market one day in Baltimore? That errand somehow sparked a lifelong friendship between a black man from the big city and a white businesswoman from the rural Eastern Shore who was the daughter of a Southern-sympathizing slave owner and the widow of a Confederate veteran. The boy's name was Robert Downs, and he served as the chef at the Plimhimmon for more than 40 years.

The Plimhimmon burned down in 1962. As you might expect in Ocean City, remnants of those "Petticoat Regime" days are few and far between. The last time I did an overnight at the beach, I opted to pay tribute to all those female entrepreneurs by staying at the Lankford Hotel, which stands on the boardwalk in the 800 block. Built by Mary Quillen in the 1920s, it's among the best preserved old-school hotels in town. Like Trimpers Rides and Angler Restaurant, it remains an all-in-the-family affair, still operated by Quillen descendants. Sitting on the Lankford's grand old porch with a cup of coffee and watching the waves roll in, it's easy to let your mind get to wandering, not just about those days gone by but also the ones up ahead as well. What revolution will the next generation of entrepreneurs bring to Ocean City?

CONNECTIONS
• Worcester County Tourism
visitworcester.org; 800.852.0335
• Ocean City Tourism
ococean.com; 800.626.2326
• Trimpers Rides
trimpersrides.com; 410.289.8617

700 S. Atlantic Ave., Ocean City, Md.

• Jolly Roger at the Pier

jollyrogerpieroc.com; 410.289.3031

401 S. Atlantic Ave., Ocean City, Md.

• Ocean City Life-Saving Station Museum

ocmuseum.org; 410-289-4991

813 S. Atlantic Ave., Ocean City, Md.

• Angler Restaurant

angleroc.net; 410.289.7424

312 Talbot St., Ocean City, Md.

• Lankford Hotel

lankfordhotel.com; 800.282.9709

807 N. Atlantic Ave., Ocean City, Md.

NEARBY TRIPS: A list of other trips on the lower Delmarva Peninsula is on page 7.

Way Back Machine
The 'Miracle Cure' of Ocean City

The entrepreneurial zeal that pops up time and again in the history of Ocean City wasn't just the province of hotel builders. Case in point: Francis Townsend Sr., a native of Snow Hill, Md. who was the first physician in the town's history, practicing between 1900 and 1945.

Doctoring in Ocean City was a tough gig then. The nearest hospital was 30 miles away along dreadful roads. There were no ambulances until 1939. Typhoid fever was a recurring challenge, thanks to a sewage system that dumped raw waste into Sinepuxent Bay, the source of the town's drinking water.

Early on, Dr. Townsend famously made his way to and from house calls by riding a bicycle up and down the boardwalk. He found time to feed his entrepreneurial appetite as well, opening a pharmacy at Caroline and Baltimore streets. Near that store, he built the town's first boardwalk bandstand with his own money. It wasn't just an act of civic do-gooderism—the soda fountain in the pharmacy was jam-packed on concert nights.

The small print in an old newspaper ad for the pharmacy hints at another of Townsend's business endeavors: "Magice Prescription No. 22" offered "speedy and unfailing" relief from sunburn to "thousands upon thousands of satisfied users." Invented by Townsend in 1912, this cream was a mix of camphor, menthol, phenol, eucalyptus, and other ingredients.

There are several versions out there of the next chapter in this story, and I haven't been able to figure out which is true. One says Townsend was eager to see his sunburn cream help more patients, so he shared his recipe with a Baltimore physician, George Bunting, in no-strings-attached fashion. Another says that Bunting took Townsend's recipe for Magice Prescription No. 22 and claimed it as his own, later denying that Townsend was involved. Then there is the in-between version, which has Bunting coming up with a new and improved variation on Townsend's original recipe.

In any case, "Dr. Bunting's Sunburn Remedy" soon became a big hit in Baltimore. By 1920, it was being called Noxzema, apparently in reference to its effectiveness against eczema as well as sunburn. That was also the year when the Noxzema Chemical Company opened its first factory. By the 1940s, the "miracle cream of Baltimore" had gone nationwide.

Back in Ocean City, Francis Townsend did just fine, even without a Noxzema fortune in the bank. Early on, he and his wife, the former Anna Rayne, lived above their drugstore, but they eventually moved into a sweet Victorian a few blocks away. The family was among the first in town to buy a newfangled automobile. Townsend was rich in more important ways, too: All of Ocean City held him in the highest regard. His funeral fell during the height of the tourism season—on July 4, 1945. In spite of that timing, every business in Ocean City closed for three hours that afternoon in homage to the many good works performed by the town's first doctor.

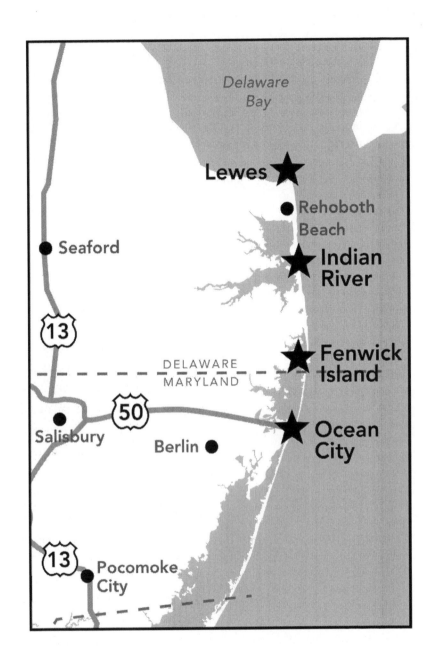

ROAD TRIP #20

THE ROUTE 1 SHIPWRECKS TOUR

Much as you might wish otherwise, you can't spend every waking moment of your beach getaway sweltering in the sand and splashing in the sea. Sometimes, it rains. Sometimes, you need a break from the baking. The break I have in mind here will take you into the forlorn depths of that sea, by way of the string of museums and historic sites that lie along Route 1 between Lewes, Del. and Ocean City, Md.

In the moment they occur, shipwrecks are tragic affairs, full of desperation and death. But as decades go by and then centuries, these disasters take on a magical aspect. I suspect Hollywood is to blame. Having served up so many sunken-treasure plots filled with scenes of shimmering, submerged beauty, the big screen has trained us to imagine old shipwrecks as otherworldly places where time stands still and artifacts from days gone by are laid out for eternity in a perfect drowned tableau.

Storm Clouds at the Cape

The Atlantic coast of Delmarva is thick with shipwreck lore, with the waters around Cape Henlopen at Lewes being especially infamous in this regard. Lewes was quite the commercial crossroads during parts of the 1700s, as vessels from Europe, the West Indies, and other far-flung locales stopped by or passed through on their way into the Delaware Bay and up to Philadelphia.

At this cape, which juts up from the mainland like a crooked right index finger, those vessels needed to navigate perilously close to shoals so dangerous that they relied on expert local "pilots" to take over the helm and steer them clear of danger. That's what Andrew Allen was up to when he climbed aboard the British sloop of war *DeBraak* on May 25, 1798. On an ordinary ship with an ordinary captain, Allen's piloting gig that day might have turned out to be a routine affair, never mentioned in history books.

But there was nothing ordinary about that day. The story of the *DeBraak* is the focus of exhibit materials and artifacts on display at the Zwaanendael Museum on the outskirts of downtown Lewes. During warmer months, the Delaware Division of Historical and Cultural Affairs offers a lecture/tour combo that begins at Zwaanendael and then gives curious onlookers a chance to get up close and personal with a massive chunk of the *DeBraak*'s hull, which spent nearly two centuries in the depths before being raised from the bottom of the sea in a salvage operation so slipshod that it inspired a new federal law designed to protect wreck sites (more on that in the Way Back Machine section at the end of this chapter).

DeBraak is Dutch for "The Beagle." Built in Holland in 1781 as a single-masted "cutter," she served the Dutch for 14 years, at which point she had the misfortune to be in an English port when war broke out between the two countries. The British navy seized *DeBraak*, then overhauled her from prow to stern, adding a second mast to turn her into a square-rigged sloop of war and installing an array of then-newfangled "carronade" guns — short, stubby affairs that were usually fired at point-blank range to rain death on the decks of an enemy vessel in advance of boarding.

That second mast proved problematic. While working the English Channel in 1797, the *DeBraak* lost a main-mast in a storm. Her captain, James Drew, later complained in a report to his bosses that the reconfigured boat was "overmasted" and susceptible to gathering in more wind than she could handle.

Drew had a checkered naval career. As a young British lieutenant, he had served at the Battle of Bunker Hill early in the Revolutionary War. A post-battle investigative report from a committee headed by future President John Adams fingered Drew as one of the guilty parties in unspeakable atrocities committed in the aftermath of one skirmish.

> Drew, after walking for some time over the bodies of the dead, with great fortitude, went up to one of our wounded Men, and very deliberately shot him through the Head. ... In a day or two after, Drew went upon the Hill again and opened the dirt that was thrown over [the body of American patriot Dr. Joseph] Warren, spit in his Face jump'd on his Stomach and at last cut off his Head.

A little while after that, Drew won a promotion to the command of a big ship, but he lasted only two years in that gig before getting demoted to a smaller vessel. Historians do not seem to know the reason he fell into disfavor, but he remained stuck in the lower ranks of naval commanders for the rest of his long career. The *DeBraak* was tiny by the standards of the British navy. She had 16 guns; an average-size warship had 74.

There are signs in the historical record that Drew could be a prideful, cantankerous man. He became obsessed over the years with winning his first-ever "prize," the term used to describe enemy ships captured at sea. The booty commandeered from such vessels got divvied up among officers and crew, so prizes led to both personal riches and professional acclaim.

In 1798, the *DeBraak* was ordered to sail across the Atlantic as an armed guard for a convoy of merchant ships, which were at risk in those days from both pirates and the French navy. Drew's orders specified that he stick as close as possible to the convoy, but early on he and the *DeBraak* went gallivanting off, presumably in pursuit of that elusive prize he craved. For 10 long weeks, the *DeBraak* was nowhere to be seen. When she finally re-emerged to meet up with the convoy off of Cape Henlopen, she had a Spanish prize in hand.

On that fateful day, May 25, Drew may have been over-celebrating this turn of events. That local pilot, Andrew Allen, later described the captain as "in a hilarious mood" and said that Drew had clearly been drinking when he came up to meet Allen, and that he headed back below decks to drink some more afterward.

Allen spied threatening clouds on the horizon. He told the crew to take down some of the *DeBraak*'s sails as a precautionary measure. But when Drew reappeared on deck, he was furious to find a stranger ordering his men about. He ordered the sails back up. Then he barked at Allen:

You look out for the bottom, and I'll look out for the spars.

Allen never got a chance to steer the bottom of the *DeBraak* clear of those dangerous shoals. The storm rolled in, carrying a devastating and "sudden flaw of the wind" that knocked *DeBraak* over on her side — she went all the way under in a matter of minutes. Was that wicked piece of weather alone to blame? Did that retrofitted second mast Drew had complained about play a role? There is no telling now.

Allen was among the thirtysome survivors. James Drew and 46 others lost their lives. A number of *DeBraak* victims are believed to be buried under the parking lot outside the Cape May-Lewes Ferry. More *DeBraak* victims are likely buried somewhere near a basketball court at Cape Henlopen State Park.

Captain Drew rests in a nobler spot, in a vault under St. Peter's Episcopal Church in Lewes. A monument to the captain stands in the adjacent graveyard. If you visit, you will be right on the main downtown drag, which is chock full of interesting shops and restaurants (see Chapter 18).

Home of the 'Storm Warriors'

More shipwreck lore awaits south of Lewes, along Coastal Highway. After passing through Rehoboth Beach and Dewey Beach, you will enter Delaware Seashore State Park. There, on the oceanside, stands the old Indian River Life-Saving Station.

Constructed in 1876, the station is now restored to the way it looked in 1905. What I like about this facility is its engaging simplicity. You will not find much in the way of bells, whistles, and extraneous displays, though I do recommend trying out the well-done cell-phone tour. Instead, you will walk through a bunk room, a dining area, and a pantry that communicate in quite genuine fashion just how spartan a lifestyle the "surfmen" who worked here endured.

Those men trained by day and patrolled by night. They were always on the lookout for ships in trouble, and that work took on added urgency during bad weather. Here is how longtime station keeper Washington Vickers described one such night, Feb. 13, 1899:

> The ice is now packed in here from off shore for a mile, such a time I never saw, on the beach or anywhere else. Snow drifting in every direction. At times you can't see 50 yards. … We have run a [rope] line from the station to the beach, so the watch can find their way back and forth from the surf to station. The watches will go as far as they can, and keep [as good a] look out as possible.

The surfmen at Indian River responded to more than 60 wrecks and saved more than 400 lives over the years. Along with their compatriots up and down the East Coast, they were lionized in the national press as heroic "storm warriors."

Check the calendar of events at the station before you go. Several times a year, Indian River conducts re-creations of old-school "breeches buoy" style rescues using a method that resembles a modern-day zip line. Surfmen would use cannon-like "Lyle" guns to shoot lines equipped with leg harnesses and pulleys as far as 600 yards.

One last note here at Indian River: There is a bit of irony to the story of how the station came to an end. The famously brutal Ash Wednesday storm of March 1962 left the station buried in sand up past the first-floor windows. For a few years afterward its roofline stuck up out of the beach like a landmark out of the closing scene in the original "Planet of the Apes." The building was restored in the 1970s.

'A Most Intemperate Carousel'

Back in your car and headed south again, you will soon come to the bridge over the Indian River Inlet. Here are the expansive stretches of beach that make Delaware Seashore park such a popular summertime destination. Here, too, is "Coin Beach," where centuries-old pennies have been drifting ashore for as long as anyone can remember.

The joy that today's beachcombers feel upon unearthing those old pieces of copper is rooted in another nightmarish wreck. On Sept. 1, 1785, the *Faithful Steward* pulled up here after crossing the Atlantic with nearly 300 passengers, the bulk of them Irish immigrants bound for Philadelphia. In its cargo hold were barrels filled with some 350,000 freshly minted pennies sent from England to help ease a shortage of currency in the former colonies.

Alcohol played a role in this wreck, too. Relieved to be across the ocean after months at sea, the captain approved a request from a couple of passengers who wanted to throw a party to celebrate their wedding anniversary. That bash became "a most intemperate carousel" and ended with both the captain and his first mate passed out and "borne insensible to their cabins."

A wicked wind kicked up that night, driving *Faithful Steward* much closer to shore than planned. The ship's second mate discovered the problem eventually, but it was too late. The ship thwacked the bottom with a dreadful shudder that sent passengers flying from their cots. The wind grew even more fierce. Waves washed up on deck. The vessel keeled over sideways.

Nearly 200 immigrants died that night. Locals back then knew the place where the *Faithful Steward* ran aground as Mohoba Bank. The Irish called it Mahogan's Bay. There were eight members of the Elliott family aboard, but just two survived. That pair and their descendants embarked on a true American journey in the decades that followed, making their way up into Pennsylvania and then across the mountains into the then-wild frontier territories of Ohio and Illinois.

Among the family history items that now reside on the website of the historical society in Indian Hill, Ohio is this little poem:

> The Elliotts and the Lees
> And Stewarts of great fame,
> They may lament and mourn
> For the lands they've left behind.
> They may lament and mourn
> As long as they have days,
> For their friends and relations
> Lie in Mahogan's bays.

'Shaking Hands with History'

Continuing south on Coastal Highway, you will make your way into Bethany Beach, which has diversions aplenty on a boardwalk and along a beachy little stretch of Main Street. Below that is Fenwick Island, home to the DiscoverSea Shipwreck Museum. Most museums on the Delmarva Peninsula fall into one of two categories, a traditional nonprofit or a government-run facility. DiscoverSea is different—it's a privately run labor of love put together by the diver, treasure hunter, and amateur archaeologist Dale W. Clifton Jr.

I haven't had the pleasure of meeting Clifton as of this writing, but I've read quite a bit about him. He caught the shipwreck bug as a boy after hearing about that "Coin Beach" near the Indian River Inlet. He spent most of a year combing through the sand there on a regular basis before he finally found a piece of what he was looking for. He started thinking about the fact that no human being had touched that coin for 200 years. And then he started wondering who back then might have been the last person to touch it before him.

It was like shaking hands with history.

That is kind of the mission statement for his museum. Housed on the second floor of a retail building, it might look a bit dicey on the attractiveness scale from the outside. Inside, however, it's quite a beautiful showcase for what may rank as the largest private collection of shipwreck artifacts in the country. On display are coins, weapons, china, keys, gold bars, and much more. If you're lucky, perhaps Clifton himself will be working the joint when you arrive. From what I've read he seems like the kind of guy who can gab in spellbinding fashion for hours on end about something as small as a thimble.

The final stop on the shipwreck tour is across the Maryland line. The Ocean City Life-Saving Station Museum is a little different from the one up at Indian River—in addition to stories of surfmen and shipwrecks, this one also focuses on the broader history of Ocean City.

The town was still just a tiny blip on the map in 1891, when the U.S. Life-Saving Service put up the building that now houses the museum. Originally located up on Caroline Street, it stands today at the lower end of the boardwalk, near the Ocean City Inlet. It's quite the kid-friendly affair, thanks in no small part to a couple of giant 250-gallon aquariums.

In an area dubbed "Davy Jones' Locker," you'll be able to see artifacts from two dozen local shipwrecks. Another exhibit, "Wreck in the Offing," showcases one of the country's best collections of vintage lifesaving equipment. The surfboat here is the item that really captured my attention—I couldn't get my head around just how small it is, considering the size of the waves and the ferocity of the storms that those surfmen had to deal with. There are regular breeches buoy lifesaving reenactments here, too, so check the calendar of events before you go.

CONNECTIONS

• Southern Delaware Tourism (Lewes, Bethany Beach, and Fenwick Island)
visitsoutherndelaware.com; 302.856.1818
• Lewes Chamber of Commerce
leweschamber.com/visit; 302.645.8073
• Zwaanendael Museum
history.delaware.gov/museums/zm/zm_main.shtml; 302.645.1148
102 Kings Hwy., Lewes, Del.
• Delaware Division of Historical and Cultural Affairs (*DeBraak* shipwreck tours)
history.delaware.gov; 302.736.7400
• Town of Bethany Beach
townofbethanybeach.com; 302.539.8011
• Indian River Life-Saving Station
destateparks.com/history/irlifesavingstation; 302.227.6991
25039 Coastal Hwy., Rehoboth Beach, Del.
• Fenwick Island
fenwickisland.delaware.gov; 302.539.3011
• DiscoverSea Shipwreck Museum
discoversea.com; 302.539.9366
708 Coastal Hwy., Fenwick Island, Del.
• Worcester County Tourism (Ocean City area)
visitworcester.org; 800.852.0335

• Ocean City Tourism
ococean.com; 800.626.2326
• The Ocean City Life-Saving Station Museum
ocmuseum.org; 410.289.4991
813 South Atlantic Ave., Ocean City, Md.

NEARBY TRIPS: A list of other trips on the middle and lower Delmarva Peninsula is on page 7.

Way Back Machine
Treasure Hunt Catastrophe

The story of the HMS *DeBraak* didn't end with her sinking. In fact, the aftermath of that disaster is a case study in how shipwrecks can take on an almost mythical quality over decades and centuries. This second chapter begins with a Lewes resident named Gilbert McCracken, who was among the locals who pitched in to help on that awful day in 1798.

When a trio of Spanish prisoners from the *DeBraak* floated ashore on some sort of chest, McCracken invited them into his home and gave them a meal. The Spaniards talked vaguely about bits of fabulous and expensive cargo they had seen aboard the *DeBraak*. In the years that followed, that conversation turned into a legend of fantastic proportions.

Seven years after the ship went down, McCracken took his son out to a stretch of beach and showed him landmarks that would help nail down the wreck's location. The notes the pair made that day were discovered years later tucked inside a family Bible and became a treasure map that proved irresistible to an endless parade of get-rich-quick dreamers.

The first dreamer to chase after the *DeBraak* was Charles Sanborn, whose 1867 permit application to search for the wreck mentioned an "immense amount of treasure, consisting of gold and silver bars and precious stones." Sanborn died before his operation got under way, but many others followed: Officially approved salvage operations took place in 1880, 1886, 1889, 1932, 1933, 1935, 1937, 1952, 1955, 1962, and 1965.

Still, the *DeBraak* remained hidden. In 1967, a pair of maritime historians wrote a journal article arguing that the legends about riches on the vessel were almost certainly false. No one listened. New searches were launched in 1970 and 1980. Then, in 1984, Harvey Harrington stepped up to the plate. He had convinced himself that the *DeBraak*'s treasure was worth half a billion modern-day dollars.

Using newfangled sonar and magnetometer technologies, Harrington's firm, Sub-Sal, finally located the *DeBraak*. This turn of events became a national media circus that ended in archaeological disaster, thanks to a mix of haste, greed, and carelessness.

Ironically, just like on the day the *DeBraak* went down, some storm clouds on the horizon played a key role. By the time Sub-Sal set out to raise the *DeBraak* from the depths on Aug. 11, 1986, Harrington and his firm had sunk $3 million into the project. Under considerable pressure to stop spending so much money, project engineers declined to wait out some bad weather in the forecast.

Instead, they tried to beat the storm. In their haste, they failed to properly cradle the wreck and then lifted it from the bottom at a speed far faster than recommended. A crane malfunctioned. The *DeBraak* emerged from the sea in an almost fully upright position. Artifacts poured from the vessel like beer from a tap. When the cables attached to that crane tore through the waterlogged hull, that flow of artifacts turned into a torrent.

In the end, Sub-Sal spent $3 million to bring up a paltry $300,000 in artifacts. Historians and archaeologists were aghast, as opportunities to raise ships like the *DeBraak* whole and intact don't come along often. Their outrage helped spur the passage of the federal Abandoned Shipwreck Act of 1988, which clarified ownership of wreck sites and gave states the power to set stricter rules over salvage work.

The coolest thing about the lecture/tour packages offered through the Zwaanendael Museum is the way attendees get to board a shuttle bus after the lecture for a short ride to a nondescript storage facility in Cape Henlopen State Park to view the surviving hunk of the *DeBraak*'s hull.

The long run of jagged timbers on display there barely resembles a ship. The wood is so soft now that you could probably stick a finger through it. The bottom half of the vessel's remains is sheathed in the copper that was used back then to protect against shipworms and barnacles. The room is damp, drab, and cramped, but still, the sight of those timbers and that old copper pack quite a punch when it comes to inspiring thoughts and visions about shipwreck days gone by.

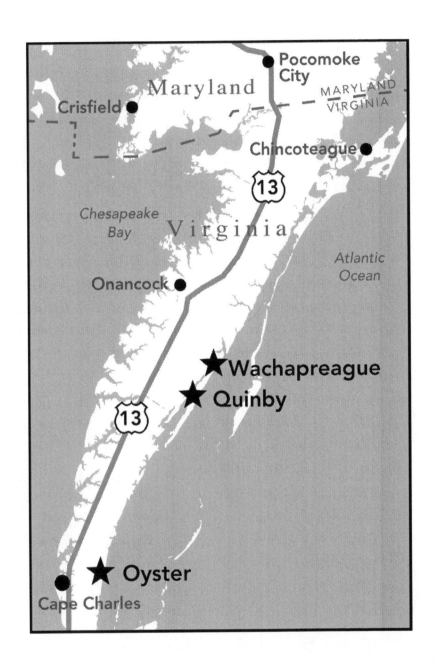

Road Trip #21

Oceanside Virginia

At the risk of going all Buddhist on you, here is a piece of advice when it comes to wandering the backroads of Virginia's Eastern Shore: Stay in the moment. Travel guides like this tend to send you over to this town and down to that waterfront and across to a pretty park, so you end up traveling with a checklist of an itinerary.

Here in this oceanside ramble, for example, the first official item on the list is Wachapreague. I'm going to suggest taking a roundabout way there to demonstrate the mindful point at hand. Jump off the Route 13 highway at Accomac and find your way to Drummondtown Road. Turn south and you'll be 10 winding miles from the storied "Little City by the Sea."

Perhaps you'll have a podcast going. Maybe you'll be gabbing with the spouse or friend in the passenger seat. That's all well and good, until you zip through Locustville with thoughts elsewhere. It's a classic blink-and-miss-it crossroads, a smattering of old houses with no shops or restaurants. But give the place a smidgeon of attention, and you'll see that it has a time-capsule quality. The historian Kirk Mariner once described Locustville as the closest thing left to the way things looked on the Eastern Shore of Virginia before the Civil War.

A legend hints at the kind of place this was back then—not rich or important, more like just another stagecoach stop. According to that tale, a Locustville man traveled to Baltimore in the early 1800s looking for a wife. When he found a woman to his liking, he wooed her with talk about his glorious "Southern plantation." She married him up in the city. When she got here to Locustville and took a look at her new home, she had this to say:

Southern plantation, humph! Shabby Hall!

The name stuck. Everyone in town started calling that place "Shabby Hall." It's still standing, but not here, oddly enough—it was moved across the Chesapeake Bay a while back, to a spot outside of Prince Frederick, Md. By the way, that couple apparently lived happily ever after in Shabby Hall, 'til death did them part.

Keep an eye out for 28251 Drummondtown Rd. That building started life as a general store in 1844 and remained open into the 1990s. Two doors away, at 28269, is the former Locustville Hotel, which began serving stagecoach passengers in the 1820s. The Folk Victorian-style Locustville Academy at 28055 opened in 1859 as a sort of prep school, with girls studying downstairs and boys up on the second floor.

Many smaller houses date from that period as well, so it won't take much effort to block out the pavement and the electric lines, leaving a view straight out of the mid-1800s stagecoach days. So it goes along these Virginia backroads: Be on the lookout for sweet, off-the-checklist rewards.

Fishing for Stories in Wachapreague

Five more winding miles on Drummondtown Road takes you into the "Little City by the Sea." Head straight to the waterfront: In front of you is Wachapreague Channel, which heads into Finney Creek, which runs into the ocean. The barrier islands called Parramore and Cedar are in the distance, the former straight east and the latter up a bit to the north.

White people didn't arrive in Wachapreague until relatively late in the game, the mid-1700s. Even after that, the place was just a family farm for decades. The first business came along in 1788 — a gristmill that ran its waterwheel not in the traditional way, via the current of a flowing stream, but by way of tidal flows that roll through here with uncommon speed and force. A shipping dock went up in the early 1800s. Shipyards popped up as the town took shape. Oyster-packing outfits thrived. Steamboats came along in time. There is a street today called Ice Plant Road, because that's what used to be there.

In 1881, a man named Alfred Kellam surveyed this working-class enclave — it was called Powellton then — and decided it would be a first-rate tourist attraction. He built a hotel and commenced advertising:

> Powellton as a sea side resort has many attractions for lovers of gunning and fishing. ... Bathing unsurpassed a short distance of the hotel.

The ads worked. Outdoorsmen started arriving from Baltimore, Philadelphia, and New York City. As the 20th century dawned, a man named Gordon Mears took that campaign to another level. He replaced Kellam's hotel with a four-story, 30-room affair bedecked with expansive porches, stained-glass windows, and an elegant dining room. The opening-day gala at Hotel

Wachapreague on Sept. 18, 1902 had guests riding boats out to Cedar Island, where a sumptuous meal was served on the beach. Actor Ronald Coleman and former President Herbert Hoover were among the many notable visitors in the years that followed.

The hotel burned in the 1970s—it used to be where the waterfront Island House restaurant stands nowadays. As you stroll up Main Street today and see only a couple of little stores, think about how the Little City by the Sea might have looked during the Roaring '20s, when there were a dozen shops, as well as a movie theater and a pool hall.

Every one of the old buildings in town must have stories to tell from those days. Consider one example: the Eva Stevens House at 17 Main St. Parts of the building date to the late 1800s. In one of those anomalies that pop up in small towns like this, there used to be a general store located *in the backyard*. During Prohibition times, the legendary Eastern Shore character Southey "Sud" Bell lived here. He had a secret compartment built under the kitchen floorboards, where he kept a whiskey barrel hooked up to a sink so that one tap poured water while the other released something a little stronger.

Before coming to Wachapreague, Sud Bell earned a measure of fame as the last-ever full-time resident of nearby Hog Island—the guy who stayed after storms and eroding shorelines had driven everyone else onto the mainland. With the population down to one, Bell proudly, and loudly, proclaimed himself the "governor" of Hog Island. He was also a musician. This description of his performance style comes from an old issue of a newsletter put out by the Barrier Islands Center museum:

This wonderfully outrageous entertainer with his trademark cigar would stroll into towns singing at the top of his voice. People could hear him coming 15 minutes ahead of his arrival because of the parade of children following him as he strummed his banjo and sang. Some swear that he could not finish a song without stopping to tell a joke or a story. Walter Chrysler and Governor Tuck of Virginia were among the prominent people who invited Bell to entertain in Richmond and New York.

Alas, the decades that followed those glory days brought one bit of bad luck after another into Wachapreague. There was the Depression, of course. There was a hurricane in 1933, then a fire in 1935. The town took another hit when the infamous Ash Wednesday storm rolled through in the spring of 1962. But you will see evidence nowadays that the Little City by the Sea is still plugging along. A good number of outdoorsmen and women still visit for the fishing and the hunting. There are bait shops, boat rentals, and charter vessels. The carnival grounds spring into action come summertime, thanks to a local fire company that's been running those rides since the 1950s.

Fishing Villages and Island Views

As Main Street heads out of town, its name changes to Wachapreague Road. Don't go all the way back to the big highway. Turn left at Seaside Road instead. That will put you southbound on a two-lane road that runs 50 or so miles down to the bottom of the peninsula. Food and restrooms will be in short supply, but the highway will always be a quick detour away.

The route number on Seaside Road changes from 605 to 600 as you cross a couple of little waterways, the Machipongo River and Frogstool Branch. Take Quinby Bridge Road (Route 182) east over a channel to enter the first of the three sweet oceanside fishing villages on our checklist. Quinby dates its history to the late 1800s when a bridge first went up over that channel, making it easier for watermen and seafood processors to get goods to the then-new railroad line in the middle of the peninsula.

The main part of town lies along Upshur Neck Road. Turn left at Harbor Drive to find your way to a marina set on Upshur Bay. Parramore Island is out in that pretty distance again. Stick with Upshur Neck beyond town, all the way to a dead end, so as to savor all the waterfront scenery Quinby has to offer.

Headed back down Seaside Drive, the next fishing village on the list is Willis Wharf, which you can reach by turning east on Willis Wharf Road, which then bends to the right past the striking old E.L. Willis store building and winds over a bridge and into the far part of town, known as Little Hog Island. Six of the eight houses on Hog Island Lane were moved here as that barrier island depopulated in the face of erosion and storms during the early 1900s.

This is as good a place as any to pause and consider the natural and historical marvels just offshore. Barrier islands are sandy affairs that take shape along coastlines and protect the mainland from storm damage. Birds and other critters love the rich mix of salt marsh, tidal mudflats, and maritime forests out there. When it comes to "birds of conservation concern" — the ones experts keep an eye on because they're at some level of risk — the barrier islands here have the highest diversity of species and density of population in all of Virginia.

In fact, Virginia's barrier islands are the longest stretch of undeveloped oceanfront land on the whole East Coast. They are mostly owned nowadays by the Nature Conservancy. Visitors can get out there only by boat, of course. There are charter captains hereabouts you can hire, but be sure to check the rules first—in some seasons, visitors are restricted to the beaches on the outskirts of islands to protect nesting birds raising their young farther inland.

These islands weren't always undeveloped. For centuries, people lived out on Hog, Cobb, and other islands. Most of those folks put food on their tables by fishing, hunting, and gardening, while others worked at coast guard stations, lighthouses, and hunting lodges.

Those lodges drew their share of rich and famous visitors. When President Grover Cleveland visited Hog Island, Willis Wharf was his departure point. In *True Tales of the Eastern Shore*, the historian Kirk Mariner relates a charming bit of oral history that sprang up around one of Cleveland's visits:

> Mary Anna Doughty came out of her house to call her four young sons to dinner only to find them shooting marbles in the lane with the President. When she called them in, Cleveland is said to have asked if he too could come, and happily joined the family for a meal of fried pies and milk.

Those days came to a close in the early years of the 20th century, thanks to a run of wicked storms that wreaked such havoc on the islands that the site of the original Hog Island Light, which once stood on terra firma, is now nearly a mile out to sea. Pretty much everyone had moved to the mainland by the 1930s.

Heading back out Willis Wharf Road, you could choose to go past Seaside Road and into Exmore if you are in need of conveniences. The town, which sprang up in the wake of the railroad line's arrival, has some shops, restaurants, and gas stations, both on the highway and in an old downtown. A classic dining experience there is the Exmore Diner, 4264 Main St.

When you get back to southbound Seaside Road, it will be a lengthy but lovely run down to Nassawadox, a community where local history buffs are working hard as of this writing to turn the old Nassawadox Sawmill, 10150 Mill St., into a museum that tells the story of the important role forest products played in this area. If you're in the mood to stretch your legs, find your way to the Brownsville Preserve, a 1,250-acre Nature Conservancy property east of town at 11332 Brownsville Rd. The William B. Cummings Birding and Wildlife Trail there runs through woodlands and marsh on a three-mile round trip.

Back on Seaside Road, another lengthy run leads to the last fishing village on our checklist, Oyster. On the way there you will come to Machipongo Drive, which runs west into the town of that name. If you want to learn more about the history and culture of the barrier islands, find your way to the first-rate Barrier Islands Center on the far side of the highway, at 7295 Young St.

Another possible detour en route to Oyster is eastbound Indiantown Road, which leads out to Indiantown Park. This 52-acre stretch of green space and woodlands stands on a piece of the only Indian reservation ever established on Virginia's Eastern Shore. The Gingaskin tribe (also known as the Accomacs) lived hereabouts between 1640 and 1813.

The route into Oyster is six or so miles below Indiantown Road, at Sunnyside Road. Home to fewer than 100 residents, the town dates its history to a plantation established in 1737. The back part of the Methodist church, Travis Chapel, was moved from Hog Island. Be sure to wind your way up and around Crumb Hill Road to the Oyster Boat Ramp, where you can get out of the car, check out a couple of historic markers, and enjoy the views—that's the tip of Mockhorn Island out toward the ocean.

Return to southbound Seaside Road one more time to get down to the bottom of the peninsula. That road ends, after taking a big right turn, at the Eastern Shore of Virginia National Wildlife Refuge, located on the former site of an air force facility, Fort John Custis. You can choose here from among several hiking trails and an auto loop to wander through the 1,100 acres—the place is especially popular with birdwatchers.

CONNECTIONS
• Eastern Shore of Virginia Tourism
visitesva.com; 757.331.1660
• Accomack County
co.accomack.va.us/visitors; 757.787.5700
• Town of Wachapreague
wachapreague.org; 757.787.7117
• Northampton County Chamber of Commerce
northamptoncountychamber.com/our-area.html; 757.678.0010
• Nassawadox Sawmill Museum
peninsulatractor.org/nassawadox-sawmill
10150 Mill St., Nassawadox, Va.
• Brownsville Preserve
nature.org/en-us/get-involved/how-to-help/places-we-protect/brownsville-preserve; 757.442.3049
11332 Brownsville Rd., Nassawadox, Va.
• Barrier Islands Center
barrierislandscenter.org; 757.678.5550
7295 Young St., Machipongo, Va.
• Eastern Shore of Virginia National Wildlife Refuge
www.fws.gov/refuge/eastern_shore_of_virginia; 757.331.3425
32205 Seaside Rd., Cape Charles, Va.

NEARBY TRIPS: A list of other trips on the lower Delmarva Peninsula is on page 7.

Way Back Machine
'No More Kindly Heart Ever Beat'

Here is how the writer Hunter Alexander described Harriet Doughty, one of the most famous characters on Hog Island at the time he wrote an 1876 article about the place for *Forest and Stream* magazine.

The people of Hog Island number, all told, some seventy souls ... all of whom are ... rough, uncouth, and uneducated, but honest and hospitable. The prevailing genius, oracle, and general authority is old Aunt Harriet, and it is worth sailing twenty miles any day to meet her....

No frightened children who were hushed into a shuddering silence by the wind, or strange tales of the nursery maid, ever imagined the face of an ogress or warlock more fearful than hers; the forehead is low, the eyes of a dark green, protruding from her head; her nose flat, with wide open nostrils, and her mouth cruel and savage looking, occupies half of her face, and is garnished with teeth as large as those of a two-year-old colt.

The countenance is that of a wolf, and her short, squat body completes the illusion. She is for all the world like the Weir Wolf, with the grandmother's nightcap on, who lay covered up with bed clothes when little Red Riding Hood came home from her errand.

Yet, looking so bad, no more kindly heart ever beat than Aunt Harriet's and were I to fall sick in a strange place, I know of no one whom I would rather be tended by than the old woman of Hog Island.

The Doughtys were among the oldest of Hog Island families. Aunt Harriet lived for another 20 years after this article was published, passing away in 1896.

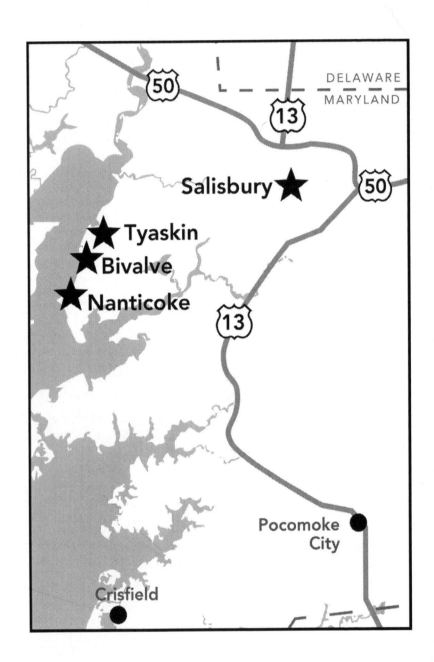

ROAD TRIP #22

WICOMICO WANDERINGS

Considering how few people live along the backroads of southwestern Wicomico County, Md., the run of traffic troubles I've encountered while wandering that way is pretty laughable. Inspired by spectacular clouds one Saturday, I veered off the highway and got caught up in the stop-and-go mess of a triathlon. Another time, my drive slowed to a crawl thanks to the one-two punch of a construction detour and a jam-packed school bus.

No worries: Both trips worked out just great in the end. The road at hand here runs alongside a pair of postcard-pretty rivers, the Wicomico and the Nanticoke. Time and again, you'll get the opportunity to commune with sweet waterfront scenery as you make your way into one out-of-the-way little park after another.

From Indentured Servant to Plantation Builder
The ride through the western outskirts of Salisbury along Pemberton Road passes a bevy of suburban-style housing

developments, but again, no worries: The long, gravel, tree-lined lane that leads into 262-acre Pemberton Park is bound to put you in the proper middle-of-nowhere mindset.

The story behind the old plantation house that comes into view along that lane is an up-by-the-bootstraps affair. Back in the 1670s, a young man named Samuel Handy paid for his voyage from England by signing on for a bunch of years of indentured servitude. When that term came to a close, Handy started into tobacco farming. By the time he died in 1721, he owned 2,000 acres and ranked among the area's leading citizens.

Isaac Handy, the 13th of Samuel's 14 children, built Pemberton Hall in 1741. The folks who restored his house in more modern times paid attention to the details. That run of distinctive wooden "snake" fencing is straight out of the history books. So, too, are the outbuildings, including a stand-alone kitchen, a milk house, and a wood-lined well.

The landscape here is another story—that was quite different in Handy's time. The forestland now standing between the house and the Wicomico River wasn't there, for instance. When Handy built his house, he had a clear view of the river from his front door, which faced the water because that's where all the action was—overland roads were iffy and little-used in his day. Across the water, an old Tondotank Indian village was still standing.

Tobacco was falling out of favor by the time Isaac started farming his 1,000 acres at Pemberton. Corn, wheat, and oats were his preferred crops. He planted fruit trees, too—today, a picturesque grove of apple trees pays homage to that aspect of his operation. Of course, to say that *he* did all the work involved here isn't quite accurate—the Handys owned as many as 16 slaves.

Like his father, Isaac ascended to the top of the social ladder. Most of his neighbors lived in clapboard homes that were about the size of the Great Room alone in Pemberton Manor. He served as a justice of the peace and as a colonel in the local militia. He belonged to the committee of five men who famously laid out plans for a brand new "Salisbury Town."

The grounds at Pemberton Manor are open every day, but the interior is open only on occasional weekends, so you will need to check that schedule if you have your heart set on touring the inside. The volunteers who walked me through pointed out some clever design touches. The house was built at an angle that would catch every possible bit of cooling breeze in the summer and every last ray of warming sunshine in the winter. With five fireplaces, it's no wonder so few trees stood between here and the river.

If the weather cooperates, you'll want to dawdle for quite some time along the park's 4.5 miles of hiking trails. They run through shaded forests, along itty bitty streams, and atop elevated wooden walkways. If you take the History Trail, keep an eye out for the remains of an ancient wharf on the river that dates to Handy's time — it's still visible sometimes at low tide.

Sweet Nanticoke Vistas

When you're done with the trails at Pemberton, take a left (west) onto Pemberton Drive, then a right onto Crooked Oak Lane. Turning left onto Nanticoke Road (Route 349) will connect you with the main drag for the westward journey ahead. Early on, this landscape will be dotted with tracts of new housing. I wonder sometimes whether folks off in the future will be seeking out the remnants of developments like these in the same way we go looking for old wharves and general stores.

Soon enough, those developments give way to roadside scenes that are mostly trees and telephone poles. Little country churches and old family graveyards pop up now and again as well. If you are intrigued by the signs pointing to the Whitehaven Ferry and Upper Ferry Road, that's a detour covered in Chapter 16.

Nanticoke Road crosses one little creek after another—first comes Gum Mill, then Dennis, Wetipquin, and Tyaskin. That last creek puts you on the outskirts of the town of Bivalve. Just ahead is Cedar Hill Park and Marina, a popular spot with boaters and anglers. A bathroom break will be available here in the warmer months, though the water gets shut down in the winter, alas.

A bench and picnic tables await up a little rise overlooking two stone jetties stretched out into the wide Nanticoke River. A 36-mile-long beauty that starts up in Delaware, the Nanticoke takes its name from an Indian tribe—roughly, the root words involved mean "people of the tidewater." Naturalists and historians often use the word *unspoiled* in describing the Nanticoke today. In some spots, it's as close as we can get to seeing the sort of place Captain John Smith encountered on his famed voyages of exploration in the early 1600s.

From Cedar Hill, Nanticoke Road runs right into the town of Bivalve. During the winter trapping season, the West Side Volunteer Fire Company here famously holds community suppers featuring a main course of muskrat. Outside the firehouse is the restored hull of an old log canoe, the *Wm. McKinley*, which was rescued from a state of decay as the fire company's way of celebrating the centennial of Wicomico County back in the 1960s.

Pretty Bivalve United Methodist Church stands at a bend in Nanticoke Road. If you stay straight there on Bivalve Wharf

Road instead of following the turn with Route 349, you will see where the road gets its name. A picturesque park bench awaits out at the end of the long pier. If anglers are hanging around, they're most likely on the prowl for perch, pickerel, catfish, or rockfish.

Back along that bend on Nanticoke Road is the ramshackle little Bivalve post office. When this village took shape in the late 1800s, this village was known as Waltersville and boasted two stores, a blacksmith shop, a wheelwright, an oyster-packing operation, and a vegetable cannery. Steamboats stopped here regularly into the early 1900s.

Next up along Nanticoke Road is the town of that name, where a gas station and country store were up and running on my most recent visit. Aside from admiring the smattering of pretty houses, your main order of business here should be paying a visit to a pair of Nanticoke beaches. The first, Cove Beach Park, is accessible by turning onto Cove Road.

To reach my favorite, Roaring Point Park, watch for the sign at Red Hill Lane that points the way to a parking area. A short trail soon opens up onto an extraordinary scene, even by the standards of a Delmarva region blessed with an abundance of beautiful spots. The thin stretch of sand here runs for nearly a full mile. Distinctive little trees and large hunks of driftwood make this spot a favorite of professional photographers. If you stroll all the way out to the point, you'll be able to see where the Nanticoke widens as it approaches Pocomoke Sound and the Chesapeake Bay.

If you continue down to the end of Nanticoke Road, the pavement narrows as you move through the town of Waterview and comes to a dead-end turnaround full of pretty marshland scenery, though no place to get out and stretch your legs. After that, you'll need to backtrack up through Bivalve.

Keep an eye out for the left (north) turn onto Tyaskin-Nanticoke Road, which comes up just past Cedar Hill Park, and then keep angling left (north again) when it ends at Tyaskin Road, which runs into the town of that name. Tyaskin, too, dates to the late 19th century—in 1877, it contained a dozen homes, a general store, and a blacksmith shop. Today, the town has 50ish homes and a population of a couple hundred, but no stores or other visitor-friendly businesses to speak of.

Tyaskin Road comes to an end at small-but-sweet Tyaskin Park, where the steamboat used to land on Wednesdays and Fridays back in the day. A picture on one of the historic signs there shows what a bustling waterfront this was a century ago, with seafood houses, a cannery, and a sawmill all crowded around the wharf. The town settled into a much quieter state of affairs after the steamboats stopped coming in 1924.

There is one last waterfront park to visit. On the way back through town, take the left onto Tyaskin Church Road, passing that church and its graveyard, and then left again on Wetipquin Road. A little way up is tiny Wetipquin Park, which is dominated by a boat ramp that drops into one of those little creeks you passed over while traveling along Nanticoke Road. The remains of an old dock on one side of the bridge here make this spot another favorite of professional photographers.

Back into the Heartland

If you have time, I suggest taking a slightly roundabout way back to Salisbury. Cross the bridge over Wetipquin Creek and find your way back to Nanticoke Road. Head east there, backtracking through familiar territory for a while, until you get to Quantico Road, Route 347.

The town that gives that road its name lies a little north of that intersection. Quantico may well have the best Indian-inspired name on the Eastern Shore—its root words mean "the place of dancing." Quite a bit older than the other towns on this trip, it was up and running in the early 1800s. A stagecoach used to stop here along a route between Cambridge and Princess Anne.

Several famous Methodist preachers called at Quantico in its earliest days, including Freeborn Garrettson and Francis Asbury. The latter kept a diary of his travels in which most entries feature extended snippets of information about the homes he visited and the people he met. But Asbury's mention of Quantico is as brief as can be:

I found no lack of anything in Quantico, except religion.

Continue north on Route 347 into Hebron, and you will have come full historical circle. Do you remember how Isaac Handy oriented his Pemberton Manor plantation house toward the Wicomico River because that's where all the traffic was in the 1700s? Similarly, Bivalve, Nanticoke, and Tyaskin were oriented to the steamboat traffic of their heydays.

Hebron sprung up around a transportation hub too—the railroad. When the Baltimore, Chesapeake & Atlantic railroad set up a little loading station here in 1890, this was an empty crossroads. The BCA executive who christened the place after a Biblical city did so before a town even existed.

By the 1920s, that town boasted five shirt factories, a flour mill, a lumber mill, and a cannery. Today, the town is most famous for an annual fireman's carnival that dates to 1926. You will pass those carnival grounds while traveling through Hebron's modest little downtown on your way out to the Route 50 highway, the transportation hub of our modern day.

CONNECTIONS
• Wicomico County Tourism
wicomicotourism.org; 800.332.8687
• Wicomico Recreation & Parks
wicomicorecandparks.org/parks-and-facilities/family-
recreation-parks; 410.548.4900
• Pemberton Historical Park
pembertonpark.org; 410.548.4900 ext. 108
5561 Plantation Lane, Salisbury, Md.

NEARBY TRIPS: A list of other trips on the lower Delmarva Peninsula is on page 7.

Way Back Machine
Tight Fit in Tyaskin
In his 1922 book, *Delaware and the Eastern Shore*, Edward Noble Vallandigham recounted the scenes and events of a trip around the Chesapeake aboard various steamboats.

The return voyage from Salisbury to Baltimore begins at noon, and on a day in late Spring or early Summer the run down the Wicomico is like a magnificent panorama, a glorified moving picture [for] the delighted eyes of the voyager. Over head is the sapphire sky, with cloud mountains on the horizon, sun-smitten to dazzling whiteness as if snow-capped. Unbelievably green marshes … stretch for miles along the vessel's course. Now a farmstead shows with its lawn falling in natural terraces to the river. Now the staunch brick gable of an Eighteenth Century church peeps out from its oak grove.

[On the Nanticoke] the scene changes [again as] … the boat nears a little wharf ministering to the convenience of a huddled hamlet. Tyaskin is a highly picturesque and difficult little harbor of the Nanticoke voyage, starred on the time-table with a foot-note that says, "Tide permitting."

The captain, more than 40 years a seafarer, and, for a full generation familiar with the Nanticoke, knows the harbor as intimately as he knows the furnishing of his own bedroom at home. He knows that when the tide is favorable he can count on a few feet of clear water either way, bow or stern, and is assured of an inch or so between the bottom of his vessel and that of the harbor.

For him, getting in or out of Tyaskin is a mere matter of backing off when the rudder stirs up too much mud, and going forward when the keel trades on the bottom. So he tinkles his signal bell every other minute, backs and fills, gains a foot now, an inch then, knowing all the while that the little crowd ashore, for whom he provides the sole amusement of the community, is watching, some half hopeful perhaps that this time he will stick till the next tide, all however, ready to applaud his triumph should he escape misfortune, and now and then someone calling encouragement.

"You kin do't, Cap'n Johnny! you kin do't!"

Captain Johnny always does it, and it is a point of professional pride with him never except in case of dire necessity to take advantage of that phrase, "Tide permitting."

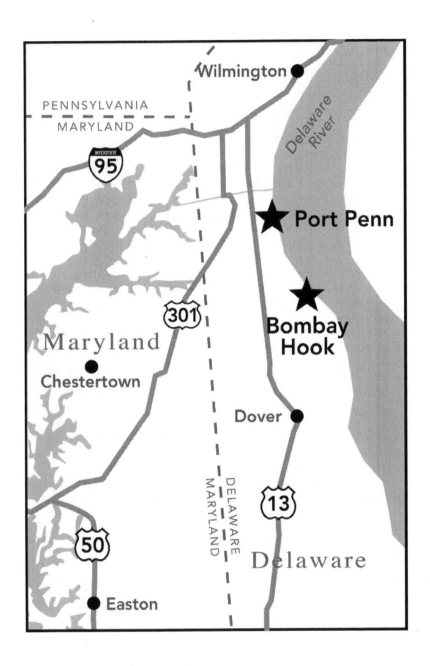

ROAD TRIP #23

BAYSHORE BYWAY

Hop on the winding Bayshore Byway below Delaware City, Del. and you will see straight away why the powers that be in the First State have been working so hard in recent decades to preserve the magnificent stretches of marsh, forest, and farmland that unfold along two-lane Route 9 as it tracks the Delaware River.

Scenery is the star attraction on this trip. Right from the get-go, views of the 3,000-acre Augustine Wildlife Area will take your breath away. And even though you've barely started, you might as well turn west onto Thorntown Road and then north at the signs for Augustine's Ashton Tract.

A half-mile up is an observation platform with a commanding view of the "Thousand Acre Marsh." That name falls short of the mark, actually—this marsh covers 1,300 acres. The deck here serves up a glorious first taste of the array of rich natural habitats along the byway, where some 400 species of birds make their home on a seasonal or permanent basis in an officially designated Wetland of International Significance.

Fish Tales in Port Penn

The scenery hits keep on coming all the way down into the old fishing village of Port Penn. You can stop to get your bearings here at the Port Penn Interpretive Center, housed in an old schoolhouse where Route 9 meets Market Street. Exhibits inside are open for viewing on summer weekends and holidays as of this writing, but the outside signage will be helpful even if those hours don't match your plans.

For instance, check out the evocative portrait on one marker of a group of workers at the old Kemp Canning Company, which went up in the 1880s and stood across the street from here, in what's now an empty stretch of swaying grass. Though it had various different owners and names along the way, the operation provided jobs to generation upon generation of locals, lasting into the 1960s.

Next, lace up the walking shoes. Across Route 9 is the starting point on the mile-long Port Penn Trail, which heads out into that gorgeous Augustine marshland and rises up for a stretch onto an elevated walkway. The last time my wife and I took this trail, we found our way to some connecting paths and extended our stroll by a couple of miles. (Public service announcement: During hunting seasons, it's best to wear some blaze orange out there.)

When you make it back into Port Penn, you'll find yourself in the real historical deal when it comes to Delmarva fishing towns. All eight blocks of the town—its population is just 250—lie within a national historic district. Fully 80 percent of the buildings in that district are more than 150 years old. The oldest of those dates to 1755 and can be found hiding behind the Methodist church at 10 Stewart St. That road takes its name from the guy who built the house, David Stewart.

Back when it went up, this was all farmland. Stewart is the one who got Port Penn started, by building a wharf out on the river and then starting to sell off lots so as to grow a town instead of crops on his farm. That wharf used to stretch into the water at the end of Market Street, beyond the tiny parking area where the street now comes to a dead end. In its heyday, the wharf was quite a bustling affair — and a colorful one, too. The historian Henry C. Conrad had this to say about those days in his 1908 *History of the State of Delaware*:

> [Port Penn] was generally thronged with sailors and was very immoral. Although at that time containing but about one hundred and fifty inhabitants, there were five inns or taverns, and these were generally filled with transient guests.

Things slowed down at that wharf once the Chesapeake & Delaware Canal (see Chapter 14) opened in 1829, drawing traffic up into Delaware City. Railroad lines came next, taking away more commercial traffic and leaving Port Penn to settle into the fishing-village role it has played ever since.

Looking at the town's timeless streetscape through modern-day eyes, it's easy to imagine day-to-day life here through all those decades as a simple and unchanging affair, each new day passing just like the one before. Nothing could be further from the truth, as the work of Port Penn's watermen has always changed with the seasonal rhythms of nature. Consider this bit of oral history from one local, Carl Morris:

> I'd trap [muskrats] from the first of December til the tenth of March. ... Soon as this was done you started rock fishing or net fishing on through April; then when the

shad hit you shad fished; then when the shad were done you went on down the Delaware Bay crabbing. We also used to sell eel through the fall … to the buyers from New York. That was our Christmas money.

Actually, Morris didn't mention a few items that could have been tacked onto his list. Watermen fished for sturgeon in the spring back when those prehistoric creatures were still running strong. They dug for turtles in the summer and hunted ducks in the fall. They fished for carp in the winter, and went oystering, too. If a slow stretch materialized, they sometimes put in a few land-bound shifts at that old Kemp cannery. Most of those seasonal sub-specialties had their own tools of the trade, leading to yards and outbuildings full of various types of boats, nets, lines, traps, decoys, and firearms.

Of Resorts and Fumigation Facilities

During the steamboat era, Port Penn managed to find a measure of fame as a getaway destination, too. That history is something to put in your mind's eye while wandering sweet little Augustine Beach, which pops up just below town. A man named Adam Diehl got the ball rolling here when he decided to switch his professional focus from cattle farming to tourism. He built the old Augustine Beach Hotel in about 1815, and yup, that's his building still standing a little way inland.

Business at the inn really took off after the Civil War, when the place landed in the hands of a Philadelphia entrepreneur named Simeon Lord. He rechristened the place "The Piers" of Port Penn, erecting a slew of bathhouses along the beach and putting up a dance pavilion as well. City folks arrived in droves aboard the steamboats *Pilot Boy*, *Ariel*, and others. The fare from Philadelphia was 30 cents a pop.

The tourism business took a dip as the steamboat era began to wane after World War I, then plunged even further during the Great Depression. By the 1940s, the only thing still running in the old Augustine Beach Hotel was a "taproom." Various business people have tried this and that in the old place since then, and various others will likely keep trying in the years ahead. Here's hoping one of them hits an entrepreneurial sweet spot and gives the old inn a fuller life as the 21st century progresses.

Before leaving Augustine Beach, cast a glance out into the river and take note of 50-acre Reedy Island, just to the north. There's nothing much out there today, but it was once a stopping place for immigrants full of hopes and dreams for a new life in America. Back in 1893, the United States government built a quarantine station out there so as to inspect every international boat bound for Philadelphia for signs of passengers with cholera, tuberculosis, smallpox, or other infectious diseases.

The island had a sprawling disinfecting chamber set on a 200-foot-long pier. Some arriving ships were fumigated with sulfur dioxide. A little hospital stood out there, too, along with housing for workers. When the station closed in the mid-20th century, several buildings were moved onto the mainland in Port Penn and turned into private homes. The Commodore's House is at 4 N. Congress St. A barracks house for unmarried workers and an officer's house are next to each other at 111 and 113 S. Congress St.

Below Augustine, Route 9 runs through still more of that gorgeous marshland, bending away from the Delaware River after crossing Silver Run at the southernmost tract in the Augustine Wildlife Area and then winding back riverward again as the Cedar Swamp Wildlife Area appears. Keep an eye out here for the Delaware Aquatic Resources Education Center, where you can stop and stroll a 940-foot-long boardwalk that leads through tidal salt marsh.

A little farther south, turn east at Woodland Beach Road for one last view of the river, and one last bit of resort history. The beach at the end of this road is quite popular nowadays with lovers of sea glass and shells—something in the currents out there seems to bring more treasures onto land at this spot than at other beaches. (If you find yourself getting angry at me when you arrive and asking, "What beach?", well, this stretch of sand tends to shrink to almost nothing when the tide is running high, so study the tide tables if you have your heart set on beachcombing.)

A large fishing pier juts into the river from the parking area, serving up a pretty view of the river. Off on the horizon is a miracle of modern-day technology, the Salem Nuclear Power Plant on the New Jersey side.

The story of Woodland Beach dates to right after the Civil War, but the glory days of the resort that once stood here didn't arrive until the 1880s, when one of the owners of a steamship line took control of the place and started promoting trips from Philadelphia aboard the *Thomas Clyde*.

Imagine the scene: In addition to a big hotel, there were 50 summer cottages, a two-story music pavilion (topped by a glass observatory), a waterfront boardwalk, and a 20-acre grove of trees. Amusements abounded, from billiards and shuffleboard to archery and amusement rides. The *Thomas Clyde* was a steam-powered behemoth—it could pack in more than 1,000 passengers. Alas, a wicked storm in 1914 tore up Woodland Beach and set the place on the path to its modern-day status as an isolated and unincorporated outpost on the Bayshore Byway.

From here, you will need to choose between two happy alternatives. One option is to keep wandering to the south along the byway, finding your way into the 16,000-acre Bombay Hook National Wildlife Refuge—the name is a bowdlerized version of the Dutch "Boompjes Hoeck," or "little-tree point." You can follow a 12-mile auto-tour route through the refuge. That route leads past a number of short walking trails and observation towers. Just below the refuge is Bowers Beach, another sweet little fishing village that's well worth a visit. The Bowers Beach Maritime Museum, open on summer weekends, is a great starting point there.

The second option is to seek out a measure of civilization in nearby Smyrna, a town of 10,000 or so that has been on the revitalization march in recent years, adding coffee shops, restaurants, boutiques, a brewery, and even a distillery. The pretty downtown here boasts the little Smyrna Museum, as well as the historic Smyrna Opera House, which has been putting on shows since the 1880s.

CONNECTIONS
• New Castle County Tourism (Port Penn area)
dscc.com/newcastlecounty.html; 302.655.7221
• Kent County Tourism (Smyrna area)
visitdelawarevillages.com; 302-734-4888
• Delaware Bayshore Byway
delawaregreenways.org/portfolio_page/bayshore-byway;
302.655.7275
• Augustine Wildlife Area
ecodelaware.com/places.php; 302.834.8433
• Cedar Swamp Wildlife Area
ecodelaware.com/places.php; 302.653.8080
• Sussex County Tourism (Bombay Hook area)

visitsoutherndelaware.com; 800.357.1818
• Bombay Hook National Wildlife Refuge
www.fws.gov/refuge/bombay_hook; 302.653.6872
• Town of Bowers Beach
bowersbeach.delaware.gov/visitor-information; 302.572.9000
• Bowers Beach Maritime Museum
bowersbeach.delaware.gov/museum; 302.222.6341
3357 Main St., Bowers Beach, Del.
• Town of Smyrna
smyrna.delaware.gov/77/points-of-interest; 302.653.9231

NEARBY TRIPS: A list of other trips on the upper Delmarva Peninsula is on page 7.

Way Back Machine
'A Remarkably Ugly Fish'
That was perhaps the kindest phrase the environmental historian Nancy Langston employed during a 2019 talk she gave about the sturgeon. The phrases "sort of like zombies" and "basically dinosaurs" came into play as well. Langston wasn't kidding about that last one. You've heard of the extinction event that wiped out the dinosaurs some 250 million years ago? The sturgeon was one of the few survivors of that cataclysm, so the creature comes by its prehistoric appearance and sometimes monumental bulk quite naturally.

Native Americans along the East Coast did some sturgeon fishing, which was quite a trick, considering the rudimentary technology available to them and the fact that the fish could weigh in at between 500 and 600 pounds while stretching to a length of 14 feet. One description I came across makes this bit of angling sound like something from a high-speed scene in a Saturday morning cartoon:

Some tribesmen working the East Coast rivers would attempt to lasso the sturgeon using ropes made of twisted grapevines. Others preferred to attach a harpoon to the grapevine rope. As often as not, the sturgeon would bolt to the bottom after being speared, leading the fisherman who was holding the rope on a wild ride.

It's interesting, the way early Europeans on these shores turned their noses up in disgust at the thought of fishing for sturgeon. They borrowed a bevy of dietary tidbits from the Indians—corn, oysters, potatoes, and more—but along rivers like the Delaware people regarded these dinosaur fish as nuisances that deserved to die for tearing through their nets and rocking their boats during spring migration season. Sturgeon meat was regarded as food fit only for slaves.

But money is a powerful motivator. In the 1840s, a Philadelphia newspaper reported an oddity—an unnamed immigrant from Russia had begun offering Delaware River fishermen a dollar per live sturgeon. That Russian then kept those sturgeon in a river pen, something fishermen still do in Russia today while waiting for the most productive moment to extract roe from the fish and sell it as caviar.

The Russian operation didn't become a big deal, but not long after, a German immigrant, Bendix Blohm, managed to launch a sturgeon gold rush. After a decade's worth of fishing trial and error, Blohm finally perfected a caviar operation on the Delaware River—it was housed in an old sawmill on the New Jersey side, in Penns Grove.

Other entrepreneurs followed his lead. By the late 1800s, Philadelphia had become the "caviar capital of North America," and fishermen in river towns like Port Penn were chasing the old dinosaurs with reckless abandon. In 1897, sturgeon once valued at 25 cents apiece were fetching a price of $30.

> Nowhere else in the whole annals of commercial fisheries is there a parallel to this case of the sturgeon, rising as it did in less than a quarter of a century from a fish despised and ruthlessly destroyed to the highest rank of commercial value.

This turn of events did not end happily for the sturgeon population. The fish were nearly exterminated from our area. They remain quite rare today, though a good number of scientists are working to try and help boost the population to a more sustainable level in the rivers of both the Chesapeake and Delaware bays.

I can't resist leaving you with one last sturgeon scene here, which comes from a late 19th-century piece by a writer named James Fennimore. Imagine yourself aboard a steamboat named *Sally* on the Delaware River:

> On each side, near her bow, were two large round windows which in the summer time were often open. One day when the *Sally* was on one of its trips up the river, a large sturgeon, in jumping, made such a leap that it passed clear through one of these windows and landed in the vessel, where it was killed.

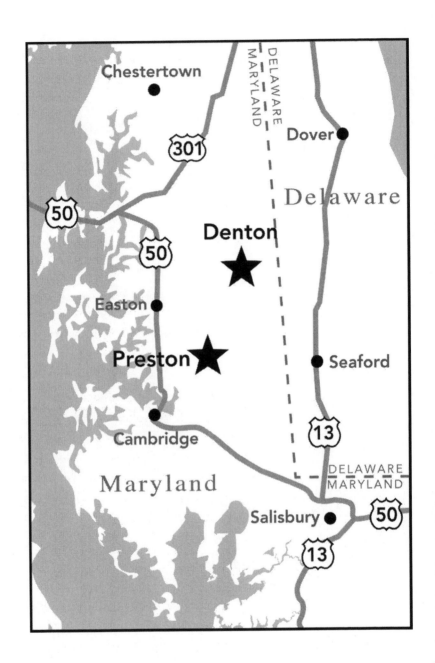

ROAD TRIP #24

CAROLINE COUNTRYSIDE

To some travelers, the two-lane roads that crisscross the vast inland farmland of the Eastern Shore and Delaware seem like blank and even boring slates, a never-ending run of barns and farm fields. But intriguing stories await out here in the middle of nowhere, too, often in surprising abundance.

Caroline County, Md. is the only landlocked county on the Delmarva Peninsula. On a ride from Preston up to Denton that's dotted with tiny towns and pretty old buildings, we will find ourselves brushing up time and again against the big sweep of American history, from the arrival of European settlers through revolution, Civil War, industrialization, and more.

An End to 4,000 Years of Drudgery

Linchester Road runs like a sliver of moon off of Main Street in Preston, which has a population of just 800 but ranks nonetheless as the biggest town around. This is where you will find a two-plus story structure clad in weatherboard and painted an ageless red.

The grounds at Linchester Mill, 3390 Linchester Rd., are always open to wanderers. Out back are the remains of the old waterwheel that powered this gristmill, along with a short nature trail and a couple of outbuildings. As of this writing, the interior is open just a handful of days a month — you'll need to check those hours or schedule an appointment if you want to make sure and get inside.

This building went up in 1840, but the place has stories to tell that are much older. The first clear mention in historical records of a mill on Upper Hunting Creek dates to the 1750s. But even in the 1680s, the property was owned by a man whose occupation was listed as millwright. Another reference from that period describes a nearby property as located "above the mill dam."

In other words, enterprising entrepreneurs were almost certainly grinding grains here shortly after Europeans first arrived in this Delmarva heartland. Gristmills don't get their due in history books. For about 4,000 years before they came along, farming families made flour by hand in laborious ways that ranked among the most time-consuming of their tasks.

Gristmills wiped that drudgery away. In doing so, they set off an interesting game of geographic dominoes that can still be traced on today's maps. Overland roads were in awful shape in the 1600s, which is why most everything moved by water then. But once farmers needed to drive wagons full of grain to newfangled mills, new and improved roads took shape. After that, if someone wanted to build a church or open a blacksmith shop, it made sense to do so along one of these better roads. In time, little towns like Linchester popped up — a smattering of houses and shops were here decades before Preston appeared.

These gristmills, by the way, weren't the rickety, backwater operations you might imagine. According to one historian,

The mills [located] upon the Delaware and Chesapeake [bays] were probably the finest at that time in the world.

That proved a lifesaver during the Revolutionary War. In the darkest days of that conflict, George Washington's army famously spent a hungry, freezing winter at Valley Forge, Pa.

Vegetables were nonexistent and meat and bread in short supply. In the early weeks, most of the nourishment for the soldiers came from "firecake," a tasteless mixture of flour and water cooked over open fires.

At one point during that winter, officials working on the revolutionary cause in Annapolis received assurances that flour would be available "at the head of Hunting Creek." Some of the staples that helped the army survive that ordeal probably came from here in Linchester.

A revolution of a different sort was under way when the current mill building went up in the mid-1800s. A Philadelphia inventor, Oliver Evans, had developed ingenious ways of employing the force of gravity to drive the milling process, with grains now getting loaded up top of a multi-story building and then making their way down through an almost fully automated process of cleaning and grinding.

A crew of just six men could convert 100,000 bushels of grain into flour every year. Incredibly, those six men spent most of their workdays simply closing up barrels at the end of what amounted to a precursor to the modern assembly line, which wouldn't come into full flower until much later. According to economic historian Victor S. Clark,

[These gristmills] may have been the first instance of an uninterrupted process of mechanical manufacture, from raw material to finished product, in the history of industry.

Mill improvements were just one element in that agricultural revolution. The cast iron plow appeared in the 1820s. The mechanical reaper came along in the 1830s. New railroads and canals popped up in the decades after that, serving as matches that ignited what another historian calls the "prairie fire spread of wheat farming."

This mill at Linchester kept chugging along right up into the 1970s, long after most other mills in the region had shut down. As a result, according to the mill's description on the National Register of Historic Places, Linchester retained a wealth of historical treasures that had disappeared from other mills.

Inside ... is a virtual museum of early milling technologies, ... a vast and dizzying maze of machines, grain bins, chutes, and elevators. ... Linchester Mill is a key to both the understanding of early milling technologies and bygone patterns of life in rural Eastern Shore communities.

There is one last big sweep of history to think about before moving along on the Caroline County backroads. During the years before the Civil War, Linchester Mill stood in the midst of a hot spot along the Underground Railroad, the line of secretive "stations" and "conductors" that runaway slaves followed in search of freedom. At least four such stations operated nearby, one of them run by the parents of Harriet Tubman. Historians suspect that the conductor at another of those stations, Daniel Hubbard, worked at Linchester Mill.

Might some runaways have made it from one side of Hunting Creek to the other along this milldam? Might there have been a rendezvous point in nearby woods? There is no telling for sure, but slaves were definitely making runs for freedom across this landscape during the 1850s and early 1860s.

From Canneries to Cabins

As you make your way into Preston along Main Street, you will see that there is nothing very big about its downtown aside from the civic slogan: the "Biggest Little Town in the USA." Preston earned that designation about a century ago, in the days when the vegetable canning industry dominated the economy of Delmarva's heartland.

Those boom times kicked into gear after the Baltimore, Chesapeake and Atlantic Railway arrived in 1890. At one point in the years that followed 16 canneries operated within seven miles of Preston. During the World War I years, more than 20 freight cars were getting loaded up here on a daily basis with canned tomatoes, as well as freshly harvested apples, wheat, and watermelons.

Preston boasted box companies, warehouses, hardware stores, and blacksmith shops as well. The downtown had multiple grocery stores and restaurants, even a hotel. The city's coffers were so flush with cash that Preston became the first town of its size in the country to pave its sidewalks with concrete. You can learn more about life in the "Biggest Little Town" at the Preston Historical Society, which is tucked inside an old house off of the intersection where Main Street meets Harmony Road.

Head north along Harmony Road (Route 16), and you will find the Webb Cabin a mile or so to the west at 23459 Grove Rd. This tiny 1852 structure may be the best place on Maryland's Eastern Shore to get a sense for the day-to-day lives of black families in slavery times, when this area was home to a mix of free and enslaved blacks. Though James H. Webb was legally free, he had to grapple with slavery nonetheless, while cobbling together enough money to buy his wife and children out of bondage. Built with hand-hewn logs set on a foundation of heavy ballast stones that Webb somehow liberated from nearby rivers, the cabin is a one-room affair with a loft accessible by rickety ladder. He shared this tiny residence with his father, Henry; his wife, Mary Ann, and their children—there were at least two of them, and there may have been four.

The cabin is probably quite similar to the one that a man named Ben Ross built a few miles away, in an area below Preston called Poplar Neck. That cabin played a key role in two of the most dramatic escapes engineered by Ross's daughter, the famous Underground Railroad conductor Harriet Tubman.

Tours of the Webb Cabin are self-guided affairs. You pull up, park, wander around the grounds, and then enter the house through the back door. There is no evidence that this cabin ever served as an Underground Railroad station, but you should still be sure to lift up the trap door in the floor that opens onto a little below-ground compartment used for storing perishable foods. Slaves on the run in those days were known to hide out in such "potato holes" when bounty hunters were hot on their trail.

As small as the cabin is, Webb's story is still quite remarkable, given the many obstacles that blacks faced during and after slavery times. He never learned to read—the documents he signed all seem to be marked with an "x." But in addition to saving the money he needed to liberate his wife and children, Webb managed to buy 54 acres of farmland around this cabin, a holding that eventually grew to 80 acres in the years after the Civil War. He lived in the cabin for more than half a century, selling it in 1906, when he was in his 80s.

Head back northbound on Harmony Road and you will come into the town that gives the road its name. Here, a small country store serves up sandwiches and sells life's essentials. If you are in the mood for a waterfront picnic, grab a snack, then head west on Gilpin Point Road until it meets up with Holly Park Drive.

The tiny Gilpin's Point Landing park along that side road presents a quiet, almost meditative scene today, but it was once a noisy, bustling affair that housed a busy wharf on the Choptank River. A marker tells the story of how 40-year-old Joseph Cornish escaped from slavery by boarding a vessel that stopped here.

Off in a nearby corner is the final resting place of Colonel William Richardson, who lived near here in the years after the Revolutionary War. He served during that conflict with the 5th Maryland Regiment, made up of soldiers from four Eastern Shore counties. The unit famously acquitted itself with flying colors at the 1776 Battle of Harlem Heights in New York City. That battle unfolded early in the war, at a time when things were not going well for George Washington's team. His army had barely escaped destruction on Manhattan Island. Then, his soldiers had made an ignominious flight from another engagement with the British, at Kips Bay.

Thanks in no small part to Richardson and his Eastern Shore comrades, the good guys stood their ground and fought hard at Harlem Heights. They didn't win, exactly, but they didn't lose either — the Brits were the first ones to start withdrawing from the battlefield that day. Historians regard the skirmish as a notable early confidence booster on the long road to victory.

Back northbound on Harmony Road, you will pass postcard-pretty Williston Lake, which came into existence because of another old gristmill—this one no longer standing, alas, as it burned down a few years back. But beyond that is gorgeous Williston Church, tucked away in a small grove of trees at 8270 Harmony Rd.

Do you recall the famous painting, "American Gothic," by Grant Wood? That's the one where a farmer is holding a pitchfork, his wife at his side. The title refers to the architectural style of the house behind that couple, which is the style of this church, too. I actually prefer an alternate phrase, "Carpenter Gothic," because it gets more accurately at the notion that this style was all about local craftsmen out in the boondocks striving with homegrown materials to create their own take on the monumental stone structures of the so-called Gothic Revival.

The church is all wood; only the foundation is stone. Built around 1870, it was probably based on a book of patterns that the architect Richard Upjohn put together after deciding that his mission in life was to help small churches strive for architectural excellence despite having limited budgets and needing to rely on local materials. This little church captures beautifully the feeling that Upjohn was going after. In his own words, he wanted to help remote congregations like this erect a structure that was

> in all essential features, a church—plain, indeed, but becoming in its plainness.

Northbound again on Harmony Road, the intersection to watch for is Detour Road, which leads into a 4-H park that's full of corrals and barns used during an annual midsummer county fair. Way off to the right here, beyond a tree line, is another little cabin that dates to the days of slavery. It's not the exact building, but rather a surviving example of the sort of place that Levin and Sidney Steel probably lived in during their time in Caroline County.

That was back in the late 1700s. Both Levin and Sidney were enslaved, but Levin managed to get enough money together to buy his own freedom. He left for New Jersey after that, presumably hoping to cobble together more funds so he could come back and buy his family out of bondage. Sidney didn't want to wait. She managed to make a successful run for it, though she was only able to bring two of their four children.

The couple had an astounding 14 additional children while in New Jersey, where the family changed its last name to Still. One grew up to become a towering figure along the Underground Railroad. As head of the Pennsylvania Anti-Slavery Society, William Still served as a gatekeeper, welcoming new runaways into town and helping them make the transition to life in freedom in towns farther north. The detailed records Still kept about his activities have served as a priceless resource for historians trying to pin down the facts about Harriet Tubman and others who worked on the Underground Railroad.

As of this writing, the William Still Interpretive Center, 8230 Detour Rd., is still a work in progress and not open to the public on a regular basis. Some informational signage stands outside the cabin, touching on a few of the many incredible twists and turns that unfolded in the life of a family that deserves to receive much more attention than it has gotten so far in our history books and at our travel destinations.

Fire and Kidnapping in Denton

By the time you find your way into Denton, the town will seem like a big-city nirvana. With a population of 4,500, the seat of Caroline County is big enough to offer interesting shopping and dining diversions, so you'll want to get out and stroll around.

The Museum of Rural Life is just across from the town's pretty Courthouse Square. All or part of four historic houses are displayed inside, with the range running from the cabin of a poor farmer to the estate of a wealthy planter. Another of those houses is a survivor of the devastating fire that tore through downtown Denton on July 4, 1865. That blaze began when jubilant citizens celebrating the end of the Civil War made the unfortunate decision to create a fireworks show by flinging balls of candlewick and kerosene into the air.

Another fire survivor stands a couple of blocks away, on 4th Street between Gay and Market streets. Nehemiah Fountain built his little cobbler shop in 1818, then toiled away inside for more than 40 years, making and repairing shoes. Across the street is a third fire survivor, the Richard Potter House, 9 N. 4th St. A marker there tells the story of a 10-year-old free black boy — he was the son of a popular blacksmith in town — who was kidnapped by a man who planned to sell him into slavery in the Deep South. Historians often refer to criminal conspiracies like this as the "reverse Underground Railroad."

Potter's kidnapper took him into Delaware and hid him for weeks before the boy finally escaped and found his way to some local white farmers, who believed his story about being free and kidnapped. They called in the authorities on his behalf. Potter himself recalled the scene that unfolded when he finally arrived back home:

As the news spread people came from every direction. I was welcomed by a great public reception on the streets of Denton.

As you wander downtown Denton, keep an eye out for the interesting Fiber Arts Center of the Eastern Shore, 7 N. 4th St. Locals rave about the pastries at the Turnbridge Point B&B, 119 Gay St., which also offers occasional cooking classes. The county visitors center offers swell views of the Choptank River — it's off of Gay Street, down the slope leading into Daniel Crouse Memorial Park. Outside of town are three sweet parks that I wrote about in my first collection of *Eastern Shore Road Trips*: Tuckahoe State Park, Adkins Arboretum, and Martinak State Park.

CONNECTIONS
• Caroline County Tourism
visitcaroline.org; 410.479.0655
• Caroline County Historical Society
(Linchester Mill, Webb Cabin, William Still Interpretive Center, Museum of Rural Life)
carolinehistory.org; 410.479.2730
• Preston Historical Society
prestonhistoricalsociety.com
167 Main St., Preston, Md.
• Greensboro Historical Society (Lady Eglantine story below)
greensboromdhistoryc.ipage.com; 410.482.2100
111 S. Main St., Greensboro, Md.

NEARBY TRIPS: A list of other trips on the middle Delmarva Peninsula is on page 7.

Way Back Machine
On the Trail of Lady Eglantine

Pretty little Greensboro, Md. lies just a few miles north of Denton. That this place is chock full of interesting stories, too, will become apparent to anyone who steps inside the town's historical society and checks out the old photos and displays the about shipbuilding, canneries, and numerous other topics.

My focus here, however, is on one specific item, the taxidermied carcass of a century-old chicken. Lady Eglantine was born on April 15, 1914. While her name has the ring of European royalty, it's actually a reference to a farm outside of town with an abundance of the wild pink roses that go by that name.

Addison A. Christian, the man who owned Eglantine Farm, was a hobbyist from Philadelphia who liked playing around with the latest developments in growing crops and raising farm animals. One of those games was a chicken-and-egg affair. Lady Eglantine stood just 14 inches high and weighed in at less than 4 pounds, but she had been bred for fertility stardom. Christian had high hopes when he entered her in an egg-laying contest.

Run-of-the-mill hens back then laid about 70 eggs a year. Lady Eglantine laid 314 eggs in the calendar year of that contest, a feat that earned her a place in the *Guinness Book of World Records*. It's comical, how much attention this generated in newspapers and trade publications. When I plugged "Lady Eglantine" into a database of old newspapers, the query generated hundreds of hits from scores of papers stretching from Maine to California and pretty much everywhere in between. This fowl lady had nicknames aplenty in those stories — "The $100,000 Hen," for one example, and "The Wonder of the 20th Century," for another. Her eggs sold for $60 apiece.

Lady Eglantine went on a victory tour after setting that new record. Her most famous stop was the Empire Association Poultry Show in New York City, held at the Grand Central Palace exhibition hall. In advance of this December 1915 show, Christian brought Lady Eglantine to Philadelphia and made a big deal of putting her up in a suite at the Hotel Walton. The next morning, Lady Eglantine was escorted from the hotel to the train station by a cadre of motorcycle police. Spectators lined the streets. When Lady Eglantine passed by, the men in that crowd removed their hats in a show of respect for her fertility prowess. As she entered the train station, an orchestra performed from the balcony.

Lady Eglantine traveled to New York with an entourage that included no fewer than 21 men, including several security guards and a private chef. The journey from Penn Station there to Lady Eglantine's accommodations at the Hotel Imperial involved a special coop awash in pink roses, a fancy car owned by a vaudeville actress, and a sightseeing bus for her entourage. In its reporting on this VIP visitor, the *New York Times* described the events as

> more factitious fuss than is customarily accorded the prima donna of a royal opera company.

Lady Eglantine died on Aug. 6, 1916. Christian took her body to a Philadelphia taxidermist and then gave her a resting place on his library table, which is where she stayed until he died in 1926. Somewhere in the years since then, she found her way to the Greensboro Historical Society, where you are welcome to stop by and pay your respects.

ROAD TRIP #25

CRUMPTON AUCTION

Dive right in. Do it headfirst. That's often the best way to experience the unique subcultures and traditions that still flourish in such abundance here on the Delmarva Peninsula in the 21st century. Dixon's Crumpton Auction along the backroads of Kent County, Md. is a great case in point.

Here, such a dive will land you in the middle of a mecca for modern-day treasure hunters. This weekly auction draws big crowds of expert collectors, professional pickers, antiques dealers, and interior designers from all over the Mid-Atlantic region. Take a moment on your way in to notice the various states represented on license plates in the parking lot. But don't be intimidated: A good number of curious onlookers and rank amateurs will be hanging about as well.

Americana in Abundance
This trip is a little different, as the auction is held only on Wednesdays in a small, unincorporated town set amid the endless run of farmland that straddles Route 301 between

Queenstown, Md. and Middletown, Del. There is just one stoplight in Crumpton, and that's probably one stoplight too many on every day except auction day.

The action starts at 8am and runs well into the afternoon. The first thing you'll want to do upon arriving is simply wander about. Fair warning: You could blow pretty much the whole day just browsing through the thousands of items on display inside a big barn-like warehouse and outside on a pair of sprawling open fields.

I am not a knowledgeable man when it comes to antiques. Without the magic of Wikipedia, I could not fathom a guess as to whether a piece of furniture qualifies as Rococo or Renaissance. Nor am I a shopper. If my wife keeps me in the same store longer than six minutes, I tend to break out in hives.

But I am a history buff, and I enjoy taking journeys through times gone by. This auction has its share of flea-market-level junk out in distant reaches of the outdoor fields, but all in all it showcases a pretty spectacular array of Americana. I never know while wandering through the Crumpton auction which of the old dolls, ornate lamps, oddball board games, and century-old oil paintings are worth real money to collectors, but those items grab my attention nonetheless. Did I really just see a matching pair of unopened red-white-and-blue cigarette packs from 1988, one adorned with an image of Michael Dukakis and the other with one of George H.W. Bush?

Another plus: The auction is as much a people-watching paradise as it is a product-watching one. The characters prowling about the auction grounds run the gamut, from bearded hipsters and big-city shop owners to overall-clad farmers and wide-eyed newcomers.

The auctions here are nothing like the fancy affairs you may have seen at charity functions. For starters, there are often three sessions going simultaneously, one inside that barn and others in each of those two outdoor fields. There's a rugby-scrum aspect to how things unfold, with an auctioneer and an assistant making their rounds from lot to lot seated in a glorified golf cart and surrounded by a shuffling huddle of the day's most serious bidders.

As each new item is sold, the auctioneer invites the dealer in charge of the lot at hand to hold the next item aloft and shout out a brief description. There are no printed programs. There are no paper trails documenting the official provenance of products. And while the auctioneers do speak in the high-speed chatter of their field, they do not engage in any idle chit-chat or cocktail-party banter.

Nor is there much in the way of coaxing extra bids. You're either in or you're out. You have half a second to make up your mind.

It's fascinating stuff to watch, especially when that occasional item pops up that captures the fancy of the professional dealers. Those items often climb past $500 and then zoom into four-figure territory. Imagine what that price tag is going to look like when the item goes on display in a high-end shop in the likes of Old Town Alexandria, Old City Philadelphia, or Fells Point in Baltimore.

Building an 'Empire Out of Honesty'

The Crumpton auction traces its history back to the 1940s, but its roots go back much further, to the bustling "trade faires" of medieval times in Europe, which evolved on these shores into ramshackle "trading posts" where early American colonists shelled out all manner of goods to Indians in exchange for furs and other salable goods.

The Dixon family took over the Crumpton auction in 1961, when family patriarch Norman Dixon bought the operation at a point in life when he was flat broke with a wife and three kids. How did the family take a then-fledgling little operation and turn it into one of the biggest markets of its kind on the East Coast? In the words of a magazine writer from back in the 1990s, what the Dixons did was build an "empire out of honesty," making sure to do right by customers at every turn.

The hours pass quickly at Crumpton. Mealtime will arrive before you know it. When it does, you're in luck, as Amish merchants set up shop in several stalls along one wall of the big barn, serving up first-rate breakfasts, lunches, and snacks. Among Crumpton aficionados, the pretzel dogs here have achieved the status of culinary legend.

If you pick up a treasure or two, you may need to visit the office in that big barn. Set behind glass windows, it's pretty much straight out of a 1950s television show, only with computers.

On your way out, take a run into Crumpton proper. The town is perhaps a mile up the road from the auction house, and it has some sweet old houses that are worth a look. You'll also catch a few glimpses of the Chester River, which is pretty as can be up here.

There isn't any especially notable place to stop in Crumpton, but do take note of the old-style historic marker identifying this as the location of "Callister's Ferry" back in the mid-1700s, as the story of English immigrant Henry Callister is quite a good fit with the mood of the modern-day auction.

One of seven sons of a widowed mother from the Isle of Man, he ranked as a lowly indentured servant at the time he was assigned to serve as ferry operator by a Liverpool company that owned some land hereabouts. In short order, Callister paid off his term of servitude and became a paid employee. The ferry operation soon grew to include a wharf and a granary. Eventually, Callister bought the place and became the boss.

He had deep ties to nearby Talbot County, Md. as well. A prolific correspondent, his impressions of life on the Eastern Shore and in colonial America are quoted quite often by historians. Dubbed by one friend as "Botanist, Florist, Philosopher [and] Musician," Callister was quite the interesting character, which is the way it usually goes with entrepreneurial treasure hunters—something you can see even nowadays in the crowds that descend on the auction house in Crumpton every Wednesday.

If you want to turn your Crumpton visit into a daylong run of wandering, you could make your way into one or both of two small nearby towns, Millington or Galena. Bigger towns within striking distance include Chestertown to the west, Smyrna to the east, and Middletown to the north.

CONNECTIONS
• Kent County (Md.) Tourism
kentcounty.com/visitors; 410.778.0416
• Dixon's Furniture Auctions
crumptonauctions.com; 410.928.3006
2017 Dudley Corners Rd., Crumpton, Md.

NEARBY TRIPS: A list of other trips on the upper Delmarva Peninsula is on page 7.

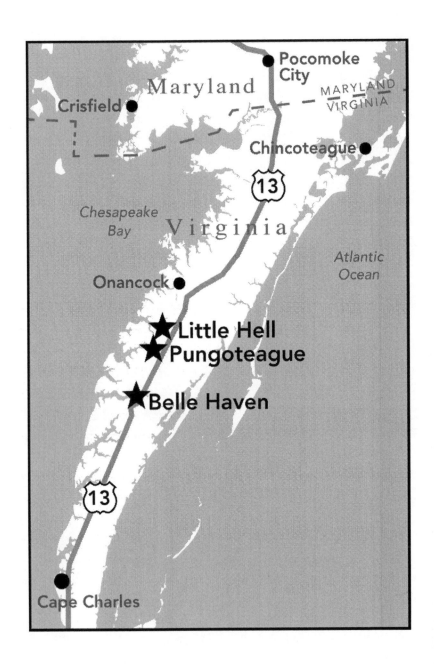

Maryland

Pocomoke City

Crisfield

MARYLAND
VIRGINIA

Chincoteague

13

Chesapeake
Bay

Virginia

Atlantic
Ocean

Onancock

★ Little Hell
★ Pungoteague

★ Belle Haven

13

Cape Charles

Road Trip #26

Bayside Virginia Loop

Different people treat books in different ways. Mine tend to be a wreck of dog-eared pages, abundant underlining, and makeshift bookmarks. The honor of most tattered volume in my collection goes to Kirk Mariner's *Off 13: The Eastern Shore of Virginia Guidebook*. The crumpled cover has about a gallon's worth of coffee stains on it. Scraps of paper towel or junk mail are tucked inside every third page to mark various items of interest.

I laugh every time I pick the thing up. Published in 2000, it's one of a dozen or so books that the Eastern Shore native and Methodist minister wrote about Virginia's Eastern Shore before his death in 2017. If memory serves, the trip I have outlined here—a backroads semi-circle that runs from Exmore to Onancock (or the other way around, if you prefer)—was the very first time I set *Off 13* down on my passenger seat to follow Mariner's lead. The first few coffee stains probably date to that afternoon.

Sprinkled through these pages are the names of a score or more writers and historians who have inspired and informed me in my travels. But no one's name appears more often than that of Mariner, who had a magnificent eye for short anecdotes and fascinating facts. I never got a chance to meet Rev. Mariner before he passed. I am feeling an urge to take a moment here to say thank you, and rest in peace.

Across the Occohannock to Guinea

Pretty little Belle Haven is the civic equivalent of a "transition zone," the term naturalists use for the border areas between different ecological territories with different populations of plants, animals, and soils. Here on shady Belle Haven Road, the sunbaked busy-ness of the highway through Exmore starts to fade and then gives way in time to the sparsely populated, history-laden countryside of this off-the-highway loop up to Onancock.

Home to 500 people, Belle Haven gets its name from a tavern that operated here in the late 1700s. Turn left at King Street (Route 178) to cross the Occohannock Creek atop Shields Bridge. Steamboats used to stop at a wharf that went up here shortly after the Civil War. Pedestrians paid 5 cents apiece to cross an earlier bridge. The rate was double for a horse and buggy.

The first town of any size beyond that bridge, Craddockville, pops up where Route 178 turns to the right and becomes Boston Road. In colonial times, a man named Abel West ran a plantation in the countryside north of here. That farm was so successful that he owned more slaves than anyone else in Accomack County at the dawn of the 19th century.

Then he started freeing those slaves. He started with a man named Adam in 1805. He freed eight others early in 1806, and then 24 more later that year. The last three slaves he owned gained their freedom in the will West left at his death in 1816. I haven't come across any biographical details that offer hints at his motivation, but freeing slaves through the legal process known as manumission wasn't unheard of back then. Some slave owners did it out of newfound religious belief, others for any number of legal and business reasons, and still others out of sincere gratitude for services provided.

What makes this case unusual is something else West did: He gave a gift of 200 acres to his former slaves "and their heirs forever" to be held "in common amongst them all as a place of Refuge." The community that developed on that land came to be called Guinea, presumably after the country in West Africa, which may have been the family homeland of some of those freed men and women.

Beyond Craddockville, Route 178 leads into the African-American town of Boston that grew out of this Guinea settlement. Boston was the first community in Accomack County to set up a school for black children after the Civil War. The original Boston School building is no more, but its replacement, which dates to the 1920s, stands empty at 32168 Boston Rd., near Fairview Road.

Two historic Baptist churches come up next. First is Shiloh Baptist, a congregation that traces its history to 1875. The current building at 31559 Boston Rd. dates to 1907 — it was six years old when the educator and champion of black entrepreneurship Booker T. Washington gave a talk inside. A little farther up is Holy Trinity Baptist, 14191 Trinity Ln., where the congregation dates to the early 1900s.

To Angola on the Pungoteague

The town of Pungoteague gets its name from an Indian phrase meaning "place of fine sand." From the mid-1600s through deep into the 1800s, it ranked as a thriving little metropolis full of commercial activity and busy with shipping traffic. Things slowed down when the railroad arrived down the middle of the peninsula, changing everything about the area's transportation patterns.

Quite a few buildings here date to the town's heyday, so the streets are worth a little strolling time. The place is full of fascinating stories, with the most incredible of those set in the farmland north of town in the 1630s, when a black man named Antonio came on the scene. He hailed from the southwest African nation of Angola, where he had gotten sold off to Arab slave traders and ended up aboard a ship bound for colonial Jamestown.

He arrived in 1621, so early in the game that slavery had not yet been defined as a legal institution. Instead of being sold as a slave for life, Antonio went off with the tobacco-farming Bennett family as an indentured servant. The next year, Indians attacked the Bennett farm, killing 52 people—Antonio was one of four survivors.

A happier turn of events unfolded the following year, when an African woman named Mary arrived at the Bennett farm. She and Antonio soon married. They would have four children together.

When the Bennetts moved to the Eastern Shore, Antonio and Mary went with them. In those mid-1630s, Antonio emerged from legal servitude and took a new, free-man name, Anthony Johnson. He bought 250 acres of land somewhere to the north and east of Pungoteague, where he raised tobacco, cattle, and hogs.

This is an odd, fascinating period in Virginia history—and American history, too. For a brief window here on the Eastern Shore, blacks and whites alike landed in the roles of slaves, servants, and masters. Johnson became one of the latter. He and his sons built the family holdings up to nearly 1,000 acres. They had servants. They owned slaves. They called their plantation "Angola." In fact, historians at the Jamestown Settlement believe that a dozen other families from that country were living in the Pungoteague Creek area in Johnson's day.

In 1653, fire swept through Anthony Johnson's farm. He and Mary spent the next decade trying to re-establish things, but they eventually gave up and moved up the road to Somerset County, Md., where they started over by leasing land. Some historians have suggested that the move coincided with the slow-but-sure subjugation of blacks in Virginia. Others suspect that the land on the family's Pungoteague farm was simply worn out, and the Johnsons left in search of greener pastures.

Johnson died in 1670. Mary followed him to the other side two years later. Historians have not been able to pinpoint the location of the Johnson farm beyond the general notion that it was on or near Pungoteague Creek. One way to get out into that formerly Angolan countryside is along Harborton Road, which leads into a waterfront town of that name. There is a long wharf at the end of Harborton Road—steamboats used to stop at an earlier incarnation of that structure.

For a run of 25 years starting in 1914, the famous James Adams Floating Theatre stopped here on a regular basis. That big old barge really was a full-fledged theater—it had dressing rooms, a 19-foot stage, and a seating capacity of 700. Two powerboats towed that vessel up creeks like the Pungoteague. After docking, the theater troupe's musicians would board one of those powerboats and commence cruising along one neighboring creek after another, playing happy tunes to announce that the show was in town.

Back on Boston Road (which soon changes its name to Bobtown Road), two more Pungoteague stories await. The first comes up at St. George's Episcopal Church, usually described as "the oldest church building on Virginia's Eastern Shore." That is mostly true, but slightly complicated. The building that went up here in 1738 was even prettier than the one you'll see at St. George's Circle today. Built in the shape of a cross, it had a mahogany pulpit, hand-carved woodwork, and lots more artsy bells and whistles.

During the Civil War, the Union Army was not impressed by all that beauty. During a lengthy occupation of the area, soldiers used St. George's as a horse stable. They tore out all that fancy woodwork and used it for kindling. They yanked bricks out to use them in the construction of a flimsy cookhouse.

The place was a wreck by the time they left. St. George's stayed vacant until the 1880s, when locals finally got about rebuilding it. They saved what they could, but much of it was either gone or beyond salvaging. The main piece of the building that deserves the title of oldest church on Virginia's Eastern Shore is the arms of the cross, or the transept. The churchyard is worth wandering — in addition to a pretty graveyard, you will find a sweet memorial to Edmund Scarborough, a local man who made the ultimate sacrifice during the Vietnam War and was awarded the Distinguished Service Cross for the heroism he displayed in his final battle.

Back on Bobtown Road, things will take a dramatic and somewhat mysterious turn just past the intersection with Michaels Hill Road. There, a marker notes the probable location of Fowlkes Tavern in the 17th century. Believe it or not, this was the site of the first known theatrical production in colonial America.

"The Bare and Cubbe" was presented here on Aug. 27, 1665, but no one has any idea what the play was about. The main reason we know about that show happening is that the playwright, William Darby, and a couple of actors, Cornelius Watkinson and Phillip Howard, were hauled into court in the wake of a complaint lodged against the production by a local Quaker man. No one has any idea what the complaint was all about, either—they didn't keep very detailed records about court cases in those days.

Formal courthouses were few and far between then. Instead, itinerant judges would roll into towns like this now and again and hear cases in local watering holes that doubled as courtrooms. Ironically, the "Bare and Cubbe" trial unfolded in … Fowlkes Tavern. The judges made the actors perform the play from start to finish, then exonerated them and ordered that nitpicking Quaker to pony up all costs associated with the case.

Back on Bobtown Road (which is now Route 718), you will pass through (you guessed it) Bobtown. The road's name then changes to Savageville Road, which runs through (you guessed it) Savageville. This little Bayside loop comes to a close when you arrive in Onancock (see Chapter 2).

CONNECTIONS
• Eastern Shore of Virginia Tourism
visitesva.com; 757.331.1660
• Accomack County
co.accomack.va.us/visitors; 757.787.5700

NEARBY TRIPS: A list of other trips on the lower Delmarva Peninsula is on page 7.

Way Back Machine
The Legend of Little Hell
On the last leg of this loop, between Bobtown and Savageville, there is a stretch of farmland that goes by the name Little Hell. Here is Kirk Mariner's summary of the local legend behind that name.

The northernmost of [the homes here, 27488 Bobtown Rd.] occupies the spot where once a tavern stood. This story is that an old black preacher, widely known for his excessive sanctimoniousness, used to pass by regularly between his churches in Onancock and Pungoteague, and he always let it be known that he disapproved of the riotous activities at the tavern.

One day the tavern folk could take his criticism no longer, and they forcibly invited the preacher in. "Drink with us," they offered, and when he refused they held him and poured liquor down his throat. "Dance for us," they insisted, and when he refused one of them produced a gun and shot bullets at his feet until he "danced." "Sing for us," they commanded, and when he would not someone twisted his arm until he "sang."

And then they let him go. When he arrived at his church in Pungoteague, the preacher preached an unusually forceful hellfire and brimstone sermon, and in it he told his flock: "I don't know what Hell is like, but I sure have been to Little Hell—and you'd better mend your ways if you don't want to go there." The name stuck.

ABOUT SECRETS OF
THE EASTERN SHORE

Thank you so much for spending time with this book!

The husband-and-wife duo of writer Jim Duffy and photographer Jill Jasuta created Secrets of the Eastern Shore to celebrate and share the joys of the Delmarva Peninsula in words, pictures, and products. Their pair has lived near the Choptank River in Cambridge, Md. since 2004.

Duffy started out in newspaper journalism in his hometown of Chicago, then moved into magazine writing and book projects after moving east. Jasuta started as a newspaper writer, too, before transitioning into graphic design and photography. Both have won numerous awards for their work over the years.

Visit the Secrets of the Eastern Shore website to see what the pair have been up to lately. That site has an ever-changing array of interesting tales, sweet photos, and travel tips, along with the full line of Secrets of the Eastern Shore books, Delmarva-themed greeting cards, and other fun products. Sign up for the newsletter while you're there to get advance word on upcoming events and happenings all over the peninsula.

More Delmarva Stories & Trips
secretsoftheeasternshore.com
facebook.com/secretsoftheeasternshore

Feedback
secretsoftheeasternshore@gmail.com
443.477.4490

GETTING PERSONAL

Here's to my wife Jill Jasuta, a paragon of patience, for her advice, support, listening, and love.

Here's to my two wonderful families, immediate and in-law, remembering most especially those who are gone—Terry, Marty, Joe, Helen, and Cele Duffy on one side; and Al and Dolores Jasuta on the other.

Here's to countless friends old and new. None better than you, Geoff Brown.

Here's to all the readers I've met at book signings, events, and presentations, as well as in random encounters and online exchanges. Your generous way with compliments, complaints, suggestions, and encouragement is appreciated more than you know.